THE HOUSE
BEAUTIFUL

*An Unabridged Reprint of the Classic
Victorian Stylebook*

Clarence Cook

DOVER PUBLICATIONS, INC.
New York

Bibliographical Note

This Dover edition, first published in 1995, is an unabridged republication of the work as published by Charles Scribner's Sons, New York; 1881. In the Dover edition the original frontispiece, in color, appears in color on the front cover and in black and white in its original location, facing the original title page. The original half title has been eliminated to accommodate the Dover title page. Apart from these minor modifications, nothing has been altered in this edition. The original title was *The House Beautiful: Essays on Beds and Tables, Stools and Candlesticks,* and the book had been published earlier, by Scribner, Armstrong & Co., New York, 1877.

Library of Congress Cataloging-in-Publication Data

Cook, Clarence, 1828–1900.
    The house beautiful : an unabridged reprint of the classic Victorian stylebook / Clarence Cook.
            p.   cm.
    Originally published: New York : Scribner, 1881.
    ISBN 0-486-28586-3
    1. Interior decoration—History—19th century. 2. Victoriana.
I. Title.
NK1960.C66   1995
747.2'048—dc20   94-48289
                                                                                    CIP

Manufactured in the United States of America
Dover Publications, Inc., 31 East 2nd Street, Mineola, N.Y. 11501

ART.

Give to barrows, trays, and pans
Grace and glimmer of romance;
Bring the moonlight into noon,
Hid in gleaming piles of stone;
On the city's pavèd street
Plant gardens lined with lilacs sweet;
Let spouting fountains cool the air,
Singing in the sun-baked square;
Let statue, picture, park, and hall,
Ballad, flag, and festival,
The past restore, the day adorn,
And wake to-morrow a new morn.

So shall the drudge in dusty frock
Spy behind the city clock
Retinues of airy kings,
Skirts of angels, starry wings,
His fathers shining in bright fables,
His children fed at heavenly tables.

'T is the privilege of Art
Thus to play its cheerful part,
Man on earth to acclimate
And bend the exile to his fate.
And, molded of one element
With the days and firmament,
Teach him on these as stairs to climb,
And live on even terms with Time;
Whilst upper life the slender rill
Of human sense doth overfill.

EMERSON.

"MY LADY'S CHAMBER."

The House Beautiful

Essays on Beds and Tables

Stools and Candlesticks

By Clarence Cook

Charles Scribner's Sons

1881

[original title page]

TO HER

WHOSE HAPPY UNION

OF

HEAD, HANDS, AND HEART,

HAS MADE

ONE HOUSE BEAUTIFUL

THROUGH MANY CHECQUERED YEARS,

TO MY WIFE,

THIS LITTLE BOOK

IS,

WITH FULL AFFECTION,

DEDICATED.

"MAN and wife are equally concerned to avoid all offences of each other in the beginning of their conversation; every little thing can blast an infant blossom; and the breath of the south can shake the little rings of the vine, when first they begin to curl like the locks of a new-weaned boy; but when by age and consolidation they stiffen into the hardness of a stem, and have, by the warm embraces of the sun and the kisses of heaven, brought forth their clusters, they can endure the storms of the north, and the loud noises of a tempest, and yet never be broken: so are the early unions of an unfixed marriage; watchful and observant, jealous and busy, inquisitive and careful, and apt to take alarm at every unkind word. After the hearts of the man and the wife are endeared and hardened by a mutual confidence and experience, longer than artifice and pretence can last, there are a great many remembrances, and some things present, that dash all little unkindnesses in pieces.

"There is nothing can please a man without love; and if a man be weary of the wise discourses of the apostles, and of the innocency of an even and a private fortune, or hates peace, or a fruitful year, he hath reaped thorns and thistles from the choicest flowers of Paradise; for nothing can sweeten felicity itself but love; but when a man dwells in love then the breasts of his wife are as pleasant as the droppings upon the hill of Hermon; her eyes are as fair as the light of heaven; she is a fountain sealed, and he can quench his thirst and ease his cares, and lay his sorrows down upon her lap, and can retire home to his sanctuary and refectory, and his gardens of sweetness and chaste refreshments.

"No man can tell, but he that loves his children, how many delicious accents make a man's heart dance in the pretty conversation of those dear pledges; their childishness, their stammering, their little angers, their innocence, their imperfections, their necessities, are so many little emanations of joy and comfort to him that delights in their persons and society."—JEREMY TAYLOR.

Contents.

2

"How far that little candle throws his beams!"

List of Illustrations.

The designs are all engraved by Mr. Henry Marsh, with the exception of Figures 14, 15, 28, 32 and 99 by Guillaumot, Jr.; 7, 9, 26, 64, 72, 74, 76, 86, 87 and 98 by F. S. King; 8, 27 and 79 by G. A. Avery; 47 by Adolph Will; 50 by C. J. Wardell; and 92 by Felix LeBlanc.

PREFACE.

THE articles of which this book is made up were originally
published in " Scribner's Monthly," and it is by the permission of the editor that they now appear in an independent form.

All that the author has to urge in defense of his book has
been said in the Introduction, and in the book itself. He is aware
that such purpose as he had in writing it is not clearly understood
by some of those who have amused themselves with hastily glancing over his pages; but he does not see that much could be gained
by attempting to make his meaning clearer. Those whose occupation and pleasure it is to pick flaws would continue to show their
ingenuity by finding new objections as soon as the old ones had
been answered; and the author likes too well to enjoy himself in his
own way to deprive others of their means of enjoyment. Even since
the book was finished there comes a letter,—the hundredth or so,—
asking to know when it will be published, as the writer hopes
to find in it that practical information in which the articles, though
well enough in their way, were sadly wanting,—information, namely,
as to the prices of the different things described, and their dimensions in feet and inches. But if the writer of this letter had
reflected he would have seen that such information, if given, would
have been practically useless, since no two people ever want
things of the same size or of the same shape, and that in the
competition of the shops the same price is never asked for the
same article in any two places. The author of these pages never
offered to give any such information. He has only asserted what

is strictly true: that when people are spending money in furnishing their houses, they will find it costs no more to get pretty things than ugly things, things that are in good taste than things that are in bad taste. The point is, has the buyer taste? If he have, this book may perhaps be of some service to him in showing him how to use his taste in furnishing his house. If he have none, the author confesses, with humility, that he knows no way of inoculating him with it.

The multitude of readers who every month enjoy the woodcuts in "Scribner's Monthly" are not expected to be aware how much of the beauty with which this costly illustration is set before them is due to the care bestowed upon the printing. But while the most careful printing cannot make a bad cut tolerable, careless or unskillful printing can spoil a cut on which designers and engravers have expended great skill and labor, and it is greatly because the cuts in "Scribner's Monthly" are so well printed that the excellence of their drawing and engraving tells as it does in a success that has carried the magazine from one end to the other of our own country, and made it sought for in Florence and Paris, in Edinburgh and London. It is to the long experience and to the patient skill of Mr. A. W. Drake that this excellence in the presentation of the wood-cuts is chiefly due, and designers and engravers whom misfortune in other quarters has made weary of the world, and the maimed and splintered wrecks of whose work are scattered along inhospitable shores, smile in pleased content when they drop anchor in the safe harbor of "Scribner's Monthly.

The author cares little for his book except so far as it reminds him of the pleasant circle in whose company he has written it, and of the friendships that have grown up and been strengthened while it has been in progress. It is a satisfaction to him to be assured that, while it is not possible his own share in the work should please for longer than a fleeting hour (happy if, in this rushing world, it please so long!), his book must long be dear to lovers of art and to all who are interested in the growth of art in our America, because it contains the drawing of Francis Lathrop and the engraving of Henry Marsh. And he is far prouder of his part in bringing a wider public acquainted with their work than he ever could be made by any praise bestowed upon his own work in any quarter whatever.

This prefatory note would be incomplete without grateful mention of Mr. Daniel Cottier, to whom, as friend and artist, the author has been constantly indebted for advice and practical help since he first began to write these pages. Without him and his House, represented here by Mr. James S. Inglis, the book would have wanted much that has helped it to win the favor of the public.

With all its shortcomings, the book is offered to those who are interested in the subject, with the hope that they may find something in it useful. If it should give to any reader half the pleasure the author has had in writing it, he would consider himself well paid.

INTRODUCTION.

A MONG the smaller facts that must be taken note of in drawing the portrait of these times is the interest a great many people feel in everything that is written on the subjects of house-building and house-furnishing. There never was a time when so many books written for the purpose of bringing the subject of architecture—its history, its theory, its practice—down to the level of the popular understanding, were produced as in this time of ours. And, from the house itself, we are now set to thinking and theorizing about the dress and decoration of our rooms: how best to make them comfortable and handsome; and books are written, and magazine and newspaper articles, to the end that on a matter which concerns everybody, everybody may know what is the latest word.

When those who have attempted to instruct the public on so intimate and personal a subject have looked about for authorities and models, they have turned back with one consent to the past, and either adopted the usage of old times as a whole, or made it a basis for their suggestions, a text for their sermon. But, if we ask where the old-time people found their models, we certainly do not get for an answer, that they ran to this or that book for them, or that they sought the advice of this or that architect. Whatever they did, were it good or bad, came out of their own minds, and was suggested by their own wants, and represented their own taste and sense of fitness.

Now, we have the same faculties that the men who lived before us had, just as we have the same desires and needs, and we have only to go to work in the same way in order to produce the same results.

Just let us consult our own desires and needs, and refuse to be governed by those of other people. And let us refuse to take what is offered to us, if it does not suit our needs or our purses, and learn not to fear being sent to Coventry for our refusal.

The best plan is to know first, as near as may be, how we ought to live externally, and then to surround ourselves with the things best suited for that mode of life, whatever it may be. This, however, commonplace as it sounds, is so seldom done, that it must be thought a thing extremely difficult to do. Look about you, reader, and ask yourself, how many people you know who live as they really like to live, and let the world go by. There are such people. I know such in my own circle, but there are not many of them, and it certainly is not the way of the world at large. But, whoever will try the experiment will find the reward in peace, and serenity, and real comfort, so abounding, that it will be no longer a query with him whether he shall continue it or not. And he will find that the question of furniture will disappear from the catalogue of vexations, because there is always provision in the world for every reasonable want. Every country, too, has its own models, and was at one time satisfied with its own — that is, the mass of the people were satisfied, though in every country, at all times, the rich have preferred something borrowed and exotic.

> " I would give thilke Morpheus
>   *   *   *   *   *
> If he woll make me sleepe alite,
> Of downe of pure doves white
> I woll give him a feather bed,
> Raied with gold, and right well cled
> In fine black sattin *d'outremere ;*
> And many a pillow, and every bere,
> Of *cloth of raines* to slepe on soft,
> Him there not need to turne oft."

Their satins must come from over seas, and homespun will not do, but they must go for cloth to some foreign town of Rennes, else they cannot rest in their beds. But the charm of every house is to find the people in it self-contained, and taking their pleasure and their comfort where they can, in the things that come to them, rather in what they have had to seek painfully and far.

Yet it is not worth while to ignore the fashion altogether, nor to insist on having things entirely different from those our neighbors have. I know there is a great deal of ridicule expended upon people who follow the fashion; but we ought to reflect that not to follow the fashion (the question is now of ways of living, of dress, and of manners) is found, in the long run, to be expensive, not only in money, but in time, and really takes away our attention too much from matters better worth while. The young man who gave his whole mind to the tying of his cravat could not, of course, give any of his mind to higher things; and if we fuss too much, or fuss at all, for that matter, over our coats, and trowsers, and gloves, and hats, we soon find we are on the wrong road. It is no better to worry ourselves over our house-furniture, and to insist upon having ideal and faultless surroundings. If we have things about us different from what the way of the world provides, it ought to be because we came across them naturally, and liked them, not because we were trying to be peculiar.

This is the good general rule, and the following it would help settle many difficulties that we hear people complaining of every day. Much of the trouble we have in getting furniture to suit us comes from our wanting things that do not suit us. We must have something that somebody else has or has not. We must either follow the fashion or lead the fashion. The last thing we think of is to please ourselves. A young couple heroically determined that when they were married they would live as comfortably as they could on the smallest income that would be theirs; and that for no fashion's sake, nor for any fidgety conventional friend's sake, would they go to any expense that would give them a minute's uneasiness. The husband was a professional man, fond of books and pictures; the wife was womanly, pleased in her own work, in her books and stitchery, and could touch the piano; and when evening came was pleased with what pleased him. "Flats" had not yet been introduced, and between a "whole house" and a boarding-house (the latter the last resort of despairing young married people) there seemed no middle ground, nor was any, until it occurred to one of them—they never could tell which one it was to whom the happy thought was due—to take a whole house and live in the upper floors, and, reserving a corner of the cellar for coals, to let the rest of the house to somebody else. This they did, and straightway went to work to furnish their floor with the best-looking furniture they could get without hunting too far. In the artist circle, and the circle of young lawyers and budding literary folk, and architects, and the Utopians generally, this upper floor became a synonym for domestic paradise; and, indeed, a prettier place had not then been seen in New-York. But it soon became whispered abroad —that is, in the course of two years or so—that anxious friends, moving in the upper circles of society, and sadly missing the aid and comfort these two were to have brought to those benighted regions, had so fretted and worried these happy young people, and had teased them so about the world, and what it was saying, and what it was thinking about doing, that at last they wearily succumbed, and let a fine house be bought for them, as ugly and anti-domestic as a New-York brown-stone front knows so well to be; and there they went, and there a charming and successful experiment came to a common-place ending.

Suppose this an imaginary story; but it is a type of the trouble everybody finds in living in his own way. Society does not regard with approval such departure from the common road, and the ruts are made so easy for us all to roll along in, there is small temptation to risk upsetting by trying unaccustomed paths.

However, my purpose is not to recommend eccentricity, nor even a modified Bohemianism. I have no mission to preach a crusade against luxury and bad taste; nor have I a hope that anything I can say will bring back simplicity and good taste. I am not at all sure that my own taste is good, or that I can depend upon its being good at all times. If I am pushed to the wall with a question as to my right to be heard in this matter, I can only say that, after much tribulation, I have reached a point where simplicity seems to me a good part of beauty, and utility only beauty in a mask; and I have no prouder nor more pretending aim than to suggest how this truth may be expressed in the furniture and decoration of our homes.

THANKSGIVING FOR HIS HOUSE.

Lord, thou hast given me a cell,
　　Wherein to dwell;
A little house, whose humble roof
　　Is weather proof;
Under the sparres of which I lie
　　Both soft, and drie;
Where thou, my chamber for to ward,
　　Hast set a guard
Of harmlesse thoughts, to watch and keep
　　Me, while I sleep.
Low is my porch, as is my fate,
　　Both void of state;
And yet the threshold of my doore
　　Is worne by th' poore,
Who thither come, and freely get
　　Good words, or meat.
　　　　Like as my parlour, so my hall
　　　　　　And kitchin 's small:
　　　　A little butterie, and therein
　　　　　　A little byn,
　　　　Which keeps my little loafe of bread
　　　　　　Unchipt, unflead;
　　　　Some brittle sticks of thorne or briar
　　　　　　Make me a fire,
　　　　Close by whose living coale I sit,
　　　　　　And glow like it.

Lord, I confesse too, when I dine,
　　The pulse is thine,
And all those other bits, that bee
　　There placed by Thee;
The worts, the purslain, and the messe
　　Of water cresse
Which of thy kindnesse thou hast sent;
　　And my content
Makes those, and my beloved beet
　　To be more sweet.
'T is Thou that crownest my glittering hearth
　　With guiltlesse mirthe,
And givest me wassaile bowls to drink,
　　Spic'd to the brink.
　　　　Lord, 't is thy plenty-dropping hand
　　　　　　That soiles my land,
　　　　And giv'st me, for my bushell sowne,
　　　　　　Twice ten for one;
　　　　Thou mak'st my teeming hen to lay
　　　　　　Her egg each day;
　　　　Besides my healthful ewes to bear
　　　　　　Me twins each yeare;
　　　　The while the conduits of my kine
　　　　　　Run creame for wine:

All these, and better thou dost send
　　Me, to this end,
That I should render, for my part,
　　A thankfull heart;
Which, fir'd with incense, I resigne
　　As wholly Thine;
But the acceptance, that must be,
　　O Lord, by Thee.

HERRICK.

CHAPTER I.

THE ENTRANCE.

A FEW words, in the beginning, about the "Hall," as, in our American love of fine names, we are wont to call what, in nine cases out of ten, even in houses of pretension, is nothing but an entry or passage-way. A hall *(aula)* must be a large room, large at least in proportion to the size of the house; and such a hall it is rare to see in our modern city houses. Our old-fashioned houses had often halls; I remember some in houses about the Common in Boston, and some in old towns like Gloucester and Hingham, that were handsome, and that. seen to-day, give a pleasant idea of the comfort and substantial elegance enjoyed by many not over-rich people in old times, when the population was not so thick as it is to-day. In city houses, particularly in New-York, where I believe we are more scrimped for room, and where even the richest people are obliged to squeeze themselves into a less number of square feet than in any other city in the world calling itself great, there is often a sufficient excuse for these dismal, narrow, ill-lighted entry-ways, but there is no excuse for them in our country houses. As in meeting a man or a woman, so in entering a house, the first impression generally goes a great way in shaping our judgment.

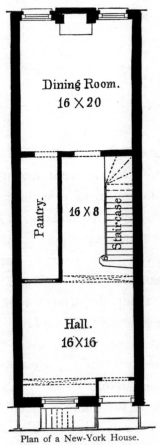

Dining Room.
16 X 20

Pantry.

16 X 8

Staircase

Hall.
16 X 16

Plan of a New-York House.
No. 1.

If, on passing the door, we find ourselves in a passage six feet wide, with a hat-stand on one side reducing it to four feet, and the bottom step of the staircase coming to within six feet of the door-way in front of us, and a gaselier dropping to within a foot of our head, we get an impression of something that is not precisely generosity, and which is not removed either by finding the drawing-room overfurnished, or by the fact that the hat-rack was made by Herter, that the carpet on the stairs is Wilton, and that the gaselier is one of Tiffany's imported masterpieces.

Of course, none of us are to blame for the smallness of our entry-ways. Our landlords must be called to account for this defect, and all they can say in excuse is, that house-building is a thing partly of necessity and partly of fashion. "When there was ground enough," the landlords will say, "when lots 25 x 100 were the rule, and not, as now, the exception, we built good-sized

"She 'll be down in a minute, sir."
No. 2.

houses and gave wide enough halls; now that people are
obliged to be content with two-thirds of a lot (houses sixteen
feet wide being common in New-York), it is not possible to

have anything but narrow entry-ways—a hall is out of
the question." This is not exactly as the landlords say.
There are houses in New-York—I once had a friend who
lived in one, and I always recall the little box with pleasure
—which, though among the very smallest, are better
provided in the way of hall than many of the largest
dwellings. The house I speak of had an entry that might
fairly be called a hall, for it was sixteen feet wide, and
nearly as long: the accompanying plan (No. 1) will show
how it was obtained. The house was sixteen feet wide,
and, as will be seen, the first floor was taken up with the
dining-room, pantry, staircase, and the hall. The second
floor had two rooms, one in front and one at the rear,
with a large open hall (not a dark room) between them,
and above were the bedrooms in two stories.

All I am concerned with now is the arrangement of the
first floor, which seems to me, if we must have small houses,
one that met satisfactorily the demands both of comfort
and of good looks. On entering the front door—the house
was what is called an "English basement," and the sill of
the front door was only eighteen inches from the sidewalk
—we found ourselves in a narrow vestibule, the outer door
of which was always wholly or one-half open. The inner
door being passed, there was a generous, hospitable space,
which was thus disposed of. The vestibule was, as the
reader will see, taken off this open space, and the recess
formed by the left side of the vestibule and the left wall
of the house was used as a bay-window to be filled with
plants. Against the right-hand wall there was nothing

placed, in order that the line from the front door to the stairs might be unobstructed, but some framed engravings were hung there, while against the opposite wall, was a table with a generous mirror—for, to parody Emerson, "All mankind loves a looking-glass"—and pegs for hats, and a rack for umbrellas. A settee stood against the end wall of the pantry, and this was all the little hall contained. With its ample space, its dark painted and shellacked floor shining beyond the edges of one of those pretty rugs made in Philadelphia of the clippings of tapestry carpets, its box of ivy in the window, its shining mirror, and its two Braun autotypes, I am sure there was no hall in the city, no matter how rich the man it might belong to, that had a more cheerful, hospitable look than that of my friend's house.

Even there, however, pains were taken to keep everything down. Sixteen feet square is a sizable hall, but it may be made to look small—as any room may—by being furnished with things out of proportion. Heavy-framed pictures or engravings on the walls, or sprawling patterns on the oil-cloth or the carpet, large pieces of furniture, fashionably clumsy, gawkily designed *à-la-mode*, and a bouncing gaselier in mid-air, will make a mere cubby-hole out of a room which by judicious treatment could get full credit for all its cubic inches. Remembering this, the hall I speak of was furnished with only those things that were really needed (the plant-stand and the prints must be excepted), and these were made to suit themselves to the situation. The mirror was a large, generous-looking affair (almost a horse-glass, as the English cabinet-makers of the last century translated *cheval*-glass), and the shelf under it was rather long and narrow,—a shelf of mahogany

A Bit of Regnault.
No. 3.

supported on brackets of the same wood.   The hat-and-umbrella-rack was an affair of the same sort as the Moorish gun-rack shown in cut No. 3, with pegs for the hats, and rests for the umbrellas and canes.   This Moorish gun-rack, Mr. Lathrop has copied from a photograph of one of Regnault's pictures, "The Guardian of the Harem," an Algerian subject. It would make, with the shelf above it, a most convenient hat-and-umbrella-rack for the entry; but, of course, its pleasantest use would be to support some choice arms on the rack, and vases, or casts, on the shelves. With the Turks and Algerians these shelves are common enough, and they are painted all over in bright, harmonious colors; flowers and ornaments on a blue or green-blue ground—the same sort of decoration that is seen on their camphor trunks, and on cradles and family chests and cupboard doors in Germany. If it could only be done well by our ordinary painters—if they had the natural eye and feeling 'for it which even these rough Turks and rude Fatherland peasants have, we could get a little more color and cheerfulness into our rooms.

These racks look coarsely made, seen near at hand, and the decoration is rather coarse also, but they are well designed, and the painting on them is effective. I wish they were more easily to be had. What a difference it shows in the taste of the two peoples, that, both of them, feeling the want of a contrivance of this sort, these barbarians, as we absurdly call them, should have supplied their want by a device at once pretty and convenient (and cheap as ours, at home, no doubt), while we are content with ugly things made of tiresome walnut, with hooks of brass or iron, convenient enough, but unnecessarily ugly. However, if one prefers something with a modern European look, there is a contrivance, made in Vienna, of Russia leather—two broadish strips of leather edged with brass, with a brass ring at the end of each to hang it by, and with brass hooks projecting from its face, on which either umbrella and cane, or hat and bonnet, can be suspended. This affair is pretty enough, but it has rather a temporary appearance, and can hardly be seriously recommended for a hall or entry-way that is much used. But there is really no need to fall back on one of the ungainly structures of wood or iron that are so much in use.

If one has only a passage-way to deal with, as is the case in nine houses out of ten, all that can be done is, to study the same simplicity. The mirror and hat-rack shown in cut No. 2, with the little bench beneath it, is taken from an entry that is even narrower than is common with us. But, while these things answer all needs, they seem to take up no room at all. And they are so pretty that the glance one gives at them prevents our noticing the narrowness of the space in which they stand.

The settee in the entry of my friend's house was of Chinese make—teak-wood, with a marble seat and with a circular slab of marble ornamenting the back. At that time such settees were uncommon, as was all Chinese furniture; but it can always be found nowadays at Sypher's, where there are often some very handsome pieces. If one should find the settees too large (and they are too large for the rooms of most of us), there are arm-chairs of the same material that look well in small space, and give distinction to the most unpretending entry. Teak-wood-and-marble does not sound like a comfortable combination;

but these settees and arm-chairs are comfortable, though there is nothing soft about them. They are not recommended for the parlor or sitting-room, however, but only for the hall, where it is true their comfort will be wasted on messenger-boys, book-agents, the census-man, and the bereaved lady who offers us soap at merely nominal prices, with the falsetto story of her woes thrown in. As visitors of this class are the only ones who will sit in the hall, considerations of comfort may be allowed to yield to picturesqueness, and any chair or bench that gives us that will serve, since, being designed to sit on, there will surely be comfort enough left for the occasion. If a lighter seat is wanted, there are several sorts that may be picked up ; a Venetian chair—either the antiques themselves, or the modern copies—the seat, back, and supports (one before and one behind) all made of flat pieces of wood, inlaid with pearl or ivory, or carved with bold carving, or pierced, and the solid parts decorated with color. These chairs (unless it be the richly carved ones) are not necessarily costly, the painted ones ought to be cheap, but the finer kinds are by no means uncommon at such shops as those of Mr. Sypher or Mr. Hawkins.

Cut No. 4 is a drawing of an inlaid Italian chair— which may be recommended for the entry or hall. This example is perhaps too costly for the purses of most of us ; but it was the only one within reach,—it belongs to the Messrs. Cottier,—and serves to show the model I had in my mind. Some of these chairs are made of a lighter wood, and inlaid all over with mother-of-pearl, arranged in geometrical patterns. These are manufactured to this day in Italy, and can be bought there at reasonable prices; but such things are not regular importations, and if they are found in our shops,—in Sypher's or Hawkins's, for instance,—they have been

Ebony and Ivory.
No. 4.

bought by those dealers at some family break-up, or from some traveler parting with his old trophies, and now off for fresh fields and pastures new. Some pretty stools of wood, thickly inlaid with mother-of-pearl, were in the Egyptian and Morocco Departments at the Exhibition; but they had hardly time to alight from their journey before they were picked up by diligent seekers after things out of the common. Another variety of this chair comes from Italy, and, keeping the same general shape, varies the flat surface with much bold carving. These chairs are often met with; but, of course, they vary in quality of design. Still, I have several times seen chairs with old Italian carving at Sypher's that I, for one, should be glad to own. Such pieces will, in most cases, prove to have descended from New-York families who, thirty or forty years ago, cáme home from Europe, where they had been living, keeping house, and educating their children, and who found it not unprofitable to bring back much of their household gear with them.

Cut No. 5 is a good chair for a hall, and comfortable, too, for a writing-chair. This example came from the "Lawrence Room" of the Boston Museum of Fine Arts.

In Mrs. Oliphant's "The Makers of Florence" there is a pretty cut of Savonarola's cell in the convent of San Marco, showing his desk at which he worked, and, in front of it, a chair similar to this.

Another chair, called the Abbot's chair, from a model existing, I believe, at Glastonbury, used to be occasionally seen in our curios-•
ity shops; but, of late, I have not met with one of them.

"I took you for a Joint-stool."
No. 5.

What ought to be sought for in arranging a hall or entry is, I think, to give a pleasing look to the house at the very entrance. How many halls look as if the house had put its hands behind its back, and met you with a pursed-up mouth, and a "What 's your business?" Nobody ought to be willing to have visitors get that impression. Even the messenger-boy

will start off with more alacrity when he hears your signal,
if he remembers the Turkish gun-rack or the photograph
of Dürer's rabbit in your entry, and the bereaved soap-
vender may moderate her falsetto a little in the cheerful
company of your flowers.

Before leaving this part of my subject, I will describe
more in detail the lower story of my friend's house, at the
risk of leaving the decorator's ground for that of the architect. This floor was only ten feet in height, but even this
is too high for an easy stairs, unless more room is given
for it on the floor than is common. Perhaps, however, the
builder's wife had been a martyr to the ladder-stairs of
our city houses, and, thinking of her, he let his nineteen
steps stretch along sixteen feet, so that with risers a little
over six inches, and treads a little over ten inches, the
ascent was reasonably easy. The supports of the hand-rail
were of iron, and were screwed to the casing outside the
steps, so that the width of the stairs was not intruded
upon. This is the way the balusters are fixed to the
stairs in all the new houses in Paris, and it works well in
practice. The newel-post was made as light as possible,
consistent with its duties, instead of, as is the rule in New-
York generally, being made as heavy as can be contrived.
The passage to the dining-room, between the stairs and
the pantry, was eight feet wide, leaving three feet for the
stairs and five feet for the pantry, which was, however,
nearly sixteen feet long. This pantry contained a dumb-
waiter, a silver-tub, and a china-closet; it was lighted, or
aired rather, for the gas was always going, by a pretty

lunette window in the end facing the front door, and by a window on the side opposite the stairs.

The dining-room was sixteen feet wide (the full width of the house) and twenty feet deep. As sixteen feet is scrimp width for a dining-room, unless (as a servant said lately to a lady who wanted to hire her) "you do your own reachin'," it would have been a mistake to diminish it still further by putting a chimney-pier on either side. The builder had, therefore, carried up his chimney between the windows,—a great improvement every way, although not, I believe, an economical one in building. The end wall of the house had to be much thicker in order to prevent the air in the chimney chilling in cold weather, but, both externally and internally, the advantage was all on the side of good looks. The chimney was so managed as to be a handsome feature, and within, the thick walls gave the old-fashioned window-seat, which every young lover of reading knows the pleasure of. Besides, on entering the dining-room, in the season of fires, the family saw the welcome hearth and the bright mirror; and, when all were seated, the fire was in no one's way. The servant had room enough to go about the table without squeezing, and the served had room enough and to spare. On the whole, this was a comfortable house, in spite of its "only sixteen feet," and the wonder is, that the general plan, with whatever modification and improvement can be devised, is not more followed, since we are all the time building narrow houses.

Just a word about the way of lighting these small entries of ours. The gas-fixtures, which depend from the ceiling, are almost all too large, and are clumsy and meaningless in design.   They are inconvenient to light and to put out, and, in overcoat time, are responsible for many a scarified knuckle, the entry-ways being seldom large enough to swing a coat

Pretty by Day or Night.
No. 6.

in, and the gas-fixtures hanging low.   A simple bracket like the one shown in cut No. 6 is the best for ordinary purposes.   It is both convenient and handsome.   In one case we know of, an old-fash-ioned hall lantern has been furbished up and turned into a gas-burner; but this was partly from economy (the lantern, when all was done, costing much more than the most expensive bronze chandelier!) and partly from a desire to keep an old piece.   It will be found, however, that a gas-burner which shall meet all requirements of usefulness, right size, and good taste, is a difficult thing to discover.

It was not only the Eastern people who had the hospi-table custom of offering a guest water for washing, when he entered the house.   The custom passed over into Europe, with others as hospitable, and descended down to a time quite near our own.   Of course, the offer to show a guest to a room where he can repair any damages that may have occurred on the road between his own house and that of his host, and can put on the last touches of

preparation for dinner, is a regular part of our own ceremonial, and is perhaps our translation of the Eastern rite.
But our ancestors were in this, as in many things, more
direct than we, and this very directness made many of
their ways more comfortable. If they did not keep up the
actual servant, with ewer, basin, and towel, they put these
utensils where the visitor could get them without trouble,
and they made them so attractive to look at that even if
there were no servants to offer them, they pleasantly
offered themselves. The vignette at the side of this page
—a corner from Albert Dürer's wood-cut, "The Birth of
the Virgin," drawn from the original by Mr. Lathrop, and
engraved by Mr. King—will hint to the reader, in a rude
way, how the old people used to
contrive to do their hospitality—
one point of it, at least—by proxy.
In a niche, sometimes, as here,
but as often against the plain
wall, they suspended a hollow ball
of brass or copper from a chain,
and provided it with a cock. Below this globe there was fastened
against the wall a basin or trough,
which, in some cases, as in this
of St. Anna's House, was provided
with a pipe by which the water

A Corner in St. Anna's House.
No. 7.

that had been used could be run off. In old Dutch pictures,
these vessels are to be seen of different shapes and sizes,
and, as their use has lately been revived, we find modern

artists also painting them.   There was a pretty water-color
at Goupil's lately, in which one of these vessels, large and
handsome, and made of *faience*, was the hero.   When
pottery began to be employed in the place of metal, these
"cisterns," as they were called, were made of earthenware,
and even of porcelain, and with their bold forms and

picturesque ornamentation, they were
certainly handsome pieces of furniture,
and useful as handsome.   In Jacque-
mart's pretty little book, "Les Mer-
veilles de la Céramique," there is a
good example engraved, and they are
produced to-day as a regular article
of manufacture by the French houses
that make a specialty of reviving old
styles in earthenware and porcelain.

Cut No. 7 shows one of these
earthenware cisterns that is in actual
use in an American country-house,
where it is set up on the porch, and is
found of great use in the summer time.

Faience Cistern.
No. 8.

Cut No. 9 is a translation, by Mr. King, of the first
drawing made by Mr. Sandier for these articles.   This little
wash-stand was not intended for a bedroom, but for a
small room off a hall or entry-way, where a person might
wash his hands without the trouble of going upstairs.   It
is very simply made of four uprights cut out at the upper
ends to receive the basin, and held together by a shelf
half-way down, which holds the soap-tray, and by two braces

at the foot. There is no decoration beyond a slight molding on the edges of the shelf and a little cutting on the upper and lower ends of the uprights. The towel is on an old-fashioned roller.

Sancta Simplicitas.
No. 9.

"THE messenger made haste and found Argalus at a castle of his own, sitting in a parlor with the fair Parthenia; he reading aloud the stories of Hercules, she by him, as to hear him read; but while his eyes looked on the book, she looked on his eyes, sometimes staying him with some pretty question, not so much to be resolved of the doubt as to give him occasion to look upon her. A happy couple, he joying in her, she joying in herself because she enjoyed him; both increased their riches by giving to each other, each making one life double because they made a double life one, where desire never wanted satisfaction nor satisfaction ever bred satiety: he ruling because she would obey; or, rather, because she would obey, he therein ruling."—SIDNEY'S ARCADIA.

"Our little habitation was situated at the foot of a sloping hill, sheltered with a beautiful underwood behind, and a prattling river before; on one side a meadow, on the other a green. Nothing could exceed the neatness of my little inclosure: the elms and hedge-rows appearing with inexpressible beauty. My house consisted of but one story, and was covered with thatch, which gave it an air of great snugness; the walls on the inside were nicely whitewashed, and my daughters undertook to adorn them with pictures of their own designing. Though the same room served us for parlor and kitchen, that only made it the warmer. Besides, as it was kept with the utmost neatness, the dishes, plates and coppers being well scoured and all disposed in bright rows on the shelves, the eye was agreeably relieved, and did not want richer furniture."—THE VICAR OF WAKEFIELD:

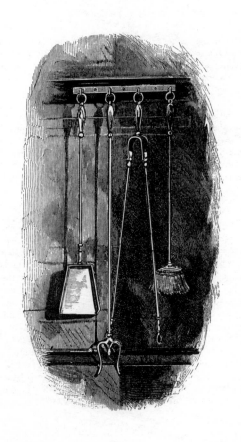

CHAPTER II.

THE LIVING-ROOM.

I USE the word "Living-Room" instead of "Parlor," because I am not intending to have anything to say about parlors. As these chapters are not written for rich people's reading, and as none but rich people can afford to have a room in their houses set apart for the pleasures of idleness, nothing would be gained by talking about such rooms. I should like to persuade a few young people who are just pushing their life-boat off shore to venture into deeper and more adventurous seas, that it will make their home a great deal more cheerful and home-like if they concentrate their leisure, in-door hours in one place, and do not attempt to keep up a room in which they themselves shall be strangers, and which will make a stranger of every friend who comes into it. Happily, the notion that such a room is absolutely necessary to every respectable family is no longer so prevalent, nor held so binding as it once was. A good many people who were children in New England fifty years ago will remember the disagreeable parlor of

the period, into which they were only permitted to go on
Sunday afternoons, though they often forgot to go there
even on that grim holiday, but preferred the nursery or,
may be, the kitchen, where there was nothing too good to
use, and some comfort might be had. The country houses
were worse in this respect than the city houses; yet

"The Young Scholar and His Wife."
No. 10.

they had this advantage, that, besides the unused parlor,
there was almost always a real living-room, and it was
oftenest on the sunny side of the house, the shady side
being chosen for the parlor, whose carpet must not be
exposed to the danger of fading by the admission of the
sun. In the country, then, one could easily forget the

existence of the parlor, and the real life of the family went cheerily on without it. The parlor was opened on Sundays, on Thanksgiving-day, for funerals, for weddings, and on the one or two occasions in the year when the awful solemnity of a formal "party" was gone through; but it was carefully shunned on more cheerful occasions, such as tea-fights, candy-pulls, sleighing-parties, and other "good times." But in the cities, the living-room was sacrificed to the social necessities, and was generally upstairs or down-stairs, the main floor being given to the dining-room and parlor.

How much money has been wasted, how much capital let lie idle, in furnishing and keeping up these ceremonial deserts! They are useless and out of place in the houses of nine-tenths of our Americans. They rightly belong to those houses where a great deal of merely formal social intercourse is carried on, where domestic life does not have time to exist, or where the position of the family is such that provision has to be made for a life apart from the domestic life. How few families among our people are in this last condition! Yet I could fill all my chapter with illustrations of the absurd way in which the comfort and domestic happiness of families have been destroyed or hindered by the supposed need of making provision for a social life outside the home life of the family. The best room in the house is taken for the use of strangers, furnished with articles that are avowedly too expensive to be used, and the cost of which makes a serious hole in the marriage-money, and a double interest has to be paid on this expenditure—one in cash, the other in just so

much subtraction made from the sincerity and naturalness
that ought to rule in our daily life.

Let us begin, then, with the frank abandonment of any
formal parlor, but, taking the largest, and pleasantest, and
most accessible room in the house, let us give it up to the
wife and children in the day-time, and to the meeting of the
whole family when evening comes.   There is not much need
at the present time to emphasize this suggestion, for it is one
which experience and necessity have already made to a good
many people; and now that the problem "How to get a
dwelling at a rent within moderate means" is being solved
by the increase of "flats" and "apartment houses," the
"parlor" must be given up, there being no provision made
for it in the common plans.   But it is by no means my
notion that the living-room should be a homely, matter-of-
fact apartment, consecrated to the utilities, while the Muses
and Graces are left to amuse themselves in the hall.   On
the contrary, we want in the living-room, for a foundation,
that the furniture shall be the best designed and best made
that we can afford, all of it necessary to our comfort, and
intended to be used; not an article to be allowed that does
not earn its living, and cannot prove its right to be there.
These wants being first provided for, we will then admit
the ornament of life—casts, pictures, engravings, bronzes,
books, chief nourishers in life's feast; but in the beginning
these are to be few, and the greatest care is to be taken
in admitting a new-comer.   The room ought to represent
the culture of the family,—what is their taste, what feeling
they have for art; it should represent themselves, and not

other people; and the troublesome fact is, that it will and must represent them, whether its owners would let it or no. After they have secured the few pieces of furniture that must be had, and made sure that they are what they ought to be, if the young people have some money left to get a picture, an engraving, or a cast, they ought to go to work to supply this want as seriously as they would the other, which seems the more necessary, but in reality is not a bit more necessary. I look upon this living-room as an important agent in the education of life; it will make a great difference to the children who grow up in it, and to all whose experience is associated with it, whether it be a beautiful and cheerful room, or a homely and bare one, or a merely formal and conventional one. All that gives dignity or poetry to this subject, or makes it allowable for a reasonable man to give much thought to it, is its relation to education. For it has a serious relation to education, and plays an important part in life, and, therefore, deserves to be thought about a great deal more than it is. It is no trifling matter, whether we hang poor pictures on our walls or good ones, whether we select a fine cast or a second-rate one. We might almost as well say it makes no difference whether the people we live with are first-rate or second-rate.

But we are not yet come to the pictures and casts. We must do with our imaginary room as we would do with the real one—get it furnished first; provide it with limbs and members before we put a soul into it. Let us begin, then, with a word or two about carpets. The camp

of young married people is divided into two factions on
the question: "Whether to have carpets or rugs?" Rugs
have novelty on their side, and that is nine points in
fashion's law, but there is, I think, much more to be said
for them than simply that "they are the latest thing out."
Carpets are associated, in the minds of many of us, with
ideas of comfort in early days; the custom of having them
came over from England, and was kept up here, partly
because of inhe.ited ideas of what was comfortable; partly
because the condition of domestic life that made them
serviceable in England existed here as well as there; and
for another reason, apart from these, if, indeed, it were not
rather the effect than the cause—I mean the poor way in
which we make our floors of planks, too wide, and badly
joined. Even in our best New-York houses the floors are
meanly laid, and in the second and third class houses they
are so bad that they must be covered with carpets whether
the occupants wish it or no.

I suppose the housekeeper's argument for carpets is
akin to her argument for "tidies" and "slips," and the
other expedients by which the great enemy, "dirt," is
imagined to be circumvented. Carpets are great hiders of
dirt and dust, and a new broom easily restores them when
too much dirt and dust are collected on their surface. But,
then, they are great holders of dirt and dust as well, and
apart from the waste of money in covering places that do
not need covering, the question of health involved in the
use of carpets is a very serious one. The large pieces
of furniture, that in all our rooms stand against the

wall—the sofas, the piano-fortes, the sideboards, the book-cases, the bedsteads, the wardrobes, the wash-stands, the bureaus—do not need the carpet under them; the carpet on which they stand represents just so much wasted money, and yet we go on putting down yards of carpet where they are never seen, where the dust collects, and is only attacked in weekly sweepings, and where it keeps a sort of color, while the rest changes color and fades. Let any one give a rug a fair trial, and he will find for himself how much less dust is made in the room, how much more easily the room is kept clean, and how much more manageable the furniture is when the time for sweeping or dusting comes round.

The principal objection to rugs is their first cost, which, for good ones, is as yet considerable. I do not like to see several rugs in a room, but prefer one large one, large enough, that is, to cover the whole floor, up to, or nearly up to, the large pieces of furniture. In no case should any one of these large pieces rest upon the rug, for it ought to be an every-day, or at least an *any*-day matter, to turn it up and brush underneath it, or to roll it up and carry it out on a balcony to be shaken or swept, and this will never be if some heavy table or piano, or book-case, has to be dislodged for the purpose. Where there are several smallish rugs in a room, or even several of good size, so long as in either case they do not cover the whole of the free floor, they are apt to prove impediments—to trip up children and old people, and they destroy the unity of the room, give it a patchy look, which is a thing important to avoid. It is better, on all accounts, to buy a rug large enough to cover all of the floor we wish to cover, even if it strain our purse a little, for a good rug will last a life-time, and, indeed, I know rugs that are well on their way to last a second life-time. The best Turkey, Persian, and Smyrna rugs are made by hand, of pure wool, and are so thick that if, as sometimes happens in their own country, a brazier of coals is upset on one of them, the charred portion, which, in the case of a Brussels carpet, could never be effaced, will disappear after a few days' wear. After much using a good Eastern rug, walking on the best body Brussels is like walking on the wooden floor to the feeling. To an artistic eye, too (and how much of this writing must be content with the judgment and approval of artistic people!), an Eastern rug that is handsome to begin with, grows handsomer with time and use, and even one that was a little staring and pertinacious at first, gets toned down and subdued by being long walked over, just as if it were a human being.

It may be remarked, in passing, that there are ugly Eastern rugs as well as ugly Western carpets. The Turks, especially, who sell a great many carpets to England, and nowadays to America, often ship a lot that are so bad, we must believe their rascally makers have learned of some French artist the phrase: "Anything is good enough for those Americans." But the Turkey carpets proper are only good when the weavers confine themselves to reds and blues, though they sometimes do a very successful thing in mustard-yellow, but the true shade of this is rare.

Just a word more as to the color of the rugs to be employed. The Eastern designers know too much, or have too correct an instinct, to use a great deal of white in their designs; they get all the light and brightness they want without it, and even when they use white it is not pure white, but gray, and used with extreme economy at that; at least in all the successful carpets. It is true, these Eastern carpets are sometimes found with what is called a white ground, and these are among the handsomest, especially when they come from Persia: but the white, in the first place, is not white, but some tint that only looks white by force of juxtaposition, and, then, what there is of it is used in so bold a way and so broken up, that all we feel, in looking at it, is, that it is cheerful and festive, whereas the Eastern rugs we are most used to seeing, and especially the Turkey rugs, are somber and rich rather than gay. However, a "white ground" carpet is rather a holiday friend, and is not to be recommended unless the room it is intended for be a darkish one, or the character of the household be such that it will not be subjected to the ravages of children and husbands with dirty boots. Otherwise, choose a thick rug with a pattern a good deal broken, and with nothing very odd or noticeable in the design, and let it take its fortunes. If it be only used and not abused, it will improve with time, and outwear more than one Brussels carpet.

If people object to rugs, there is at least the comfort left them of knowing that they can get carpets better made than ever carpets were before, and with designs that can only be matched for elegance and beauty with those of Persian rugs. These are English carpets, designed and made by the houses of Morris & Co. and Cottier & Co. These carpets are so handsome and so well made, that, if one can afford it, I would advise having squares made of them, with the borders that are sold with them.

There are, however, other and cheaper resources. They make, in Philadelphia, a pretty and serviceable rug out of the ravelings of fine carpets, and in Boston I have seen the same material. There is, of course, no set pattern, but a pleasant mingling of hues, and the texture makes it agreeable to the foot, though it is, perhaps, more comfortable as a rug over a matting in summer, than as a sole dependence in winter. Still, it is something it is well to know of. These carpets come in breadths, like common carpeting, and can be made into rugs of any size. They have no "right" side, but can be turned at pleasure, and the edges will not curl up as those of rugs made of ordinary carpeting are apt to. Those manufactured by William Pollock, carpet manufacturer, 937 Market street, Philadelphia, second door below Tenth street, are highly recommended, and they are also made by some firm in Providence, Rhode Island. They make, in Scotland and in Holland, a carpeting of a mixture of wool and jute, which is dyed a deep maroon, and is about the thickness of Brussels carpeting. A good way of using this is to make a square or parallelogram the size of the clear space of the floor when all the large pieces of furniture are in their places. This is laid down and held in its place by rings sewed to the under edge, and slipped over small brass-headed nails, driven down close to the floor. This makes a comfortable footing, and is easily removed when necessary. Then in the center of the room, or before the fire, or in front of the sofa, lay down a bright-colored Smyrna rug.

But, the reader will say: "The floor—the floor's the thing. What are we to do with our floors?" If we have a sound floor of narrow pine boards, each board well driven home to its neighbor,—a thing, it must be confessed, rare to find in an American house,—a good result can be produced by staining, and finishing with shellac. But, in ordinary cases, this is impracticable; for the floors are too badly laid in our houses to make it possible to bring them to a good appearance by any such superficial treatment as this.

With a bad floor, which it is proposed not to cover entirely with a carpet, only one of two things can be done. The handsomest thing is to lay down a parquet floor, of what is called wood-carpeting. But this, with a rug after-ward, is a very expensive way of getting out of the diffi-culty, and I therefore advise that we should meekly accept the situation, and, sending for a house-painter who knows his business, let him first fill up all the cracks, knot-holes, shrinks, seams, flaws, etc., with red putty,—it will take a good deal,—and then *stain* it (not paint it) carefully in a dark brown, warmed with a little red, and, over all, a coat of shellac. If this be done well, and allowed to get thor-oughly dried, it will last a long time; but, I believe, when it needs renewing it must be *painted*, as the shellac cannot be removed so completely as to admit of restaining. This makes a handsome floor; but when the rug is down and the furniture in its place, but little of it is seen.

The advantage of a hard-wood floor laid down originally, or of a common floor covered with wood-carpeting, is so great on the score of health and labor-saving, that it would seem as if only the prejudice that comes from old

Italian Fire-screen.
No. 11.

associations could long keep up the fashion of carpets. But, however it may be in the case of a whole house, large or small, to be furnished with carpets, there cannot be much question as to the desirableness of rugs for rooms in flats. One who has tried them will never want to use an ordinary carpet again.

Our modern rooms, especially in our cities, are so small, and, as a rule, so ill-proportioned,—too often long and narrow,—that it is very puzzling to know how to furnish them so as to get in the things we need, and yet to have space left in which to move about. It is too much the fashion, especially here in New-York, for the builders of houses (and it is, of course, only once in a thousand times that an architect designs a dwelling-house in New-York) to put in mantel-pieces, doors, cornices, and all the moldings that are about the doors and windows, by a system of contract supply that takes no account of the differences in size of different houses. Mantel-pieces are got out, for all the principal rooms, of about the same dimensions, the only difference between those for the parlor, dining-room and library, and those for the main bedroom, being, that the bedroom mantel-pieces escape the overloading with badly designed and coarsely executed carving that is bestowed upon the parlor mantel-pieces. Moldings as heavy, though not as handsome, as would be found in a cathedral are run about the doors and windows of small rooms, and moldings no heavier are used in rooms of twice the size. Our houses are treated pretty much as state-prison convicts are—clothes of one pattern and size are provided, and each convict takes his chance. The clothes handed out to him may happen to fit him, but, also, they may not. Here, in the room in which I am writing, a room seventeen feet wide by twenty-two feet long, there is a double door, *six feet wide*, opening out of a narrow passage-way, and sliding-doors, *nine feet wide*, opening into a small bedroom. It is true these big sliding-doors are useful, because, by their opening, they supply all the light that the bedroom gets; but they were not put in because

they were useful.   It is usual in this city, and has been for
forty-odd years, to have a parlor open into the next room
by folding-doors; and all parlors will continue so to open
until this generation of builders shall have passed away.
If these people could be persuaded to employ in designing
their houses a man whose business it is to think what are
the best ways to secure comfort and convenience, we might
have every room supplied with just so much door and
window as it needed and no more, and the mantel-pieces
might be made of sizes proportioned to the rooms they
belong to, and both the mantel-pieces and the doors and
windows might be put where they would be needed, and
where they would best suit the use to which the room is
to be devoted.   We might also see moldings about doors
and windows and in the cornices reduced to proper dimensions, and even, in some cases, dispensed with altogether.
But, as it is, none of these things are likely to be done
or to be left undone: we must take our room as it is, and
treat it accordingly.

Let us begin with the principle, that every piece of
furniture in the room must have a good and clear reason
for being there.   Nothing ought to be placed in the living-
room to diminish the number of cubic feet of air needed
for the support of the occupants that cannot justify its
presence by some actual service it renders to those occupants.   There must be at least one sofa, one large easy-
chair, an ample table, a book-case, a cupboard, and smaller
chairs.   It will be found good for the health, and conducive
to the freshness and simplicity of a small apartment, to get

rid of upholstery and stuffing in our furniture as far as possible. The wooden chairs, and chairs seated with rushes or cane of the old time, were as comfortable as the stuffed and elastic seats we are so fond of. And if we could

Sofa, with Movable Cushions.
No. 12.

consent to come back to something of the old-fashioned austerity, we should find it greatly to our profit in many ways. I do not believe a more comfortable chair can be found than a pattern once in universal use here, but now only seen in old country homes. The seat was of wood, hollowed, and curved as skillfully as if it had once been of soft material, and had been molded to its perfection by an owner of persistently sedentary habit. The seat sloped a little from the front to the back, as every chair-seat ought; was of ample depth, and was inclosed by a slightly sloping back and gently spreading arms. The back was composed of slender rods, and the flat arms were a little broadened and rounded at the ends, offering a pleasant and soothing

object for the hands to play with. The legs of these chairs
flared considerably, but only so much as to give the necessary stability, and they were connected by rungs. Now
these chairs, once in common use all over our eastern
country, and then despised in the growth of luxury and the
desire for stuffed furniture, are come into favor again, and
are bought up at once wherever they are offered for sale.
It is well known, too, what a prosperity the Wakefield
manufacture of rattan furniture is enjoying, and it deserves
it too. Whenever the designs obey the law of the material
employed, and do not try to twist or bend it out of its
own natural and handsome curves, they are sure to be
pleasing to look at and serviceable to use. The Chinese

The same, without Cushions.
No. 13.

make a picturesque and comfortable chair out of the large
shoots of bamboo, and their reclining chairs, with a foot-
rest that can be pushed out or in at pleasure, are almost
indispensable to a house in the country. With such a

chair, and a good hammock, a hermit might set up housekeeping. It would be hard for him to say what he wanted
next. Diogenes would have said he wanted nothing but
to throw away the hammock. And, indeed, the chair I
speak of is bed and table and chair all in one. Further
on, the reader will find a cut of one of these chairs. A
sofa, or settee, that seems to me to answer all one's
reasonable needs, is shown above, in cuts Nos. 12 and 13.
It is long enough to lie upon and take a nap, and deep
enough and low enough to sit upon with comfort. The
cushions are all movable at need, and in summer, if we
choose, we can stow them away and use the sofa as a
settee. As for the coverings of the cushions, we need not be
at a loss, for there has not been in the last fifty years such
a supply of materials for this purpose as there is to-day:
the stuffs themselves of first-rate make, and the designs as
good as ever were produced at any time. We have serges
nowadays, in colors whose delightfulness we all recognize
in the pictures that Alma Tadema, and Morris, and Burne-
Jones and Rossetti paint, colors that have been turning all
the plain girls to beauties of late, and making the beauties
more dangerous than ever—the mistletoe-green, the blue-
green, the duck's-egg, the rose-amber, the pomegranate-
flower, and so forth, and so on,—colors which we owe to
the English poet-artists who are oddly lumped together as
the Pre-Raphaelites, and who made the new rainbow to
confound the scientific decorators who were so sure of what
colors would go together, and what colors would n't. Whoever would get a new sensation, and know for the first

time what delicate or rich fancies of delightful color and softness of touch can be worked with silk and wool, must go to the Messrs. Cottier's shop and learn for himself.

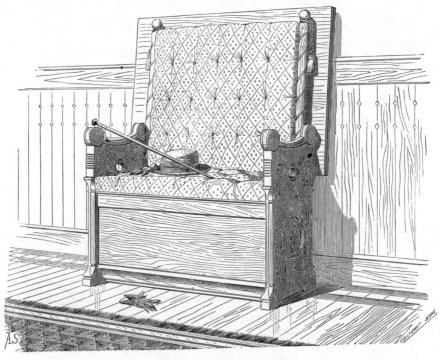

A Settle, convertible into a Table.
No. 14.

It may sometimes happen that a larger table than ordinary may be much needed when maps are to be consulted, or large books examined, or a collection of prints enjoyed by a company of amateurs. Yet, the room is not large enough to permit of such a table standing in it all the time. The common ironing-table of our kitchens, the "settle" of the old days, has served Mr. G. F. Babb as a model for a piece of furniture which may be used either as a sofa or as a table.

> "The chest contrived a double debt to pay,
> A bed by night, a chest of drawers by day."

Mr. Babb's design is more suited to a hall or an office than to a living-room, for the reason that it does not look comfortable to sit on. The seat is too narrow and too high, nor do I like the way in which he has attached the cushions to the top. The round sticks at the sides could

The same, as a Table.
No. 15.

not be secured to the table-top, nor could the cushion be fastened to them, except by a fussy contrivance of a cord twisted about them. Both the cushion on the seat and that against the back are designed to be movable. The cushion on the seat does not need to be secured: its weight and the depth of the seat will keep it always in place. It is made movable in order that the lid of the box beneath (a good place for storing magazines, pamphlets and newspapers) can be opened. The cushion at the back should be held in place by three broad straps fixed at their lower ends, but attached at their other ends to the table-top by means of a button or a buckle. The object of making this cushion movable is only that it may be occasionally beaten, and dusted, or turned; for my plan does n't approve of wrong sides. Each side of these cushions ought to be as good as the other; both of velvet, or both of chintz, or both of bed-ticking. It was all well enough for handsome Charles Brandon to have one side of his horse-cloth of cloth-of-gold, and the other of cloth-of-frieze, with the motto on the former:

> "Cloth-of-gold, do not despise,
> Though thou 'rt matched with cloth-of-frieze;"

and on the other:

> "Cloth-of-frieze, be not too bold,
> Though thou 'rt matched with cloth-of-gold;"

for this was only a quip of the Renaissance time, to show his wit and veil his suit; and, besides, he showed both sides of his jesting horse-cloth in the broad daylight of the tournament. I am sure I shall be upheld by everybody who will try the experiment, in my advice to have no "best side," and no belongings too good for daily use and service.

When this transformed ironing-table is not wanted to play the desk or book-table, as it will only be wanted now and then, it is designed to be a thoroughly comfortable seat, and should be supplied with a small cushion at either end. These cushions are omitted in the drawing, to show the construction of the sofa the better. So, in cut No. 15,

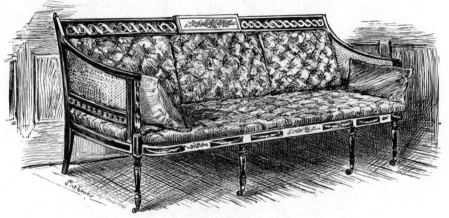

A French Settee.
No. 16.

the two cushions of the seat and of the back are omitted, but this was not intended, for they, of course, remain in their places when the back is lowered to make a table.

In a cut which will find its place later in these pages, there is a design made by Mr. Alexander Sandier (who made the drawings for cuts Nos. 14 and 15, from Mr. George F. Babb's designs) to meet my objection that a piece made after Mr. Babb's design would prove too heavy, and that, besides, it presents some inconveniences. I believe, however, that any one wanting such a combination of sofa and table would find that the common ironing-table, painted and fitted up with cushions covered with chintz or serge, will serve all purposes.

The settee represented with and without its cushions, in cuts Nos. 12 and 13, was not a real one, but was designed for me by Mr. James S. Inglis, who also made the drawings on the block. Cut No. 16 was drawn by Mr. Lathrop, from "the life," and if the reader agrees with

A Friendly Lounge.
No. 17.

me in finding the settee pretty as it is in black-and-white, he would think it far prettier in the original, with its gay decoration. The wood-work is painted with a black ground, relieved with gold, and with medallions in which are brightly painted flowers. The back, the seat and the ends are filled with bamboo woven-work, and this is gilded—a very elegant way of treating bamboo, and not more expensive than painting done as painting should be. This particular settee is furnished with cushions made of a rose-scarlet satin; but, of course, something less costly, and less liable to injury, may easily be found that will please the eye as well. The stuffs called Algériennes, made of silk and cotton, in gay but well-harmonized stripes, are serviceable, and look well to the last; there are serges, too, but probably the prettiest coverings for cushions are the stamped plushes which are now made in England, with patterns and colors that leave nothing to be desired. It will be observed that the cushions of this French settee, like those of the one which was engraved on pages 59 and 60, are movable, and it will also be noted that they are thin. Being the same on both sides, they can be turned frequently, and can be more easily dusted, beaten and aired.

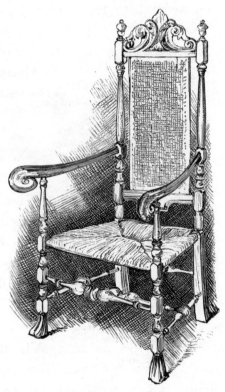

"Now, do be seated!"
No. 18.

Cut No. 17 is a drawing of a piece of furniture, the like of which used to be common in France, and which they called a *chaise longue*. It has no back, except at one end, as an Irishman might say, and it seems

narrower than it is, on account of its length, which admits
of a person lying upon it as comfortably as in a narrow
bed.   The mattress is movable, and the cushion, or cushions,
at the end are movable also; the affair is simply a frame,
either with skins of sole-leather stretched across for a
sacking, or with straps of leather or surcingle crossed and
recrossed into a stout webbing.   In some good examples I
have seen, these straps passed through slots in the edge of

Oak Chair with Plush Cushion.
No. 19.

the frame, and the ends were
riveted together with flat copper rivets, as is done with
leather belting and hose-pipe.
If the sacking is made of
skins of leather, it must be
securely fastened to the sides
with several rows of brass-
headed nails.   Once well done,
and it is done forever.   The
end of the lounge is set into
the frame-work of the seat at
a little slant, and in some
cases is carved with a good deal of spirit; the legs and
braces are also turned, and so a simple piece of furniture
takes on quite an air, while keeping its ornamentation
strictly within bounds.   This particular *chaise longue*, or
lounge, is said to be the one on which George Fox slept
at the time a convention, or "meeting," of Friends was
held in the house where it now is, and it stands where it
has always stood.   The house has been in possession of

one family for over two hundred years—an uncommon thing in our North country, though by no means unusual in the. South.

Cut No. 19 is an adaptation by Mr. Sandier, from one found in a picture. It is perhaps a little heavier than need be, but it is a comfortable shape. The chairs shown in

Oak Chairs, Embroidered in Silk and Worsted on Canvas.
No. 20.

cut No. 20 are also, as it seems to me, too heavy for the occasion; but, if any one should wish to copy them, the cabinet-maker could be instructed to lighten the supports and braces a little. These chairs are designed to be covered with embroidery of silk or worsted on canvas. Good patterns for embroidery, suited to such objects, used to be difficult to get; but the taste for the mediæval and renaissance tapestries and stuffs has so revived of late years, that designs copied from first-rate originals may now be found at several shops in New-York. These designs imitate the faded look of the stuffs they copy,—a look that

Coffee-Table with Chair, both of Black Wood.
No. 21.

really belonged to these always, and is not wholly the result of fading. No one who has familiarized his eye with the designs and tints of the old stuff will ever willingly go back to the pictures and formal wreaths and bouquets of flowers with which the tasteless German worsted-shops have so plentifully supplied us.

Cut No. 21 shows a good chair, comfortable and pretty, which was introduced here by the Messrs. Bumstead, of Boston, I believe, though Mr. Lathrop's drawing was made from one of the same lot at Cottier's. The originals were of English make; but those we get now are all made in Boston. As a rule, it may be remarked, furniture made in England or anywhere in Europe will not stand our climate, or, rather, let the blame be laid on our climate and our houses combined. The Messrs. Cottier long since found themselves obliged to give up importing furniture from England, as all the pieces that came from over seas had to be overhauled before they had been many weeks in this country. The chair shown in cut No. 22 is not a modern one, but the Cottiers have used it, or one like it, as a model, and have produced a design that takes the eye of every one who sees it. The chair is vastly more comfortable than it looks. We can sit at ease in it, now leaning against one side for a back, now against the other. Was it not a chair of this sort that Milton used? Mitford tells us "He composed much in the night and morning, and dictated in the day, sitting obliquely in an elbow-chair with his leg thrown over the arm." The old chairs of this sort are mostly made of mahogany, and were either bottomed

Coffee-Table and As-you-like-it Chair.
No. 22.

with rushes or seated with leather,—a piece of sole-leather stretched over the frame and well secured with a double row of brass-headed nails. Those made in imitation of their general design, by Cottier, are stuffed and upholstered. Stained black and polished, and with the seat covered with plush or morocco, or a square of needle-work, one or two of them will be found a welcome addition to the comfort and beauty of the living-room.

The chair in cut No. 23 is one of a pattern made some time ago by Cottier, and which seems to me perfect of its kind, both for the elegance of its lines and its comfortableness as a seat. This chair must not be confounded

Chair and Table from Cottier's.
No. 23.

with other chairs of the same general shape, but which, as a rule, are as different from it as a cabbage is from a rose. They are almost always too large,—that is their main fault; then, their curves are abrupt, and the proportions not good. This chair is small, but amply large enough for a comfortable man, and nothing could be better managed than the flow of its lines. The original chair is covered with a material of a golden-yellow color, damasked over with a floriated pattern, and around the bottom is a silk fringe of the same color, with some red introduced into it. It is so pretty to look at, that one forgets to sit down in it; but this is not to imply that it is too good to use. The stuff it is covered with is a sensible work-a-day material, looking as if it were made of silk and linen; but, in reality, the seeming silk is jute, I believe. However, the form is the principal thing, and such a chair, covered with a good chintz, might be as pretty a creature as she is in her golden gown. Next to making simplicity charming, the Cottiers have done us the greatest service, in showing us how to unite usefulness and beauty. All that they manufacture is made for every-day use, and will stand service. If they are not as much sought after as they should be, it is because they do not know how to minister to the popular desire to make a great splurge on a very little money. It is amusing to hear that when they recommend their things as thoroughly well made and good for a life-time, the modish people cry out, "Oh, we don't want things to last a life-time!" "What is life"—says one beauty, as she glances at her charming head in a Venetian mirror—"what is life without new furniture?" But the number of people increases who like sincerity even in chairs and tables.

I have left what I wrote about this pretty arm-chair as it originally stood, but I am bound to say that the chair itself is a great deal prettier than the artist has made it in his drawing, and, to do it full justice, Mr. Lathrop should have made another sketch of it. The material, too, with which it is covered does not stand wear-and-tear so well as it promised, and this is a pity, because it is beautiful to look at,—the color and the pattern, both, all that can be desired, and the stuff soft to the touch. But materials equally handsome and more serviceable can be found either at the Cottiers' or at Nicol & Cowlishaw's, a place to which we recommend our readers who are in search of covering-stuffs, curtains, and such things; they will find there a great variety to choose from, and, in chintzes especially, many patterns that I have not seen elsewhere.

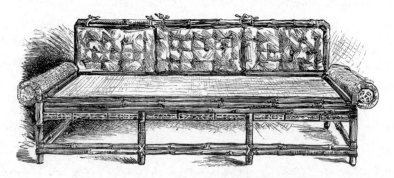

Chinese Sofa, made of Bamboo.
No. 24.

I have encouraged my little bamboo sofa, of which a cut is here given (No. 24), to believe that she will make many friends in society, and that all those who know how to value modest merit will seek for her acquaintance. She does not make the least pretense in the world,—her only claim upon our good will is, that she will do her best to make us comfortable. I found this sofa at Mr. Van Tine's, where there is always a supply of bamboo furniture,—settees, lounges, stools, chairs of various styles,—made in China or Japan, and capital stuff it is to fill up the gaps in the furnishing of a country house for a summer. Even in a city house, or in city rooms, several of these bamboo articles will be found useful, though they are often too large for our apartments. They have the merit of being strongly made and easily kept clean. The settee repre-

sented above had no cush-
ions when I bought it;
and I found the roll-over
ends not strong enough
to be depended on, and I
was therefore obliged to
have them taken off, and
upright arms made of bam-
boo were put in their
place. There are three
thin cushions that rest
against the back of the
settee, to which they are
fastened, as shown in the

Solid Comfort.
No. 25.

cut, by pieces of the braid with which they are bound. The seat is also covered with one cushion reaching from end to end. In his drawing, Mr. Lathrop has omitted this cushion in order to show that the seat is of bamboo.

Cut No. 25 is a drawing of a chair of the same age as the *chaise longue*, shown in cut No. 17, and belongs to the same family that owns that interesting relic of the great Quaker. It is of oak, and has grown very dark with age, and as I sat in it to hear the story of the ancient house that shelters it, I found it the most comfortable old shoe of a chair I had ever sat in. It takes one in like a motherly lap, and is so loose-jointed and compliant that no cushioned chair could better deserve the name of easy-chair.

It is much easier to find tables suited to our various needs than to find the right kinds of chairs;—chairs for the dining-room, chairs for the drawing-room, chairs for chat,

Small Tables for Corners.— Useful in Tea-Fights.
No. 26.

and chairs for repose. I have given only a few examples of different sorts. I have found nothing so troublesome in the playful labor of writing these pages, as the search for chairs that should be at the same time handsome and useful.

But, as I have just said, tables are another matter, and if one cannot get just what he wants at the cabinet-makers' shops, there are old-fashioned tables easily to be had. I have just had a piece of good fortune, which I speak of because the like may be any one's luck who will go to work the same way. A friend of mine who, by persistent rummagings in tumble-down farm-houses, and in the decayed dwellings of still more decayed gentle-folk, has amassed a great treasure of old-fashioned furniture and china-ware, told me where, in a certain garret, there was to be seen a large table, a centenarian at the least, and that it could no doubt be bought for a song. Bought, it accordingly was, though with some misgivings, since it was in a state of extreme depression from long neglect, and one leaf had fallen from its hinges. But, brought to town, and put into the hands of my friend, Mr. Matt. Miller, the, to me, pleasing discovery was made, that I was in possession of a table of solid San Domingo mahogany, worth a great deal more, even as wood, than I had paid for it, and with turnings of first-rate design. This was, of course, a piece of good fortune, but, after all, not of very rare good fortune; those who seek such things are continually finding them, for the garrets and barns in the older parts of the country are rich in this furniture of a by-gone time, that has been set aside to yield place to that of a more fashionable make.

In the old times to which this table of mine belonged, the furniture-makers showed a great deal of variety in their designs,— far more, as it seems to me, than is shown now. There was, of course, as there is in every age, a certain general likeness,— the " style " of the period,— but the ingenuity of the maker appeared in his adaptation of this style to a great many different uses. I have seen, in my day, over a hundred pieces of last-century furniture, of English and American make, but I never saw two pieces alike in detail. No doubt the reader is as familiar as I am with the sort of table represented in cut No. 27. They are found of many sizes, from simple lamp-stands to such

as are large enough to accommodate, rather snugly to be sure! four people united over a friendly dish of tea. The tops are almost all made to turn up, being hinged on the central support, and they often revolve, the piece to which they are hinged being in that case a separate block or light frame through which the top of the central pole passes, and on which it turns.

The Cheerful Round of Daily Work.
No. 27.

Then, again, the edge of the circular or oval leaf is treated in a variety of ways, sometimes left quite plain, but, in all the better sorts, molded, and sometimes, as here, *dentelé,*—to use the French term,—in homely English, *scolloped.* But the variety of these scollops is great, as great as the fancy of the carver could devise. The table-maker seems to have taken pleasure in his work: that is the secret of his success, as it is of all success. And he had enough of the artist in him not to allow himself to be tempted into fantasticalness by the demands of fashion. For if we are to believe the report of the fashion-prints of the day, there never was greater fantasticalness than in the dress of the time, yet even when frippery and furbelows were at the height of their absurdity, the furniture kept a staid and discreet appearance, as much as to say: "We can't both of us be giddy; it rests with me to uphold the dignity of the times."

To the eye of one whose liking for our Revolutionary furniture is not a new thing, the charm of it consists, apart from its usefulness, which is evident to everybody, in the color given to it by age, and in the simplicity with which all its ornament is obtained. Its moldings are always good and quiet; just what is needed, and no more, to round an angle with elegance, and to catch the light agreeably, and whenever any carving is attempted, or paneling, there is a certain moderation in it that is very refreshing in these loud times. Yet they are not too tame either, but their spirit is the spirit of high-bred people, and not of folks who like to be conspicuous. Even the architectural details in bureaus and clothes-presses that these old people were so fond of,—a little too fond, per- haps,—were often very delicately and adroitly managed, and we find ourselves easily forgiving them, seeing how well in keeping they are with the effect of any piece as a whole. Yet, much as these articles of furniture deserve to be praised, I would not counsel that they should be copied. In fact, I do not believe in copies, whether of furniture, of pictures, or of men and women. Nothing ever can be copied exactly, and we ought never to try to do it, unless it be for purposes of instruction, and even then its desirableness may be disputed. The least thing from a master's hand is pretty sure to be better worth studying, if we would know something about the master's method of

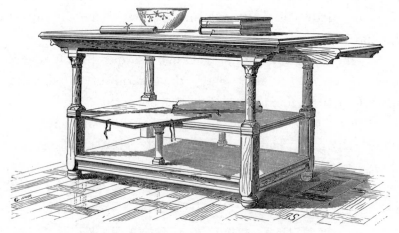

For Books, or Work, or Healthful Play.
No. 28.

working, or his way of thinking, than the best copy. And it may be said that the better artist the copyist is, the less his copy is apt to resemble his original. The French have carried the copying of old work—in furniture, in jewelry, in pottery—to great perfection; but an artist would rather have a square foot of genuine mediæval or Renaissance carving than the best copy of a whole piece that ever the skill of Récappé produced. So with old American or English furniture (for how much was made here, or how much imported, we do not know); no matter how super-ficially resembling the copies may be, they will always be wanting in something,—in proportion, in delicacy, or in spirit. And even if copies could be cast in a mold, it is not good to wish for them, for we can put all their merits into original pieces, made for ourselves to-day, that will not only give us pleasure, but will show our children that we knew how to profit by what our fathers taught us.

Cuts Nos. 28 and 29 are suggestions of designs for tables that will be found convenient for the living-room. No. 28 is rather intended to go against the wall, to write at, or hold the books and pamphlets that are being read, while the two shelves below will be found very convenient for folios, and large books of prints, atlases, etc., etc. A shelf at one end pulls out at need. In design, the lower supports of the table are heavier than need be, and the lower shelf, also, much too heavy. Cut No. 29 is intended for the center of the room, and ought to be a handsome piece if well carried out. It was designed for me by Mr. George F. Babb, who is so much of an artist, and puts so much thinking into his work, that I believe he will make no objection to my criticising his table a bit, and objecting to the three small brackets that support the projecting top at the ends. As will be seen by the drawing, these brackets are not the ends of straps that brace the two supports of the table and help to steady the top. There are no such straps, and perhaps they are not needed, but these little brackets are certainly not needed, and being useless and yet looking as if they were useful, they ought to have been omitted. But this is a small matter, and would not be worth mentioning, if it were not for the tendency there is nowadays to add to furniture just such little points as these, that are intended for decoration, yet do not decorate, and that look as if they were a part of the construction, yet, in reality, have nothing to do with the construction. This point settled, the reader will no doubt enjoy with me the skill with which Mr. Babb has

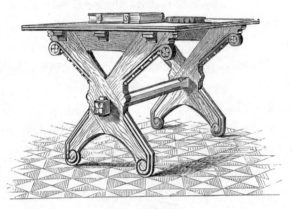

A Criss-cross Table.
No. 29.

contrived to get a variety of lines pleasingly united in the composition of his table-ends, each end made of two solid pieces halved into each other, and braced at the top by a third piece mortised into the two. The change in direction of the outer line of each support in its upper portion, the inner line left plain, the outer line decorated with a little carving, seems to me an original motive, and the ends of the supports, too, that touch the floor, are well managed: their curves are good, and they do not interfere with our feet.

The most troublesome member of the living-room ornaments, and yet the one we can least do without, is the
portfolio of prints. It is always in the way, and if it is
on a stand, the stand has to behave itself with great reti-

A Print-Stand from South Kensington.
No. 30.

cence and modesty,—keeping its back straight to the wall
and turning its toes well in,—not to be reckoned a perpetual marplot. As a rule, when the portfolio is introduced,
all enjoyment of the prints it contains is at an end, for we
are lazy creatures, the most of us, and, rather than drag

out the portfolio-stand or open the cumbersome book, we prefer to forego the pleasure of studying its contents. The print-stand, cut No. 30, has been devised to help us in this emergency, and it certainly does help us effectually. The upright pole supports as many frames (attached in the simplest way, by hooks fitting into rings) as its circumference will permit, and each frame will hold two prints. Each frame is supplied with two pieces of glass, and the prints are fastened with drawing-pins to the sides of a panel that slips down between the glasses. If need be, the frames themselves can be locked to the supporting pole, and each frame secured by a padlock; but this is rather a necessity for public institutions than for our private rooms. The possession of such.a print-case as this makes all the difference between enjoying the prints, drawings, and etchings one owns, and not enjoying them. Besides, it saves a great expense in framing, and it unites the advantages of frames and portfolios. When we want to see our possessions, we can see them framed, and see them without trouble, and when we don't want to see them, we turn the print-frame away, and forget for a while what it holds.

Another form of print-case, of which I have no drawing to offer, consists of a chest of shallow drawers, not over two inches and a quarter in depth, but large enough to hold the largest-sized print easily, with room to spare. One I have in mind is four feet long, three feet high, and two feet six inches deep. The large top makes a good resting-place for books that else would be unmanageable, and where they can not only rest at ease, but their contents be also comfortably consulted at need. Without some such contrivance as one of these two,—either the Kensington print-stand, cut No. 30, or the chest of drawers,—the possession of many prints, etchings, drawings, etc., becomes a great trouble, and, in the end, we find that we get much less than we ought to out of them, either for enjoyment or utility.

The next pieces of furniture to be considered are the cabinets, writing-tables or desks, and the like, of which, again, the last century gives us many excellent examples, some of them very rich and stately, others extremely simple, but all well designed and convenient. Of these, however, I have not had

Chinese Cabinet.
No. 31.

any drawings made, for the reason that they are so familiar to us all. I have preferred examples of styles less known, though I do not think anything could be devised handsomer than some of those used by our great-grandfathers.

Cut No. 31 is a double cupboard, with two drawers between the upper and lower divisions, and drawers within the upper division dividing it, also, into two parts. It is, I believe, a Chinese piece; the frame is made of lighter wood than the panels, which, in the doors, are ornamented with ivory figures, fastened upon the wood. It is a little over a man's height, and is of a comfortable depth. It will hold a great deal, and a piece of furniture modeled on it would be found most convenient in any house where there are books of prints, or old china, or curios, or anything of which it is not desired to make a display. It will be observed that it is of the simplest construction, and owes much of its picturesqueness to the ornaments upon the doors. But, sufficient richness and elegance could be obtained by a combination of two woods, or even by one wood alone, if the panels were selected by a carpenter with an eye.

It is not uncommon to find in old curiosity shops, pieces of painted Spanish leather. A gentleman of my acquaintance has the walls of a large room in his city house entirely covered with pieces of this leather, which, I believe, were picked up, here and there, at odd times. And I know a house in which the lower part of the parlor wall—the space between the chair-rail and the skirting-board—is hung with the same material. In this latter instance, I know that the leather was bought at several times, piece by piece. Now, the panels of a cabinet made after the design of this Chinese one would look very well, filled in with such leather as this. And, in default of leather, some member of the household might try her hand at decorating these panels with painting. With the abundant material that is put into our hands, nowadays, by the cheap German and French publications relating to art-industry, good models for such work are easy to be had, and there is no reason why, with practice, our American girls should not do this decorating work as well as their English sisters. As it is, we are driven, for anything of this sort, to the most expensive places, and whatever we get there is a luxury, and we have to watch over our purchases and dearly bought decorations as if they were croupy children.

But, even if one be willing to pay for it, it is not easy to get decorative painting done. If it be ordered from first-rate hands, it is expensive, and there is seldom any talent for this kind of work among our house-painters,— even among those of the trade who add "decorator" to their other titles. A good substitute for original decoration, and under the circumstances, a legitimate one, is to be found in the picture-books of Walter Crane, published in London and New-York, by Routledge & Sons. These books are the most beautiful children's books that were ever made; and, indeed, they are altogether too good to be confined to the delighting of children, even though these were the bonniest golden-haired kids ever raised on porridge. Those who know the Walter Crane books—the last one, "Baby's Opera," is perhaps the prettiest of all— buy them for themselves, and then can't resist the desire to give them to the children, and then have to buy more for themselves. They are, indeed, many times better than the general run of pictures that one sees by modern masters. They are better, because so much of modern art is merely mercantile, but here, the artist evidently enjoys his art, and, for the pleasure he has in his work, puts into it life, richness of color, much delicate and ingenious fancy, and a power of story-telling that hardly needs the help of the text to explain the pictures.

An acquaintance of the writer had a wardrobe made of pine, in which the panels of the doors were made expressly to be filled up with these pictures,— each picture having a panel to itself,—and then the rest of the woodwork painted to harmonize with the general color-effect. Staining pine a good black, or, with a strong decoction of tobacco (which gives a good brown and brings out the grain of the wood) and then shellac-

The Housekeeper's Friend.
No. 32.

ing, not varnishing—NEVER USE VARNISH ON FURNITURE— either of these methods will make a good background for these pictures. A useful plan for a wardrobe is to have one half closed by a door the full height of the piece, and the other half divided between, say, three drawers below, and above, a cupboard, closed by a door. In the larger closet one hangs clothes that must be hung, the drawers hold body-linen, and the cupboard above is useful to the owner, if he be a lady, for her hats and furs and other nothings of that nature. The panels should be made to hold each a single picture, and an agreeable variety may be obtained in the disposition of the panels by making some of them oblong and others square, to suit the pictures, which sometimes fill two pages, and at others only one.

Cut No. 32 is a convenient little movable, a combination of book-shelves, letter-pad, and cupboard, which Mr. Sandier has designed for me. The cupboard below is for books that are too valuable to be handled by everybody. It is capacious enough, however, to be found very useful for many purposes when one is in narrow quarters. In execution, I should, myself, prefer to have the top of this writing-case inclosed by a back and sides, rather than, as in the drawing, merely defended by the two sides carried up and formed into little gables. I would carry these ends and the back of the case up as high as the ends are carried in the drawing, and either leave this parapet solid, finishing it with a chamfer, or pierce it with some simple tracery. The ornament on the edge of the middle shelf looks a little as if it were meant to represent such a strip of leather as is occasionally fastened to the edge of a book-shelf to protect the tops of the books below from dust. In the present case no leather is used; the ornament is really a zigzag cut in the edge of the shelf. It must be remembered, that all such fancies as this add

something—it may be little, but it is something—to the cost
of the piece.   And yet the front of a shelf in so small an
article as this ought to be ornamented, if it be only with
a bead such as can be run on both edges with a plane, or
a simple reeding.   The writing-shelf in this example is
stationary, and the hinges, key-plate, and closing-ring of
the cupboard are of plain polished brass.

No Nonsense about it.
No. 33.

Another writing-table is shown in cut No. 33.   This is
of much simpler make, and, beside, does not offer to make
itself so useful.   The writing-shelf either lifts up, or, if
preferred, the space beneath it is got at by a drawer.
Then the back of the case is made useful by several small
drawers.   These can either run through, from side to side,
or they can be made only half the width of the case, and
the space opposite them can be left free for a tall book or

two. If all the space be wanted for drawers, .I would advise that they be made to run through, from side to side, with a partition dividing each drawer into two. Small drawers like these will be found to run much easier if they are made of a good length. On each side of the drawer-hole there should be fastened a hard-wood strip, and the sides of the drawers themselves should have grooves cut in them, answering to these strips, on which the drawers may run straight without the possibility of tilting. This advice applies to all drawers, especially to those which are shallow in proportion to their length. It is the want of something to steady drawers that makes them so troublesome as they are often found to be. This little case will be found a very pretty addition to the furnishing of the living-room if it be made of hard-wood and stained black, and afterward polished. This must be done by a cabinet-maker, however, to look as it should, and probably for those who cannot conveniently employ a cabinet-maker, but must depend on a carpenter, the better way will be to have the natural grain of the wood brought out by hand-rubbing with wax or oil.

In the finishing of the plainest piece of furniture everything depends upon the maker's skill in dressing the wood. I am supposing the piece to be well made, the joints perfectly fitted, and nothing shirked in the construction. Yet, with all this, a piece of pine-wood in the hands of a carpenter who knows and loves his business, may be made, by skillful dressing, to take on all the beauty of the finest satin-wood. No one knows what the difference can be between wood imperfectly dressed and wood that has been through the hands of a skillful workman, who has not seen a book-case, a wardrobe, or a kitchen table made by a carpenter like Matt. Miller, say, or by any workman as good (if one can be found!), and compared it with the work turned out of ordinary shops. To wood brought to as fine a surface as possible, a very little linseed oil should be well rubbed in, so well that the whitest handkerchief could continue the rubbing and get no stain. This treatment applied as often as time can be found for it, will soon result in bringing out all the beauty of the grain of hardwood. Pine-wood cannot be treated in this way. It must be oiled first, and then coat after coat of shellac applied until a permanently hard surface is produced.

The beautiful piece which is shown in cut No. 34 belongs to a gentleman in one of our cities, who has kindly allowed me to have drawings made from several of his choice possessions, in order to illustrate my book. This particular piece is of French make, I believe, a production of the last century: the panel in the door having been painted, it is said, by Angelica Kauffman. The brass ornamental work on the frieze, on the edges of the upright divisions, and on other parts, is in the first instance delicately cast, and has then been finished by the tool of the *"ciseleur"* with all the care that would be given to silver or gold plate.

It will thus be seen that the artistic value of this piece of furniture depends almost entirely on its decorative detail, for the form of the object, its design, is of extreme sim-

"Miss Angel" painted it.
No. 34.

plicity. There does not appear to be an inch of carved
wood anywhere upon it, and the only difficulty it presents
in construction is the rounded door.

Fault has been found with me, good-naturedly enough, but I venture to think mistakenly, for the number of elegant and costly things I introduced into the articles in "Scribner's Magazine," from which this book is made up, and I am so little penitent for what I have done that I have not left a single one of these elegant and costly things out of the book itself. This is not because it is every now and then possible to purchase a fine piece of furniture—artistically fine, I mean—very cheap, but because I think we need in this country to be made as familiar as possible with the look of beautiful things of this sort. A drawing like this is a lesson in good taste, and it happens to be, like many another in this book, a threefold lesson. We have, in the first place, a very elegant and interesting piece of furniture, and this has been drawn with spirit and picturesqueness by Mr. Francis Lathrop, and then engraved with the hand of a genuine master by Mr. Henry Marsh.

Now, the improvement of the public taste, if that be not too presumptuous an aim, is one of the principal objects of this book of mine, and it seems to me I can do something toward this end by showing beautiful things, even if they are, not seldom, out of reach, as well as by always complying with the demand that I shall show people how to get things cheap.

It happens that the piece of furniture under discussion gave so much pleasure to one reader of "Scribner's Magazine" when the cut was published there, that she determined to have one as near like it as she could contrive. She had the body of the piece made as neatly as her

favorite carpenter could do it,—and he was a skillful workman and did his best,—and then with her own hands she
painted all the ornaments, in colors, not attempting to
imitate the brass, and
filled in the panel of
the door with a paint-
ing on silk which had
belonged to a great-
grandmother, and might
have been painted by
Angelica Kauffman her-
self, so far as age was
concerned. It is true
this lady had exceptional
taste, and exceptional
skill in carrying out her
designs, but nothing ex-
traordinary, and many
a one could have done
the same. The result
of this venture was a
piece of furniture that
does not look as if it
were copied from any
model, and that deserves
to be admired for its

Chinese Étagère, with Cupboard.
No. 35.

own sake. Later, when I come to speak of the dining-
room, I shall show my readers other cupboards and
cabinets, more suitable to the uses of that room than they

would be to those of the living-room. If there be space
enough in the living-room to permit it, an *étagère*—the
fine name which we have given to a set of shelves—will
give us an opportunity to display any pretty things in the
way of *bric-à-brac* of which we may be the possessor. I
give drawings of two of these *étagères*.

Cut No. 35 has a cupboard below, and a set of shelves
above. It was purchased at Mr. Sypher's, and offers one
or two interesting points. The wood is a hard species,
which is either black naturally or is stained to as fine a
black as ebony, and takes a good polish. It stands, like
cut No. 36, upon a low bench, and this gives much lightness to the look of the lower part and brings the cupboard
more within reach. Note, too, the contrast between the
carved base of the main piece and the plainly molded edge
of the bench. Its being lifted up this way both enables
us to see it, keeps it out of harm's way, and gives it a
chance to play with the light advantageously. In each of
these pieces the disposition of the shelves is worth remark-
ing upon, as affording a useful hint to ourselves. Observe
that no one of them extends entirely across the space to
be shelved, nor is there any upright partition dividing the
shelves themselves. The object of the irregular arrangement is first, I think, to avoid monotony, but it finds a
better excuse in the accommodation it gives to articles of
different sizes and shapes. Here are places for little
things and places for larger things, and each is at home
in its own compartment, and by being somewhat isolated,—
yet not entirely, for the absence of partitions prevents

this,—does not suffer by having its beauty interfered with by that of its neighbor. The sides of the upper portion of this *étagère* are filled in with an arrangement of sticks that makes one think of a cobweb.

Cut No. 36 has an elegance of its own, distinct from that of cut No. 35. Considering the use for which it is intended, it must be admitted to be purely ornamental,—an ornamental upholder of the ornamental. It is a more beautiful piece of cabinet-making than its neighbor, the wood is of a finer and rarer kind, and the borders around the outer edge of each compartment are carved with a good deal of spirit. The fable of the fox and the grapes seems to be introduced into two or three of these borders,—at any

Chinese Étagère, with modern English Sconce.
No. 36.

rate, if this shall not be allowed, there is no doubt about there being a fox and a grape-vine. I think both these pieces are Chinese, though so far as the arrangement of the shelves is concerned, the Japanese are as fond of it as

13

the Chinese themselves. The sconce, for candles, that hangs over this *étagère*, is of modern English make, the pattern beaten out of rather thin brass. These sconces look very pretty on festive occasions, particularly at Christmas time, with a few bits of holly stuck about the brass disk.

In our small New-York—or why not say our small American—rooms, since a large room is certainly the exception?—in our small American rooms we want to leave the floor as free as possible, and to put on the walls whatever can be conveniently given to their keeping. I have already shown one device, on page 30, for making use of the walls to accommodate what ordinarily would stand upon the floor. This was in the entry-way of the house; but the need of room is as often felt in the living-room, owing to the small size of our rooms of which I have just spoken. At Herter's and at Cottier's there are several pretty hanging shelves, or *étagères*, intended to meet this want. They sometimes have little cupboards below the shelves in which frail objects of curiosity, or beauty, or both in one, can be kept under lock and key.

This clearing of the floor, and so making up somewhat for the scrimped rooms we most of us have to live in, is a point of no little importance in relation to comfort, and yet it is one we seldom give much thought to. The tendency is to crowd our rooms beyond their capacity, by which we make ourselves very uncomfortable, and destroy the value, as decoration, of many pieces, and their real usefulness as articles of furniture. What with easels, chairs not meant for use, little teetery stands, pedestals, and the rest of the supernumerary family filling up the room left by the solid and supposed useful pieces, it is sometimes a considerable

Hanging Shelf and Cabinet.
No. 37.

test of one's dexterity and presence of mind to make one's way from end to end of a long New-York drawing-room. Mignon's egg-dance was as nothing to it. In such an enterprise, these unfortunate people are much to be pitied (they are all men, of course), whose feet are not only too large for the work they have to do, but are unmanageable besides, and always throwing out to right and left, and getting their owner into scrapes. A New-York parlor of the kind called "stylish," where no merely useful thing is permitted, and where nothing can be used with comfort, is always overcrowded; things are bought from pure whim, or because the buyer does n't know what to do with her money; and as the parlor is only used on what are called state occasions, what would be the good of having easy-going, comfortable things in it? So everything bought for show goes there; and as the temptation to New-York rich people is to be all the time buying things for show, the inevitable result is, that in time the intruding camel crowds out the occupant of the tent.

One of these hanging cabinets is shown in cut No. 37. It was designed by Cottier & Co. This has a closet with plate-glass doors, surrounded by shelves above, below, and on each side. As seen in the cut, it is so much foreshortened, that the rails on either side of the top seem much higher than they are in reality. The little shelves at the sides are backed with mirrors, the edges of the squares of plate-glass in the doors are beveled, and as the wood is stained a rich black, the effect of the whole, as seen filled with India porcelain and Venice glass, with a great platter of old blue a-top, is brilliant enough. Yet, here again, as in the case of Mr. Sandier's shelves, much that goes to make this actual piece of furniture too costly for any one of moderate means to so much as think of buying it, is not essential to the design. The main elements of the design are independent of the mirror, and of the beveling of the glass in the doors. These add splendor, but splendor not of a sort to please a true taste. An artist's eye would leave all for the color of the pots and the bits of glass that are arranged on the shelves. Such a cabinet might be made a museum for the preservation of all the curiosities and pretty things gathered in the family walks and travels. The bubble-bottle of old Roman glass stirred in walking by one's own foot in the ruined palace of the Cæsars, and not bought in a shop; the Dutch drinking-glass, with the crest of William of Orange; the trilobites found in a Newburgh stone-wall, or the box of Indian arrow-heads, jasper, and feldspar, and quartz, picked up in a Westchester County field; bits of nature's craft and man's, gathered in one of these pendant museums, may make a collection of what were else scattered and lost, and which, though of little intrinsic value, and of small regard to see to, will often find its use in a house of wide-awake children.

And here one might put in a word for that heterogeneous catalogue of things for which the word *bric-à-brac* has been invented.

These objects, which are coming to play the part in our external life that they have played these many years in Europe and Asia, have really, if one wishes to find a side on which to regard them that shall commend itself to more serious consideration than trifling, however sanctified by fashion, can deserve—these objects, when they are well chosen, and have some beauty of form or color, or work manship, to recommend them, have a distinct use and value, as educators of certain senses—the sense of color, the sense of touch, the sense of sight.　One need not have many of these pretty things within reach of hands and eyes, but money is well spent on really good bits of Japanese workmanship, or upon good bits of the workmanship of any people who have brought delicacy of hand and an exquisite perception to the making of what are in reality toys.　A Japanese ivory-carving or wood-carving of the best kind,—and there is a wide field for choice in these remarkable productions,—one of their studies of animal life, or of the human figure, or of their playful, sociable divinities, pixie, or goblin, or monkey-man, has a great deal in it that lifts it above the notion of a toy.　It is a toy, a button, a useless thing, or nearly useless, but it is often as poetically or wittily conceived as if the artist had a commission from the state.　Then it is sure to be pleasant and soothing to the touch; it was made to be clasped by the fingers, felt with the finger-tips, rolled in the palm; for the general use to which they are put is being fastened to the pipe-case to serve as a button to keep it from slipping from the belt, and in this place they offer a natural rest and solace to the hand; their character has been developed by necessity.　A child's taste and delicacy of perception will be more surely fed by the constant habit of seeing and playing with a few of the best bits of ivory carving his parents can procure—and very nice pieces are often to be had for a small sum of money—

than by a room full of figures like those of Mr. Rogers, for example, or the great majority of French bronzes. Of course, a bronze by Barye, or by Fremiet, would do as much or more for the child's taste, and by all means let the money go for that if it can be afforded; but I am speaking now of trifles that, in a serious consideration of art, have no place perhaps, and which yet do nothing but help us in learning to know and admire the best art. Perhaps it is fanciful; but suppose that one of the Japanese spheres of polished crystal were put within the daily reach of a child, and that he were pleased enough with it to often look at it, handle it, and let the eye sink into its pellucid deeps, as from time to time he stopped in his reading of Froissart or King Arthur. Would not the incommunicable purity and light of the toy make a severe test for the heroes and the heroines in the boy's mind; and could his eye, cooled in such a bath of dew, get pleasure any more from discordant color or awkward form? Our senses are educated more by these slight impressions than we are apt to think; and *bric-à-brac,* so much despised by certain people, and often justly so, may have a use that they themselves might not unwillingly admit.

Another way to keep our floors more free of furniture is to make use of the corners. This was a favorite way in old-fashioned days,

"In tea-cup times of hood and hoop,
And when the patch was worn."

The corner cupboard, cut No. 38, is not a movable piece, but is a part of the construction of the room. It has a cupboard above and below, and the inside space is larger than would perhaps appear on seeing how much room is taken up by the "architecture"—the pilasters, cornices, and friezes of this bit of New England Renais-

Grandmother's Cupboard.
No. 38.

sance. I asked Mr. Lathrop to draw this one for its picturesqueness, but it is not, of course, recommended that it should be exactly copied. It affords a good hint as to how the end is to be gained by making a corner useful, which it very rarely is in our houses, the little shaky *étagères* we are so fond of,—or were so fond of, for they are a little gone off in these days,—serving no real use, but

A Cupboard of To-day.
No. 39.

only to put futile bits of glass and china on for the house-
maid to break. A corner-cupboard, however, like this one,
is useful either in dining-room or living-room. In the

dining-room it holds the prettiest pieces of china and glass for use upon the table; keeping it where it will make a cheerful show of glinting light and color. In the living-room it often serves for a book-case for books that are too bright and good for human nature's daily food; or it may be a cabinet for minerals, or shells, or birds, or for those "curios" and "objects" that the bewitched collector is often glad to hide away from the critical friendly snubs and slurs of the unappreciative members of his family.

Cut No. 39 is a design for a movable cupboard, made by Cottier & Co. after their own design, mainly to serve as a frame to the two painted panels in the doors with which Mr. Lathrop enriched it. The cupboard itself is plain enough, and its ornamentation, which is kept down as much as possible so as not to interfere with the painting, is only of arabesques painted in gold color, not in gold, on the black ground. It will be seen that there is a good deal of room in such a piece as this—two cupboards, three drawers, and four shelves, counting the top and the one that runs around the middle compartment at the back. The whole takes up very little space, and would certainly be a cheerful object in the living-room

The hanging shelf in cut No. 40 makes one point only in Mr. Sandier's interesting drawing, in which he has ingeniously contrived to group no less than four objects. But the shelf which, with all the other pieces,—the sofa, the writing-table, and the pedestal,—he has designed himself, is certainly a very pretty one. It has three shelves, counting the top, and will hold a number of good-sized objects.

Mr. Sandier has made his drawing from the original, which he designed for Mr. Herter. In that the sides were pierced with carved open-work, the back was paneled, and the panels decorated with figure subjects, painted by Mr. Sandier himself, and the top was covered with a piece of Oriental embroidery, bordered with a fringe, which hung over the front edge. Of course, all these details add greatly to the cost, as well as to the luxury of the little piece of furniture; but the only one that it would be a pity to give up would be the carving. Still any one can see that if one had pretty enough things to put on such a shelf, it would be them, and not the shelf, we should look at; and therefore, if the general form and the proportions are found pleasing, it would be easy for Mr. Sandier to devise one that could be compassed by a slenderer purse than must, no doubt, be drawn upon for this.

Besides the hanging shelf and the sofa, of which something is said further on, Mr. Sandier has cleverly brought into this cheerful drawing of his, several other objects, which may furnish useful hints to our readers. The pedestal in the corner is an ingenious provision for a much-felt need,—a pedestal for a statue, vase, or cast, being one of the pieces of furniture most difficult to find. This pedestal, made of wood, and having a small cloth laid over the top, has one shelf near the bottom, but may have another near the top, or even a little closet in the upper part. The figure on the pedestal in this drawing is Barye's "Minerva," one of the great sculptor's studies of the human figure seldom seen. A nude Minerva would have shocked a Greek, and,

Much in Little Space.
No. 40.

perhaps, puzzled him; he would have wondered what incident in the goddess's story could have given him an excuse

"To twitch the nymph's last garment off."

As I take it, Minerva has disrobed for the contest of beauty with Juno and Venus; there being nothing else left, she is taking off her sword. The other piece of furniture in this room is a writing-table with a book-shelf above and drawers at the side, and on the wall over it, Mr. Sandier has hung one of the Japanese scrolls, which we find nowadays in the shops that devote themselves to Eastern products,—Mr. Vantine's, in Broadway, or Mr. Rowland Johnson's, in Beaver street. Mr. Jarves describes some beautiful ones he owns, in his book about Japanese Art, and they are often far more beautiful than any pictures by our own men, that we with the short purses can lay hands upon. Besides the screens, there are the Japanese paintings on silk gauze, or on paper, of men and women, birds and flowers.

There is hardly anything with which we can produce a prettier effect in rooms where we want to break up the wall, and yet have nothing particularly good, as engraving or picture, to hang upon it, than these Japanese paintings of birds and flowers, and native men and women which come painted on gauze, and with which the Japs themselves ornament their screens. Secured to the wall by a drawing-pin at each of the four corners, they give a bright and cheerful look to a dull room, and are always pleasant to see, even when they are of the cheaper sort. The best ones are often much better worth having for spirited design, and the mastery of their painting, than any work done by the professed decorators; indeed, for their flowers and birds there is no decorative work of our day that can at all compare with them. One of the prettiest modern rooms I ever saw was in the house of a distinguished artist in one of the London suburbs, and the sole decoration on the walls was one of these screen pictures in each of the wall divisions; but these were of very rare beauty, both in design and execution, and the tone of the room had their color for its key.

The seat on which the lady is sitting, reading, in Mr. Sandier's drawing, is really a seat, and would probably be used as such twenty days in a month. It is the design referred to on page 65, a variation on the settle figured in cuts Nos. 14 and 15. As its main use is to serve as a low, broad, comfortable seat, the table is always ready, never gets littered with books or work, and should never be allowed to get so, because it ought not to be made troublesome, which it is sure to be if it be not principally used as a seat.

"Ah—take care. You see what that old-looking saucer is, with a handle to it? It is a venerable piece of earthenware, which may have been worth to an Athenian, about two pence; but to an author, is worth a great deal more than ever he could—deny for it. And yet he could deny it, too. It will fetch his imagination more than it ever fetched potter or penny-maker. Its little shallow circle overflows for him with the milk and honey of a thousand pleasant associations. This is one of the uses of having mantel-pieces. You may often see on no very rich mantel-piece, a representative body of all the elements, physical and intellectual—a shell for the sea, a stuffed bird or some feathers for the air, a curious piece of mineral for the earth, a glass of water with some flowers in it for the visible process of creation, a cast of sculpture for the mind of man; and underneath all is the bright and ever-springing fire running up them heavenward, like hope through materiality."

So wrote Leigh Hunt, years ago, in his "Indicator," in the article entitled "Autumnal Commencement of Fires."

I transcribe it here from my note-book as an introduction to what I have to say about mantel-pieces and fire-places.

We are just putting behind our backs the time when furnaces were all the rage, and the doctors in consequence were rattling around in their gigs with no end of business, and it required a steady stream of rich men's last-will-and-testaments to keep up the supply of hospitals that were made necessary by this, the devil's last, best gift to man, as much as by anything. It really began to seem as if the hearth-stone were a dead institution; and yet it was pathetic to see how many men and women still held on to the idea, and instead of logically leaving chimneys out of their houses, or building the piers up solid, kept on putting in expensive make-believe fire-places, and erecting mantel-pieces over them, as if they could n't bear to give up the memory of what had once been so pleasant. In those days, the kitchen came near being the only cheerful room in the house; for there, at least, there was a real fire-place with a real fire in it, giving out heat that was actually warm. Poorish people had to give up burning wood, of course, because it was too dear; but rich people, who might have kept up the delightful luxury, did n't, of course, dare to, when all the world took to burning hard coal. However, some few of them did, and there were others who wanted to, and so made a compromise by employing that funniest of all the fashionable humbugs of our time,—worse than wedding presents, than funeral flowers, or dinner parties with borrowed silver,—the fire-place with its make-believe andirons supporting make-believe logs with pieces of asbestos stuck between them and made red-hot by lighting the gas discharged by pipes hidden behind the fraudulent heap. Still, even this, vulgar or babyish as it was, was a concession to the god of hospitality, who really does not know how to make people sociably happy unless he can bring them around a fire, and, as a concession, it had an air of respectability about it. But the "furnace register" that puffed out its dusty heat at you from behind the so-called "summer blower" was not a concession at all; it was a pretense, and deserved no fair words. It was and is honester to frankly make a hole in the floor and warm yourself at that, than to pretend you still have something left of the beloved old-time fire-place, with its hospitable warmth and eye-and-heart-delighting glow.

It was noticeable, too, that all the time we were trying to thrust the fire-place and the hearth-stone out-of-doors, the traditional surroundings of the fire-place became more and more pretentious and unmeaning. The house-builders went on building chimneys, and, though we did n't use them, there seemed no way of using the pier except as supports for make-believe mantel-pieces, with mirrors over them. And then cheapness began to run riot in her delight at seeing how much finery could be got for next to nothing. This was the era of marbleized slate, by which invention Nature was taught what ugly things in the way of marble she might have made if she had been born a Yankee; and the manufacturers became at last so intoxicated with their success in the business as to overshoot the mark and produce a reaction. Now, as we know, marbleized slate, if found at all in good houses, is thrust out of sight into rooms little used; but its main employment is in cheap houses made to sell and to tickle the buyer's eye, or in "flats," where these stunning mantel-pieces are supposed to make the rash gazer, while he wipes his eye, forget to remark the cracked and blistered plaster, the gaping wood-work, and the wind that whistles through the door and window-frames for want of thought.

But marbleized slate, though dead, has let his mantel-piece fall on the shoulders of "wood," and the fashionable furnishers are trying how much vulgarity they can get for a good deal of money in that material. But not to waste words on these offensive mixtures of veneer and meaning-less moldings, let us be glad of anything almost that keeps alive the sentiment of the fire-place, especially since we see how much has been done of late to re-instate the open fire in public favor. People have been finding out that though a furnace may be an excellent thing in the long-continued cold of winter, yet there are days in early spring and late fall when a fire of logs is much pleasanter and seems to go more directly to the right spot. And then all the accompaniments of the open fire are of an ornamental character; the fire-dogs, or the taller andirons, the tiles that border the opening, the brass fender of open-work, the very shovel and tongs, with the bellows,—all these are the shining armor of the god of fire, and he likes to let his sparkling eye roam over them in the twilight, as he recalls a thousand memories of the days that are no more, or feeds a thousand hopes for the days that are to come.

It is a good plan to have the fire-place made as in
our illustration, cut No. 41, which, with cut No. 42, has
been copied by Mr. Inglis from wood-cuts in "The Architect." The two fire-places and mantels were designed by

"Aha! I am warm—I have seen the fire!"
No. 41.

Mr. Edward W. Godwin, one of the best of the rising
English architects. Mr. Francis Lathrop has added the
lady in the first wood-cut, and has kindled the flame
that Mr. Marsh has cut with such a flowing hand. The

fire in this illustration is burning on a steel basket or
cradle which rests upon the andirons. This being movable, a wood fire can be kindled on the hearth at any
time, the cradle for coals being simply lifted off and set
away. The other illustration, cut No. 42, shows a grate
set into the pier in the ordinary way, but the reader's
attention is particularly called to the plainness of this
grate, which is in pleasant contrast to the showy, over-
ornamented, pretentious things that are so much in favor
with us. There is this excuse, however, for the bad taste
shown in the employment of the "fashionable" New-York
grates: they are not intended for use, but for show.
Probably not one in fifty of them ever was defiled by
fire; yet they are almost always well made, and in the
stage scenery of our social life they may be reckoned
among the things which the slang of the theaters calls
"practicable;" they are real things, not shams. But, if
they are used, they very soon lose their elegance and
luster, or require a great deal of care and labor to keep
them neat and bright. The English grates, the best of
them, are either kept very plain, or depend for their ornamentation upon good design. The best of the modern
English grates, those designed by Mr. Morris particularly,
depend for their ornamentation a good deal upon the delicate casting of the iron, which brings out the pattern in
clear relief on the flat surface. It may be remarked in
passing, that very good ornamental casting is done here
even now, and in the old time our American casting could
not be excelled. The "Franklin" stoves, for burning wood,

were covered with excellent ornament, executed in a first-
rate manner, and the good design and workmanship were
inherited by the "Nott" stoves, that superseded them on
the coming in of anthracite; but the stoves for heating,

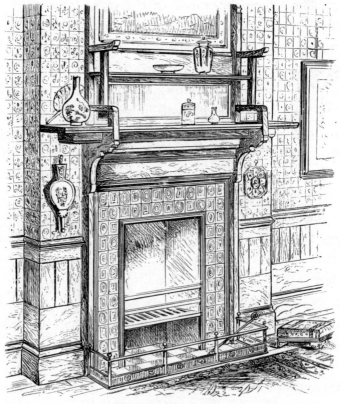

'T is home where'er the hearth is.
No. 42.

made in this country now, are as coarse in execution as
they are clumsy in form. The only handsome stoves seen
nowadays in America are the cooking-stoves, but they are
generally kept austerely plain.

The English grates I am praising come provided with the prettiest appendages in the shape of andirons, brass shovels, tongs and pokers, fenders, scuttles, and "trivets" for holding the tea-kettle; and when the grate is fairly installed with her frame and tiles (as in cut No. 42), her ministering kettle singing on the trivet, and all her shining appurtenances in order about her, a man must have an inhospitable streak in him, or be entirely given over to "social science" and the Spencer-Youmans theory of life, who does n't feel the cockles of his heart thrill a wee bit with the cheerful human sight.

But, however willing people have been to give up fire-places, they have not been willing to give up mantel-pieces, and, indeed, I suppose the keeping up even a show of fire-places has been partly owing to the liking for the shelf that has so long been suspended over them. It has long been the fashion to support this shelf in one way—that is, with two seeming posts, or piers, or pilasters, one on either side, supporting an entablature, or sometimes a simple lintel, whether of wood or marble, and the shelf supported by a molding that played the part of cornice. This is the arrangement which, whether reduced to its simplest elements in upstairs bedrooms, or concealed in the parlor with a heap of absurdities by way of ornament, obtains in nearly all our houses, and wherever in any country there are fire-places at all. In houses of the late last century or early present century, in New-York, Boston, and Philadelphia, examples may be found where the piers and the lintel are sculptured, sometimes by skillful hands, with delicately designed classic ornamentation of leaf, flower, or arabesque; but this refinement seemed tame to the next generation, and but little of it survives. In England, in the time of Queen Anne and the early Georges, there was a great deal of this sort of work done, and good sculptors did not think it beneath them to carve mantel-pieces; nor would it be a bad thing now if some of our sculptors would leave their search for the ideal and their search for a big job, and take humbler tasks in hand, that were perhaps better suited to the measure of their talent. In England, to-day, they are coming to set great store by the delicately carved mantel-piece of Queen Anne's time; and as the houses of that period are pulled down, as too many of them are, the mantel-pieces, and not only the mantels, but the wrought-iron stair-rails, the wainscoting and the paneled doors are bought up, often for good round prices. But there, as well as here, houses built thirty or forty years ago have nothing in them worth buying, except as lumber, and it will be so with the houses we are building to-day.

In cut No. 42 Mr. Godwin has discarded, even more positively than in cut No. 41, the old post and lintel system, and has devised a very simple way of framing the grate and supporting the shelf. He gets, in fact, two shelves,—the lower one with projecting ends, and, between it and the upper one, a long strip of mirror, which enables us to look at ourselves on the sly by accident whenever we want to, and also gives opportunity for all sorts of pretty reflections and glancing lights, without usurping the

room we may happen to want for our favorite picture or
print. The wood-work in cut No. 42 would look best in
mahogany, or in some hard wood stained black; but of
course this depends on the general tone of the room.

Hardly anything in the modern parlor is so uninterest-
ing as the mantel-piece. It is such a trouble to most
people to think what to put on it, that they end by
accepting blindly the dictation of friends and tradesmen,
and making to Mammon the customary sacrifice of the
clock-and-candelabra suite. I remember a rich lady who
had so much money she never could devise ways enough
of spending it, and who one day introduced us to a stunning suite of mantel-piece ornaments, fearfully and wonder-
fully made, in the very latest style, and costing all that
even the most fashionable votary could require. The handsome owner stood before her purchase, and good-naturedly
excused herself by explaining how she had been badgered
by her friends, who, one and all, to the self-same tune and
words, had assured her that she must have a set of mantel-
piece ornaments. "I did n't want 'em; never did care for
such things, and don't like 'em now I have 'em; but I 've
done my duty, and shall have a little peace from my
friends." Now, this was a person who had a strong, clear
mind of her own on most subjects, who was abundantly
able, out of her own pursuits and resources, to have made
her house delightful, by simply allowing it to reflect her
own accomplished individuality, and there was much about
the house which did reflect her own tastes and studies, and
gave a peculiar charm to certain corners, but this was

overcrowed by the conventional commonplace note of the world she lived in, and the total result was mere tameness and matter-of-fact. The mantel ornaments were the key to the whole.

A clock finds itself naturally at home on a mantel-piece, but it is a pity to give up so much space in what ought to be the central opportunity of the room, to anything that is not worth looking at for itself, apart from its merely utilitarian uses. It is very seldom worth while to look at a clock to know what time it is, and, as a rule, it would be much better to keep clocks out of our dining-room, though, for that matter, it is hard to say where they are not an impertinence. In the dining-room they are a constant rebuke to the people who come down late to breakfast, and they give their moral support to the prig-gishness of the punctual people, while they have, no doubt, to reproach themselves for a good share in the one bad American habit of eating on time. In a drawing-room a clock plays a still more ill-mannered part, for what can he do there but tell visitors when to go away, a piece of information the well-bred man is in no need of, and which the ill-bred man never heeds. So that, if a clock must usurp the place of honor on a mantel-piece, it ought to have so good a form, or serve as the pedestal to such a bit of bronze, or such a vase, as to make us forget the burden of time-and-tide in the occasional contemplation of art eternities. We get this habit of clocks, with their flanking candlesticks or vases, on all our mantel-pieces, from the French, who have no other way, from the palace to the bourgeois parlor. But they get rid of the main difficulty by either making sure that the clock does not keep good time,—the best French clocks being delightfully irresponsible in this particular,—or by having clocks without any insides to them, a comfortably common thing, as every one used to Paris "flats" knows.

Ever since Sam Slick's day, America has been known as the land where cheap clocks abound. If we were a legend-making people, we should have our Henry IV., who would have said he wished every peasant might have a clock on his mantel-piece. But, though we have cheap clocks enough, we have no pretty ones, and we are therefore thrown back on those of French make, which are only to be endured when they are mere blocks of the marble they polish so finely, of which we can make a pedestal to support something we like to look at.

The mantel-piece ought to second the intention of the fire-place as the center of the family life—the spiritual and intellectual center, as the table is the material center. There ought, then, to be gathered on the shelf, or shelves, over the fire-place, a few beautiful and chosen things—the most beautiful that the family purse can afford, though it is by no means necessary that they should cost much, the main point being that they should be things to lift us up, to feed thought and feeling, things we are willing to live with, to have our children grow up with, and that we never can become tired of, because they belong alike to nature and to humanity. Of course, if one were the happy owner of a beautiful painting,—but that is so rare a piece of good fortune we need hardly stop to consider it,—the problem would be easily solved, but we are happy in knowing that in these days there can always be procured, at trifling expense, some copy of a noble picture—the "Sistine Madonna" of Raphael, the "Madonna of the Meyer Family," by Holbein, or some one of the lesser, yet still glorious, gifts of Heaven to man. There are photographs taken now, in large size, from the originals of all the famous pictures (Raphael's "Sistine Madonna" has just been so taken), and, both for truthfulness and richness of effect, they are superior to any engravings of these pictures, no matter by what master. There is a large photograph of Raphael's "Madonna of the Grand Duke," which is certainly better to have than any copy. There are German lithographs of the "Sistine Madonna," and of the "Meyer Family," by Holbein, which, to my thinking, are much more desirable than even Steinla's engravings of the two great master-pieces, although, as engravings, Steinla's seem to me far the best that have been made.

All this, by the way. It is impossible to choose for another, and it is fortunate there is so wide a field from which to select. All is, to choose something for the living-room mantel-piece that shall be worth living with; it ought to be something that is good alike for young and old. Such an engraving, photograph, or picture, might be flanked on either side by a cast of some lovely masterpiece; but for casts there is no resource but Europe—there is small opportunity for getting them here. However, they can always be ordered from London, Paris, or Berlin,—the expense of even the very best casts of the good things is but small, the main obstacle is the trouble,—and there is hardly anything that better rewards trouble than a fine cast of a really noble or lovely piece of sculpture. Who would ever get tired of seeing on the wall, over his man-tel-piece, as he sat with wife or friend before his sea-coal fire, the mask of either one of Michael Angelo's "Captives" on one side, and the Naples "Psyche" on the other—these or any two of the many everlasting works made in the charmèd days ere sculpture was a lost art! The mask of one of the Angelo "Captives" can be found in our shops, and so can his "Julian de Medicis," and also the "Psyche."

Of course, the two or three "great" things having been installed, there is room enough for the pleasant little things that always find a hospitable place at the feet of greatness, and which, as they cannot derogate from the master's dignity, so neither does his dignity crush them, nor make us think them out of keeping. Here is the bit of Japanese bronze, or the Satsuma cup, or the Etruscan vase, or the Roman lamp, or the beautiful shell, or the piece of English or Venetian glass. Here, too, is the tumbler filled with roses, or the red-cheeked apple, or the quaintly painted gourd, or the wreath of autumn leaves. And here, too, must be the real candlesticks, with real candles to be lighted at twilight, before the hour for the lamps, in the hour of illusion and of pensive thought, casting a soft, wavering gleam over the down-looking picture and the mysterious cast, and bringing a few moments of poetry to close the weary working-day.

Cuts Nos. 43 and 44 are other specimens of the small grates I spoke of a while ago. Mr. Morris himself designed some of the patterns, and some of his prettiest poetry has got itself mixed up with this cast-iron work, and is quite at home there. These fire-places are as good as they are handsome, and give out as much heat as if they were ugly and clumsy.

Parlor Fire-place.
No. 43.

These designs for mantel-pieces are intended as hints for people who may be fitting up new houses of their own, or who may wish to get something better in the place of the mantel-pieces imposed upon them in houses taken on a comfortably long lease. The writer knows of one

Snuggery Fire-place.
No. 44.

case, at least, where a tenant renting a house removed the mantel-piece that was in the principal room to the cellar, and put up in its place a well-designed wooden one. This would certainly be worth doing under some circumstances; but, as a rule, we New-Yorkers live in any one house too short a time to make any considerable improvement, the cost of which comes out of our own pockets, seem worth while. The

An Every-day Mantel-piece, Simply Treated.
No. 45.

best is to try what can be done with the mantel-pieces
we have, and the two designs (cuts Nos. 45 and 46) are
intended to give some help in this direction. Cut No. 45
is much the simpler of the two, and, in spite of doubting

Thomases, shows an inexpensive way of treating an ordinary fire-place, one no uglier than is to be found in almost every respectable dwelling-house in our city. These two cuts are engraved by Mr. Marsh after drawings on the block by Miss Oakey, and they are both taken from actual objects. In cut No. 45 we have a frame of walnut, stained black, resting directly on the mantel-shelf, but secured to the wall in some easily detachable way. This frame incloses three mirrors, a large one (but not large) in the middle, and a smaller one on each side. Above the mirror is a projecting shelf with a railing, supported on brackets. This shelf is to hold a few pretty plates, bits of glass, or table-trinkets of any kind which the owners of the mantel may happen to be possessed of, and which are worth putting where they can be seen and not meddled with. On the marble shelf of the mantel-piece is laid a board, covered with velvet or plush, and having a narrow valance of the same material over the edge. This valance should not be more than six inches deep, and it ought to avoid any very pronounced ornaments—one of the beautiful new English gimps, or "laces," as they are called, makes the best decoration. The effect of these laces depends on the color, partly, and partly on the pattern, which is always one of the elementary patterns—alternate squares of dark and light, or round spots of gold on a ground of black or dull red. Of course the woman's deft fingers and quick eye can weave or embroider these for herself; but if she will buy them, the English make them more beautifully, as well as more substantially, than any one else. The owners

Another Way of Dealing with Commonplace.
No. 46.

of this mantel-piece have substituted a brass fender for the foolish black dust-pan that comes with our common grates. It is much easier to take up the ashes from the actual hearth than to try to keep the grate-pan clean, which plays the part of make-believe hearth. Besides, a brass fender is always a handsome addition to the belongings of the fire-place.

The other mantel-piece, cut No. 46, is more expensive than cut No. 45; it is handsome and different; but, cut

No. 45 is handsome too. This mantel ornament serves as frame to one of the circular mirrors, which, a few years ago, were reckoned common, and were on their desponding way to the garret, or the auction-room, when the new fashion set in, and some one with an eye pulled them by the sleeve and encouraged them to come back again. They are now much sought for, and fetch high prices; large ones, with all their ornaments of spread-eagles, chains, and candle-branches, have sold for two and three hundred dollars. But they may be picked up, now and then, and as they are easily made, we already begin to see the manufacture reviving. As mirrors, they are not of any use, their only object being to give pleasure by the queer distorted reflections they make, and by the clever way in which they give back a view of the whole room. A very pretty mantel wainscot, of the kind shown in cut No. 46, has been made by a person who found himself in possession of an old-fashioned mahogany cabinet, or chest of drawers, the most of which was past revamping. The pediment at the top, the pretty cornice beneath it, the handsome paneled doors,—in short, the whole front of the upper part of the bureau set against the wall made, in hands skillful at adaptation, a combination and a form indeed.

———

Next to carpets, there is no subject that comes so near to all women's housekeeping hearts as curtains, and there is no subject that bothers them so much. And they are, for the most part, rude and unfeeling as it is to say it, utterly wrong in their ways of solving the troublesome problem. They are all agreed that cornices are indispensable, and the upholsterers and furniture-people, finding this an easy and expensive way of suiting their delightfully troublesome clients, would go on putting up cornices for them till doomsday, and assuring them that there is no other way.

Now, a "cornice" ought never, under any circumstances, to be thought necessary in a private house. In fitting up concert-rooms, ball-rooms, and public places, where a certain frigid formal suggestion of domestic hospitality is to be given, it might, perhaps, be allowed; but only a commonplace designer, a sort of misfit architect, would try to get off with such a substitute for design. I suppose "cornices" for curtains to have come to be thought necessary when "cornices" for rooms began to be "the thing" everywhere. And there is as much necessity for one as for the other.

What is the use of a curtain? Part of its use is its usefulness, and part of it is its beauty, or the sense of comfort it gives. It is useful to shut out the light and to keep out the cold air, and, as in all household decoration, usefulness is the first thing to be secured, we must consider first how these two ends are to be gained. To get all the light we may ever, at any time, want from a window, we must be able to have the whole glass clear; to draw curtains, if there be curtains, completely away from the glass, and keep them well to either side. Now, if there is a cornice, the curtain is either nailed to it (on

the inside), or it runs with rings on a rod that is stretched
across the cornice on the inside.   If it be nailed to the
cornice, so that it only opens in the middle, it can never
be so drawn as to give us all the light we may need.
And, if it slides on a rod, there is no need of a cornice,
and no reason why the rod should not be shown and
acknowledged.   I may say just here, that "cornices" are

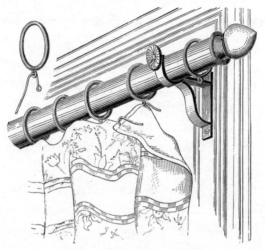

Curtains Hung by Rod and Rings.
No. 47.

almost always very troublesome to take down and put up,—
the services of an upholsterer's man or men being necessary,—and are a constant source of expense, for no end
whatever, except to give the upholsterer pleasure.

Here the housekeeper cuts in with: "But then, sir, the
room looks so bare without 'cornices.' And, how are we
to support our lambrequins without their aid?" Well, I
will be down upon lambrequins presently, and give them a

gentle piece of my mind; but first let us see whether it is inevitable that the room should "look bare" without the cornices. That it does look bare, as a rule, I will admit, but that is the fault of the room. Our rooms are so universally without harmony in their fitting-up, and the walls are so rarely (almost never) a good background for the furniture or the people, that we come to depend upon the furniture to give us some color and sense of solidity. If the carpet, walls, and ceiling of a room were once treated as a whole, and brought into proper harmonious relation, we should find that the room would not only look well with fewer and smaller pieces of furniture, but that taking out one or two things would not make such a difference as it does now.

The only sensible way to support curtains is by rings running on a brass rod. The mechanism of this is shown in cut No. 47. The rings remain upon the rod, and the curtains have long hooks of wire sewed to their upper edge, which hook into eyes soldered to the edge of the rings. With a step-ladder, a child can unship the curtain in a jiffy, and put them up in less than no time, and the upholsterer's yearly bill be easily shorn of two items at least. The rod rests upon two brass stays that are screwed, once for all, to the wall, and that need never come down. Nor need the rod and rings come down, for that matter; and, as they are made of burnished brass, they only need the dusting they can get with the long-handled feather whisk. The rods are sold, or ought to be sold, by the foot. They come of different diameters, and a button

screws on at either end to cover the openings, and prevent
dust and animated nature from seeking shelter in the hollow tube.   Perhaps we can gratify the average woman by
admitting that the real use of these buttons is to take off
the "bare" look from the rod.   We must consider, before
settling upon the rod, what are the dimensions of our
room.   We knew a lady who teased her husband into
discharging a servant because she was so tall as to be out
of proportion to their house, and a curtain-rod may easily
be too large for the room it is put up in.   Every woman's
eye will tell her whether a rod is too large or too small
for the work it has to do, and she has only to choose
what suits her case.   The rod should look as if it could
support the curtain, not merely be able to support it.
Here, as in many cases, the eye has to be considered.

Hanging curtains by rod and rings is the good old
way, and its elegance, as well as utility, has always commended it to artists and people whose tastes in great things
prove they may be trusted in small matters.   It is not to
follow Mr. Ruskin in his fetich worship of the old Hebrews,
to say that, as the curtains of the Jewish Tabernacle were
hung by rods and rings, we may think well of that fashion,
but only because it is plain from the descriptions that both
the earlier Tabernacle and the later Temple were intrinsic-
ally beautiful structures.   The Italian painters were always
hanging their curtains in this way, as the reader may see
in Raphael's "Sistine Madonna," for a familiar example.
But a dozen others come to my mind, and several in
Dürer besides.

The curtain in the "Sistine Madonna" is hung, not upon a rod, but upon a wire; and neither the means by which it is suspended, nor the way it hangs, is to be commended, for so heavy a curtain should have been hung from a

Curtains for an Every-day Window.
No. 48.

strong rod, and it should have been drawn aside, not looped up. But there is a hint in the hanging of this curtain we may make use of in our own practice, and that will sometimes be found to add just the touch that was wanted to reconcile us to curtains in a room where curtains may have threatened to be in the way. The wire on which the Raphael curtain hangs sags a little near the middle, as is natural, seeing what a weight depends from it. This lets in the light from the top, and, without puzzling ourselves over what Raphael did it for, we may try the experiment for ourselves of stretching our curtain-rod, not above the lintel of the window, or even across it, but a few inches below it, enough to let the light stream in and play about the ceiling. Miss Maria Oakey has drawn for us a curtain that is hung in this way (cut No. 48), and the effect of it is very pleasant in practice, though, at first sight, it seems a little strange. In a parlor or living-room there is never any need of shutting the light out altogether, and even if there are no outside blinds or shutters, no cold will come in at the top of the window, so that nothing is lost or given up by this arrangement, while we gain two things—a pleasant effect of light, and the additional solidity imparted by the molded lintel of the window.

Indeed, perhaps this is as good a way as can be devised for securing something of what is unconsciously sought to be gained by the device of a "cornice." If the lintel be well designed, and with good moldings, and then not left staring white, but brought into tune with the rest of the wall and curtains themselves, it will do all in effect that the "cornice" could have done, and without interfering with the play of the curtains as we move them on their rods.

Cut No. 49 shows curtains hung across the arched door-way, taking the place of the sliding-doors, which, however, are still there, to be shut when necessary, which is but

seldom. Here there can be no doubt as to the desirableness of hanging the curtains, not across the architrave of
the door-way (the arch being a mere supposed ornamental
cutting off the corners of the square, and not a real arch),
but in a line with the
spring of the arch itself,
leaving the whole arch
open for light and air.
This again, in practice,
is found to work well,
avoiding the heavy and
obtrusive effect of such
a mass of stuff as would
be required if the cur-
tain had been hung
from a rod stretched
above the top of the
door along the archi-
trave.

Curtain in an Arch-way.
No. 49.

Their length de-
pends on whether they
are to be caught back
sometimes with a band
or cord, or whether
they are at all times to be allowed to hang straight. In
case they are to be subject to tying back sometimes, they
must be made longer than when they are to hang straight.
In the latter case they should well touch the floor, but not
sensibly lie upon it. At least, this is my notion of the

fitness of things; others may think differently. If the stuff
the curtains are made of is heavy, they will hang in good
lines even when the ends lie on the floor; but I cannot
see what is gained by letting them do so. Nor should
the stuff be very heavy. It may be thick and impervious
to light and air, but it ought to be soft and easily falling
into folds. The color ought to go with the room, but
ought not to domineer or lead the rest; indeed, nothing
ought to do that in a room; but if the tone of the room
be accented anywhere, it should be by something small,—
a vase, a cushion, a bit of tapestry,—not by any large
piece of furniture, nor by any large space of wall or
drapery. The decoration of the curtain by bands across
the stuff, not by vertical stripes, has everything to recommend it—oriental usage (almost always a sure guide in
decoration), and the fact that it is always to be reckoned
on to produce its pictorial effect, since the bands cannot be
hid, no matter how many folds the curtain makes. But
stripes are continually being concealed in the folds, or else
cut in two, and so their value lost or impaired.

With all the varieties of stuffs that are in the shops
to-day, a woman with ingenuity and an eye ought to have
little difficulty in getting handsome curtains without too
much money, and at not too high a price. Give up the
cornices and the lambrequins—awkward additions to any
window, nine times out of ten; give up fringes and borders, and straps by which to hold the curtains back, and
you can then throw the whole weight of your purse upon
the main stuff of your curtains and the bands they are to

be crossed with. Any lady who can trim her own hat can trust herself to lay bands of harmonious color across the ground-work of her curtains. These should be separated one from the other by narrow bands or laces, to prevent one color affecting another. The Cottiers, and Morris, Marshall & Company of London, have been very successful with these banded curtains, and the laces and fringes they make are most beautiful in execution and texture, and telling in design by virtue of their quaint simplicity. It must be admitted that curtains made up of these bands and laces on a ground of soft woolen stuff, though most delightful to the eye and to the touch, are far from cheap; but it is not necessary, even for the enjoyment of the eye, to have the costliest; and there are simple combinations enough to be made. But the most beautiful ought to be seen once to get the eye in tune.

In connection with this subject of curtains I may remark that a delightful field is open to women, one in which they would be sure to find pleasant employment, and where certain faculties they have, peculiar to their sex, would be exercised and made useful. This is the art of embroidery. "What!" all the women will cry at once. "Embroidery, do you say? And are n't we embroidering all the year round—slippers and smoking-caps, lambrequins and table-cloths, chair-covers and foot-warmers? Embroidery, forsooth! Oh, here 's a discovery!" But this writer makes bold to confess he was not thinking of any of these unhappy productions of misplaced womanly labor when he spoke of embroidery. If he were recommending a young man to

study literature he would not expect to be put down by
the young man's assurance that he read three newspapers
every day.   There is no such waste of time, money, and
patience as the worsted-work and embroidery to which our
ladies give up so much of their leisure.   It is n't beautiful,
it is n't useful, and it stands much in the way of educating
the eye and the general taste.   Of course girls will always
make slippers and smoking-caps for young men—at least
I hope so; they enjoy making them, and the young men
are not what I take 'em for if they don't enjoy getting
them.   There is no reason whatever why these things
should not be well designed; but they never will be so
long as the girls are so wanting in taste as to put up
with the patterns they find in the shops.   I suppose, however, if the young men and maidens were not so easily
pleased, or had a taste of their own, there would be a
supply of patterns to meet a more exacting demand.   So
long as people are in the infantile state of mind that is
pleased with little imps and devils careering over slipper-
toes, or chasing one another along a lambrequin, or with
foxes' heads and tails, hunting-caps and whips, or with any
out of the whole catalogue we all know so well, not much
can be hoped for.   But the advice to take up embroidery
did not have reference to little love-and-friendship tokens
of the cap-and-slipper tribe.   It was intended to apply to
more serious works, such as coverings for furniture, hangings for doors or walls, and the like.   Since things took a
turn in England, and the arts of furniture and house
decoration began to interest artists and architects, and the

new doctrine found a sacred poet to father it and save it from sinking into trade and commonplace, the arts of embroidery have been inspired with new life, and have enlisted in their service a number of good talents, who have not only given pleasure to the public, but have found pleasure and profit in it for themselves. Some of the ladies belonging to the families of the house of Morris, Marshall & Company have distinguished themselves by the beauty and originality of their designs, and no less by the excellence of the workmanship; and they have become important members of the business, their work and their taste having not a little to do with the success of the enterprise. These ladies make their own designs for the most part, though they also execute designs furnished them either by the firm or by outsiders. Nor are they by any means the only persons in England who do this sort of work. There is an important business interest slowly growing up there in the field of designs for stuffs and embroideries, and many women are contributing to the success of the new industry. As I have said before, there has not been for a hundred years and over, such a time as ours for the beauty and excellence of the stuffs that are used in household decoration. Any one who will go into Herter's or Cottier's, and look over their plushes, silks, serges, and all the nameless materials that are being made nowadays in England, France and Austria, will easily see enough in half an hour to justify my remark. Many of these materials are very costly, and out of reach of most purses; but many of them, especially the English things, are not costlier than is reasonable in the beginning, and they have a capacity for wear in them that makes them cheap in the end. Besides, it must always be remembered that every good thing is better for showing, in moderation, signs of wear; and stuffs, particularly, never look just right till they have the gloss of newness rubbed off them. I know this is n't what is called American doctrine; certainly it is not New-York doctrine, where we cannot have things new and scrubbed enough; but it is artistic doctrine, and every artistic nature will recognize its truth by imagination, if it do not already know it to be true by experience.

A want long felt having been provided for in the success of these new stuffs and these new colors, it was natural there should be felt a need for decorators whose work should be in harmony with the new materials. I believe that, in fact, much of the proficiency of modern Englishwomen in embroidery, and much of the enthusiasm for it among them, date back to the rise of the ritualistic revival there; but it has found a wider field since then, and a more rich development in the service of household art. Besides, most of the ecclesiastical decorative work was conventional and copied, cramped in its expression and pinched to the uses of a narrow creed. But, working in the service of human love and feeling, the artist was free to express herself and follow the flight of her own fancy. The result has been, that many works of embroidery are produced to-day in England which show the old skill and taste to be still alive, and only waiting for the opportunity of exercise.

We have had but few beautiful works of this sort produced here, partly because there has been no social movement that caused the art to revive naturally, partly because there has been no market for such works if they had been produced. Some of our readers may have had the pleasure of seeing—it is now some three or four years since—a small collection of pieces of embroidery executed by a young lady in Boston from her own designs. They were every way exquisite; and, although it was evident she had been stimulated by the Japanese design, yet there was no resemblance to Japanese work except in what, for want of a better word, we call "the motive." The pieces produced were not "useful;" they were only intended for ornament—to be fastened upon a wall, to be framed, to be brought out and looked at upon occasion. Squares of silk or satin were taken, the color selected for its suitability to the design to be worked upon it. These designs were bits of external nature transferred by silk threads, instead of oil or water colors, to the lady's silk or satin "canvas." Her morning's walk, her stroll in the garden, suggested to her the day's delightful work. Now, on a pale sapphire silk, she made a flight of apple-blossom petals drift before the wind, at one side the branch that bore them, with its tips of leaves; or across one corner of a square of amber satin a geometric spider had woven her silver web, darting from tip to tip of the white rose-tree; or cat-o'-nine-tails against a blue-green water, with a rose-red mallow, or the neck and head of a duck sailing through her kingdom; or autumn leaves, sad colored, raining down against a weltering sky of gray; or hips and haws, or black elderberries, or—anything. The lady worked as she pleased and as Heaven directed, and had no fear of "schools" or of "laws" before her eyes. And she painted pictures with her needle that opened the doors of the artist guild to her as cordially as if she had n't been a woman; nor could we fairly reckon up the influences that have brought about the possibilities of a new day for us here in America, if we left out the embroideries of this Boston girl.

There is much interest felt of late among the young people in this matter of embroidery, but most of them are hampered by the difficulty of making a start. It is almost inevitable that we should be thrown upon the Japanese for our first hints and instruction; their art is so perfect as decoration, their method so varied, and their materials suited to every subject and belonging to our own time, and we so rich in its productions. Other art is strange to us—belongs to other times and to modes of life that once were those of men of our own world, but now outworn and laid aside. The Japanese live in moon-land; their ways are not ours, and it is impossible for us to put ourselves into sympathy with them. But their art comes out of themselves, and they are producing it now in our day on the models they have been following for centuries and with much of the spirit of the antique time. And therefore it has a vitality for us, and knocks at little secret doors in our own natures and gets some sort of response, though, for the most part, it is but the wind whistling through the key-hole. Still, if a woman can enjoy it, if it attracts her, she will do well to study it and base her embroidery upon it. But it ought to be done with a constant reference to nature, and it is better to fail in putting our own observation into silk and worsted, than to succeed in working up into painful perfection Mrs. German Something-or-other's conventionalities of design and eye-scratching colors.

———

How to hang our pictures is the next worry after curtains, and yet the way out of this wood is as clear or clearer than the other. Our plaster walls are not made for driving nails into, and they are easily defaced if we try to drive nails into them without the aid of a practiced hand. We have to get a carpenter to come with his hammer and we set him at tapping the wall like a woodpecker to find the solid places by the sound, and then put in his nails at a venture. And then we are the slaves of the studding timbers, and our pictures must hang where they will, not where we will. The first device for getting more liberty was that of fixing a permanent brass or iron rod along the upper part of the wall just under the cornice, and hanging the pictures from that, moving them back and forth till we had them where we wanted them. But this has a clumsy look and a mechanical, and suggests the notion that we are taking advantage of an accidental gas-pipe to suspend our pictures from. We wanted something simpler and less obtrusive than this, which is only suited to a public hall; and what seems to just hit the mark is a strip of wood shaped as described in cut No. 50, and nailed along the wall at any height desired. Ordinarily, it will be best to fasten it directly under the cornice; but this depends upon the height of the room. If the room is a very lofty one, by fixing the strip some distance below the cornice, we avoid the monotony of a number of cords or wires spreading over the wall, and we can utilize the space thus left between the strip and the cornice by hanging there some casts, or pieces of armor, or objects of

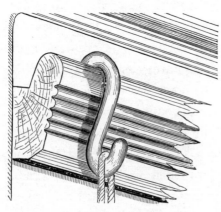

Strip and Hook for Hanging Pictures.
No. 50.

any kind that will bear being hung above the level of the eye. Very few things do bear this —I mean, of things that are of a size to bring into our houses at all; but there may be such, and while we should like to have them on the wall of our living-room, we do not want them to drive things away that need nearer looking at. No picture ought to be hung higher than the height of the average human eye when the owner of the eye is standing. It is the almost universal rule in our houses to hang pictures much above this level, and they cannot be enjoyed there. If the picture is a portrait, or if it have human faces in it, its eyes should look as nearly into ours as possible; and if there be no such simple guide, perhaps a good rule will be to have the line that divides the picture horizontally into equal parts level with the eye. If one starts in hanging pictures with the determination to place them so that they can be easily seen and enjoyed without stretching the neck the least, or stooping the body, he will be pretty sure to do well. In remote farm-houses and country taverns we often see pictures, particularly portraits, skyed as high as if their owners had been Academy Hangers, and the painters young rivals of a new school. I suppose the reason is that the simple-hearted owners think a picture such a precious thing, it can't be hung too securely out of the reach of meddling hands. They are often not clear in their minds as to what a picture is meant for, and not finding in it any practical relation to human life and society, they treat it with reverence and put it where it will disturb them as little as possible. But, as people come to enjoy pictures and get some intellectual, spiritual nourishment out of them, they want them, as they want their books, where they can see them and use them.

In connection with this part of our subject, we may deprecate the hanging pictures in places where there is not light enough to see them, which people surely never do unless a supposed necessity compels them. They have accumulated a number of pictures and framed engravings; they are attached to them and accustomed to them, and they want to hang them all up on their walls. So, some fare well and others fare ill. But it is so annoying to see a picture hung where it cannot be seen, the very end and aim of its being frustrated, that it is best to reform the practice altogether. Weed out the collection; put the less desirable ones, or the ones we have outgrown, into other rooms; start them gently on their way, by slow degrees, toward the garret, and do not try to fill their places, but give the remaining ones a chance to be seen and enjoyed. Or take the engravings out of their frames and put them in portfolios, or into the frames of the South Kensington print-stand figured on page 83, where they can be seen when we feel like it. In our effort to introduce some serenity and largeness into the furnishing and decorating of our houses, one of the main things to accomplish will be the hanging fewer pictures and objects on the walls, putting there only what is worth looking at, and that cannot be better seen by being held in the hands. A large room can be made to look small by being overcrowded with furniture, or by having the walls covered with a multitude of small pictures, engravings, and objects, the windows swathed in drapery, and lambrequins cascading over mantel-pieces and shelves. And by reversing this way of treating a room, a small room may be made to look almost large, and at any rate will tranquilize the eye and mind instead of fidgeting it. Have nothing in the room in the way of furniture that is not needed—that has not a real use, whether for work or play; and hang nothing upon the walls that does not need a wall to show it, and that is not worth being shown.

One trick of our time I should like to have a word with, and that is, the habit of over-ornamenting everything. It is not merely that we over-ornament; where ornament is advisable at all this is a natural enough fault to fall into, but we ornament a thousand things that ought not to be ornamented. It is hard to find an object of merchandise to-day that has not ornament (so called) of some kind stuck or fastened upon it. That terrible word "bare" seems to have frightened us all, and driven us to cover the nakedness of things with whatever comes to hand. We cover our note-paper with clumsy water-marks, we put "monograms" (though "many grams" would express better the multitudinousness and intricacy of these illegible devices) on our clothing, on our bed-linen, on our table-linen, on our books and title-pages, on our carriages and silver—our silver! Oh, was there ever silver like unto ours for knobs and welts, and wrinkles and spikes, and everything that silver should n't have! If the reader will look about him as he reads this, he will certainly find in his own surroundings—for we can none of us wholly escape—the justification for this criticism. The architects cannot design a house or a church but they must carve every stone, cover the walls with cold, discordant tiles, break up every straight line with cuts and chamfers, plow every edge into moldings, crest every roof-ridge and dormer-window with painted and gilded iron, and refuse to give us a square foot of wall on which to rest the tired eye. Within, the furniture follows in the same rampant lawlessness. The beauty of simplicity in form; the pleasure to be had from lines well thought out; the agreeableness of unbroken surfaces where there is no gain in breaking them; harmony in color, and, on the whole, the ministering to the satisfaction we all have in not seeing the whole of everything at once,—these considerations, the makers of our furniture, "fashionable" and "Canal street" alike, have utterly ignored, and the strife has long been, who shall make the loudest chairs and sofas, and give us the most glare and glitter for our money.

Just as I had written these deprecating words, I took down my overcoat from where it had been hanging, and, as the loop hesitated a little about slipping off, I gave a closer look at the hook. It was as ill-adapted to its use as the maker could contrive; cut out apparently from a thick sheet of brass with a dull chisel, the edges left as sharp as the tool would allow, so as to give the loop every opportunity to fray and cut itself free, and each of the branches armed with a little round at the end so as to prevent your getting your coat off in a hurry. However, as a make-weight for all this want of consideration for the utilities, the flat sides of the hook (which, to tell truth, was cast, and not cut out of a thick sheet of brass) were ornamented with an extremely pretty pattern, so that if you had plenty of leisure, or if your coat should detain you some seconds in getting it off the hook, you could improve the time in studying "how to apply art to manufactures."

The dirty people, too, who amuse themselves and make clean people miserable by squirting tobacco-juice over their own and other people's floors, must be touched now and then—for even they have sensibilities hid deep beneath their thick skins—by the perception that somebody cares even for them, when they see what taste is expended on the decoration of the spit-boxes which they are all the time engaged in making ineffectual efforts to hit. Pretty Greek *meanders* and *guilloches* encircle the sacred little vessels, and neo-Greek medallions enshrine heads of pretty women, and we see how good a thing it is to introduce Art into every-day life, and to disseminate it widely in order to elevate the masses.

Even in so small a thing as this strip of wood on which our pictures are to hang, we find an illustration of this waste of ornament. Remember, that ornament cannot be produced without time and money, and it is as foolish as it is wrong to waste these by investing them where they bring no return.

These picture-strips are sold in all our picture-frame shops, and the hooks that belong with them are sold with them. Instead of being contented with a good strong line for the profile, such as is shown in our cut, and with a simple strong hook just fitted for its work, the dealer supplies us with a strip of rough-looking wood, "ornamented" on the front with moldings out of all proportion to the size of the strip. The hook that holds the picture-cord is of unpolished brass, left rough as it came from the founder's mold, but "ornamented" for all that, by being made an exact counterpart of the molding on the stick. Nothing is gained, either for looks or for utility, by all this fussing. The "ornament" is not of the least value when the strip is nailed in its place, and the hook has no better grip for being shaped to fit the molding. It is very well to have thought of the simple device, but if the deviser had stopped when he had calculated strain, leverage, and resistance, and been content with making both strip and hook capable of doing all that could be required of them, he would have produced a much more comely-looking contrivance.

When the wall space has been divided horizontally into bands agreeably proportionate, so much for the wainscot, or for the band of color that answers for wainscot, so much for the frieze, or the band of color that answers for frieze, then, to my thinking, the pictures hung upon the intermediate space—the wall proper—look best hung in a continuous line rather than irregularly, some higher, some lower. As they are sure not to be all the same size, enough irregularity will be secured by following the suggestion that they should all be hung on the line of the eye. Also, if an exact symmetry be not insisted upon, but the pictures hung with reference to where they individually look best and can be best seen, we shall find the whole room will look better for this reasonableness.

There is one advantage this way of suspending pictures by a hook resting upon a strip has over the usual way— the picture can be easily unshipped in case of need. No doubt many valuable pictures have been destroyed by fire in consequence of the cord by which they were hung refusing to leave the nail or hook from which it was suspended. The writer knows of one very beautiful portrait by Copley—a portrait of a lovely woman painted by the artist for his own pleasure—which was burned up with the house it adorned, because no knife was at hand to cut the cord that held it, and it could not be untwisted from the old hook that held it. The hook we recommend can be unshipped in a moment if needed; but I still think it better to put the strip a foot or two below the cornice, so as both to get rid of the too-much cord, and to have the hook within broomstick-distance.

It is just as easy to hang a picture by a single line of cord as by two lines diverging from the point of suspension—the common way. A very large or long picture should be hung by a cord at each end, each cord depending from its own hook. These vertical lines are much more agreeable to the eye than the diverging lines, and make a useful contrast to the horizontal lines of the wall division. But I don't think the means by which a picture is suspended ought to be concealed, or kept at all out of sight. There ought to be a cord that not only is, but that seems to be, sufficient for its work. And it is our fault if we cannot make these cords harmonize with the wall on which they are to appear as lines.

———

Cuts Nos. 51 and 52 were drawn for me by Mr. Lathrop, to illustrate a point I want to make in reference to the treatment of rooms in country houses in the upper story, or in what is sometimes called the Mansard, where the outside wall on one or two sides slopes inward, following the line of the roof. Cut No. 51 is a corner of the bedroom in an improvised summer-retreat in the country. The building was once the carriage-house of a dwelling of which the oldest portion was built in the second half of the last century. The carriage-house was contemporary with this oldest portion, and was built—after the sensible fashion of those times—with stone walls two feet thick. The lower room is about nine feet high, and the loft above was floored with thick oak planks resting on beams of oak.

"Hail! Calm Acclivity, Salubrious Spot!"
No. 51.

At a later day, this loft was converted into a billiard-room; the roof was raised, and supported on brick walls carried up on the outer edge of the thick stone walls so as to leave half their depth available for a shelf which runs the whole length of two sides of the room, the ends being differently treated. The stone portion of the wall is cased with wood, and the brick wall above it is lathed and plastered; and the result is, not only that a pretty decorative effect is produced, but that we gain two substantial points in comfort. First, we are pushed out by the stone wall so far into the room that we can't bump our heads against the ceiling. Then we get a most useful and handy shelf along the two sides of the room, which takes the place of a dozen tables. And a third advantage is, that we get a good piece of perpendicular wall on which to hang pictures, a mirror, casts, etc., etc.

Nobody who has not seen it can have a complete notion of what a comfortable, cozy and picturesque result this arrangement produces. In its origin it was purely accidental; but it would be a good thing to copy, and seems to me the right solution of the difficulty always found in treating these rooms with sloping sides. The second cut, No. 52, is another solution of the same problem; but this belongs to a modern-built house, and the owner, who was not the builder (if he had been, such a thoughtful architect as he is would have left no flaw nor botches in his work), has been obliged to take things as he found them. The sloping ceiling starts from a point nearer the floor in this instance than in the other, leaving just room enough to put some low book-shelves against the upright portion in one place, and a sort of deep cupboard against it in another. In the corner an easel serves the purpose of a wall, and supports a water-color drawing (and in this case what a lovely, tender specimen it is of the beloved old master, Hill); while in front of the easel such a comfortable, low, roomy Chinese bamboo chair invites us to its embraces, that we can't get nearer to the sloping wall if we want to. Who but an Oriental could have devised such a combination of luxury as this chair? A low platform beneath the seat slides out on easy rollers, and we have a lounging seat. The back is lowered to a lower angle, and we have a bed; while the two flat, capacious arms, long and broad, and just the right height, are a library-shelf, a writing-table, a dining-table, or a rest for the chess-board. And all so quietly managed and so free from fuss! Light cushions are easily added, and covered by tasteful womanly hands, make the chair more easy to the invalid or old person, who has more leisure than the most of us to enjoy it; but the well person does not need such additions, for the bamboo makes a sufficiently soft and springy seat.

The owner of this sky-parlor and of its belongings has found a use for Japanese scrolls that shows how suitable they are for decoration. Yet to use them for this purpose does not oblige us to fix them permanently on the walls. One end of the roll lies on the book-case or cupboard under the sloping roof, and, being held in its place by a book or bronze laid in front of it, the other end is carried up and fastened at the angle where the sloping roof and the flat ceiling meet. The two scrolls in the drawing are decorated with colored figures on a gold ground, and they light up the corner of the room very cheerfully, and so take off from the stiffness of the ceiling-angles, giving, though

quite unintentionally, something of a tent-like expression
to the room. Of course, it would not often be desirable to
use the scrolls in this way; but rooms roofed like this are

A Harbor of Refuge.
No. 52.

common enough, and this hint may help some one who
does not know how to use the sloping wall.

There is hardly anything this time of ours enjoys less,
less knows how to value, than a clear space of blank wall.
Yet there are few things so pleasant to the eye, provided

the wall is of a good tone and has a surface that absorbs the light, or at least does not reflect it.   The early Italians, painters and builders alike, understood this, and some of them, Giotto, for instance, liked such breadths of breadth so well, that he could sometimes hardly make up his mind to put a fold or a wrinkle into the cloaks and mantles of his personages.   But all the great men knew the secret, Titian best of all; and this delight in broad stretches of blank wall, broken only, and that rarely, by the shadow of a projecting corbel, or by the wrought-iron support of a lantern, or by the sparse leaves and knotted, straggling branch of a creeping vine, is one of the most encouraging elements in the art of the new school of Italian-Spanish painters.   We must try and get something of this feeling in our house-furnishing—trust more to simplicity and unity; give the eye some repose, and put the little bits of pictures and the knickknacks away in closets and drawers and portfolios, to be looked at only when we have nothing better to do.

And here it occurs to me to meet an objection that has been made to these designs I offer—the objection, namely, that, though often very pretty and attractive in themselves, they are of no practical use, because they are not procurable by the general public; or, if procurable, are too expensive or difficult to find.   Now, this objection is valid enough, but it does not touch me, since my main object in writing these pages is not to dogmatize, nor to give definite rules for doing this or that, nor to give people precise patterns to follow.   On the contrary, it has been urged from the beginning that people should follow their own taste, and do the best they can to make their homes pretty and attractive in their own way. If everybody's rooms are to be furnished like C's, how is that better than when they were all furnished like B's? There is

A Chinese Shelf.
No. 53

always a first sheep to leap a fence, or run down a side street, and all the sheep follow their leader till a new one tries a new start. I write in the hope that people are not all sheep, and that enough will be found to look at the principle taught, and to try and put it into practice in their own way. This is all I am after, and these cuts are meant to indicate my general taste in furnishing a house, and what seems to me likely to be pleasing to many people besides myself.

As for getting these things, or things like them, there is n't any real difficulty. We have shops like Sypher's, where, in the course of a year, more good things appear and disappear than any one house of ordinary size could find room for; and, considering how really good they are, and how well made, they cannot be called dear. They would not be called dear in most cases if they were new, and careful use improves almost all furniture. Every artist or artistic person would rather have a well-kept piece of old furniture than any new piece.

A suggestion may be offered to young married people who find themselves in "a whole house," as the saying is, that they should not be in haste to furnish all the rooms at once, but that they should take the matter easily, furnishing only the rooms they actually need. I cannot, in conscience, recommend the example of a couple I once heard of, who found themselves in Paris in possession of a pretty but unfurnished flat. Intending to remain in the city several years, they concluded to get only things that pleased them; and as there was not money enough to do this all at once, they secured the few absolutely essential pieces, and then looked for the rest. But the wife, who lived to laugh at this afterward, always declared that for six months they sat on their two trunks, because her fastidious better half could n't find chairs he thought "the thing," while, as they had only a cup-and-saucer apiece, waiting till the right thing in ceramics turned up, they were obliged, having in an impulsive moment asked friends to tea, to go out and ransack the bric-à-brac shops for the "old blue" for that particular evening. I believe they enjoyed this way of getting to rights much more than if they had been what is called "better off," and could have gone to a fashionable shop and ordered their whole flat furnished at once.

A young couple may get a great deal of innocent recreation by keeping one of the parlors of an ordinary New-York house, and one or two of the bedrooms, empty for a year or so, and visiting them often in company to discuss how they shall be fitted up when times are a little easier. Besides the pleasure of anticipation, there 's the consideration that, with experience, our tastes change, and probably improve; and we may reflect that it is much easier to change pieces of furniture that we never had, and have outgrown, for others that we like better, and mean to have some day, than it is to change or modify the real things that have been bought, and paid for, and brought home. When Udolpho came home tired one night, and was taken by his wife into the parlor to see her new chairs and sofas that had been brought in only that afternoon, delighted as she was with her achievement, she did not relish seeing the weary man good-naturedly sit down on the floor, saying that white satin embroidered with gold butterflies was too fine for him to sit on. Adelaide wished at that moment that she had not believed everything the upholsterer told her, but had used her own sense and judgment. And if ever she should read this,—which is n't likely,—she will perhaps agree that it would have been as well to let her ideas of what is suitable to a parlor ripen a year or so before giving them shape.

Then there's the pleasure of "picking up" things. In my humble opinion, this is the only way to furnish a house; produces the prettiest result, and is cheapest in the end. I should n't like, for my own part, to be able to go into Maherter's, or Hercott's, or Milord's, and order suits of furniture *ad libitum.* That might do for some people, and, I dare say, when one considers the awful waste of precious time implied in the way I am recommending, it is much to be preferred by serious persons who don't like that particular way of wasting time. But it has its disadvantages, nevertheless. The main things must be searched for first, and it would n't be a bad notion to try the Paris plan of hiring furniture (you can hire it there of any quality for a month, or a year, or a life-time), and clear it out by degrees. But, in default of such a provision so suited to our human needs, let the young folks try getting the cheapest things that will hold, and using them till they can be one by one replaced,—the new installed for a long voyage and the old ones going to some poor neighbor. This suggestion is not whimsical: it has been tried and found very satisfactory. "Picking up" is an easy art in Europe, where, after all that has been carried off as spoils, there is still an immense deal of old furniture to be bought: some of it splendid, some handsome, and some only curious, but all of it useful. The getting it home is the difficulty, and unless one is well prepared to submit to all the petty vexations and small swindles of our custom-house, and to bear the expense cheerfully, it is seldom worth while,—never, perhaps, except in the case of some very lucky find.

"Picking up" at home is a much pleasanter, if it be a more difficult task, and a lady the other day hit, with a woman's tact, upon the reason. She was talking, to be sure, of china, and not of furniture; but the argument applies as well to one as the other. She said the things we come upon in our own country are soon at home in our houses, because they were used by our own ancestors or our own people. They were to the manor born. They neither look affected, nor strange, nor pretentious, but native and natural. And one reason why it is not so easy to pick up the furniture of by-gone times in America is, that those who have inherited it are learning to value it, and are less and less willing to part with it. As our readers know, old furniture is "the fashion" in some parts of our country. In Boston a polite internecine warfare has for some time raged between rival searchers after "old pieces," and the back country is scoured by young couples in chaises on the trail of old sideboards and brass andirons. It is a pursuit highly to be commended, but it is apt to become fanatically fascinating, and, in their blind admiration, the young things buy many articles that even Mrs. Toodles would have had the judgment to resist. It is surprising to learn to what strange uses things may come at last! In the suburbs of Boston, the best places in which to look for Jacobean sideboards and cupboards that came over in the "Mayflower" are found to be the hen-yards, the closets and drawers having been for years given over in fee-simple to the fowl. Several handsome oak cupboards that now adorn pretty Boston dining-rooms had to be feathered and singed before they could be made presentable. The way in which they have stood this usage is creditable to their makers; so far from being hurt by it, they are really improved by their adventures. Experience of the mutabilities of fortune has been good for them, as it is good for everybody. They are well seasoned; they have a good healthy color, and their angles are enough rubbed down to take away the disagreeable look of newness which troubles us in things just out of the shop. Besides, in most cases this newness has to be rubbed off by human beings, and its loss represents just so much wear and tear of our muscle and heart-strings; but with these latest treasure-troves of Boston, all this has been done for them by proxy—by the hens.

In the rage that has sprung up of late for "grand-fathers" and "grandmothers,"—a kind of thing till very lately ignored, if not despised, in the bumptious arrogance of our social youthfulness,—it adds inestimably to the value of sideboards, andirons, and old china, if they have come to us by descent, and have n't had to be hunted up in a chaise. But everybody can't have a grandfather, nor things that came over in the "Mayflower," and those of us who have not drawn these prizes in life's lottery must do the best we can under the circumstances. We must go to Hawkins's, or Sypher's, or Drake's, or scour our own back country, where, perhaps, we may light upon a mine of unexpected richness, with owners who cannot conceal their wonder at people who are willing to pay hard cash for chairs, and tables, and sideboards, and china, that seem to them not worth taking as a gift. I have lately known of some very handsome things, such as would cost a great deal of money to make in these days, which were found in a house lived in by people who were in squalid poverty, but who had seen better days, and were glad to sell their birthright for a little more than a mess of pottage.

This mania, as it is called by the scoffers, for old furniture is one of the best signs of returning good taste in a community that has long been the victim to the whims and impositions of foreign fashions. The furniture which was in use in this country in the time of our grandfathers (of the great-grandfathers of the girls who, I please myself with thinking, sometimes look over these pages for the sake of the pictures) was almost always well designed and perfectly fitted for the uses it was to be put to. The wardrobes, or clothes-presses, as they were called, the dressing-tables, the tea-tables, and the chairs, were often extremely handsome—the hard-wood—on which labor had not been spared to work moldings on the solid, or to carve the drawers with rounded panels — lighted up with brass handles and key-plates serviceably designed. I have before me now, as I write, two chairs, both belonging to the time of our revolution. They are both hinted at in cut No. 53, but the detail is not dwelt upon, as Mr. Lathrop wanted us to look rather at the shelves on the table between the

chairs. The one at the right is backed and seated with
cane; the other has the back and seat stuffed. The cane-
seated chair is more delicately made and designed than the
stuffed one; the carving upon it is as well done as need
be, and the proportions are so good, it takes the eye of
almost everybody. This was no doubt a city-made chair,
and out of some stylish shop. The other chair came, with
three others, from up country somewhere; when they were
bought it was said they had been given by the Indians to
a certain old-time New-York merchant. As the Indians
were never, so far as I know, manufacturers nor designers
of furniture, this story of their origin has always thrown
about these chairs a little flavor of massacre and scalp.
They are every bit as well designed as the finer chairs,
but they have been made with the rudest tools, and
all the apparent turned-work upon them has been done
with the knife. Yet, notwithstanding all their rudeness,
they are much more artistic and effective than the chairs
covered with carving which we were all admiring as antique
a few years ago. It is to be hoped that no one will let
himself be laughed out of his fancy for a good piece of
"old furniture," to the extent of letting it slip out of his
hands when once he has the opportunity of buying it. If
it be even an ordinarily good piece, it will be money well
invested to buy it; for, besides its usefulness and the
pleasure of looking at it,—elements of "interest" not often
enough computed,—it will any day sell for more than it
cost if it were "picked up," but not, perhaps, if it were
bought from a dealer.

Hardly any piece of furniture is more troublesome to bring into harmony with the conditions of our modern room than the book-case. And one may well despair of bringing any help to those who are puzzling themselves

"What do you read, my lady?"
No. 54.

over the problem. If a man be a large student and a great accumulator of books, necessity solves the problem for him. He takes a room to himself, lines the walls with shelves, and covers all his available space with books. But that is not our problem. We want to have our books in our living-room, and we want pictures, and "objects," and

furniture, and comfort too. We want our books, not necessarily as Leigh Hunt said he liked his, "where he could
lean his head against them," but in close companionship,
and where we can get at them easily, and where we shall
be often tempted to get at them.

Cut No. 54 shows how this difficulty may be met in
one case, and it is a way that is by no means the invention of the owner of this particular book-case, but one that
has found favor with many another lover of books. The
present example was made to fit into a certain room where
it was fondly hoped it would remain for a half-dozen May-
days or so at the least.   But it has since found itself at home
in two other rooms, and, on the whole, shows itself a man-
of-the-world in accommodating itself to what it finds at
hand.   It is made of plain white pine, brought to a good
surface and shellacked, and its third year finds it with a
most beautiful color, only distinguishable from satin-wood
by a richer tone. It is twelve feet six inches long, the top
and bottom being each one piece, and it is about three
feet high. The bottom of the lowest shelf is four inches
from the floor, and the ends run up nearly five inches
above the top, and are connected by a strip at the back
of the same height. This makes a low wall of protection
for whatever may be set upon the top of the book-case,
and "finishes" it, as the slang phrase is, at once usefully
and handsomely. This book-case is divided into four by
three upright partitions, on each side of which slots are
sunk for the ends of the shelves to rest in, these shelves
being plain boards, all of the same thickness, of course,

and, what is unfortunately not "of course," sliding in and out with perfect ease, whether weighted with books or not, and each one fitting like a glove into any two of the one hundred and four slots that it may be necessary to slide it into. I have found this way of supporting the shelves a very good one; and it is an additional point in its favor, when once its practicalness has been admitted, that it looks well, the front ends of the slots in which no shelves rest showing black and alternating with the uncut portion of the wood,—an effect which was not sought for in the design, but which, when the work came to be executed, rewarded the designer for having tried to solve his problem of self-support in a straightforward, natural manner. Cut No. 55 will explain this little detail to the eye. This book-case will hold, easily, four hundred books; nearly five hundred, if ordinary small octavos and duodecimos are to be accommodated—the lesser number, if one hundred and odd of them are large octavos and folios. Moreover, the shelves being a foot deep, as many more books or pamphlets that are not designed to be discarded, but are only wanted semi-occasionally, can be ranged behind the other books and pamphlets.

The top of such a book-case as this will be found an excellent place on which to set many useful and ornamental things that find their natural home in the living-room, and which yet, under ordinary circumstances, are apt to be in the way. It may be consecrated to the utilities or to the ornamental, or, as is best, no doubt, it may offer to both a fair field and no favor. Here, at one end, is the convenient Japanese chest of drawers without doors, made of unlackered wood, a capital hold for writing-paper, envelopes, etc., or for small precious objects that one likes to have at hand, and yet which must not be left about. In the other corner, next the window, is the favorite cast, too small for a pedestal, but lifted here to a convenient height and safe from all ordinary accidents, whether from four-footed cats in fur, or from two-footed cats in petticoats wielding dusters and feather whisks. Between these there is room for many pretty and curious things, to say nothing of drawings or photographs in *passe-partout* that one does n't care to hang up, but which can be easily set a-tilt against the wall, and lightly moved or changed at will; and it will be wise not to allow this tempting shelf to become too crowded, for it is a capital place to rest a book for momentary reference.

Abundant room for books; a shelf so convenient that, when once it has been tried, it will hardly be given up; and a third advantage,—all the wall space above three feet from the floor left free and unincumbered for whatever use can be made of a wall. The books, with their various bindings and their varied shapes, make a handsomer wainscoting than can be else designed, and one that gives force and richness to the decoration of the wall above. In the arrangement of this wall, dignity should be aimed at, by giving up the field to one or two large objects,—large, I mean, in proportion,—and putting in the remaining space such things as will harmonize with them or set them off. And this will be found a good rule for decorating our walls in general; there is too great a tendency to spot the wall all over with little things—little pictures, little brackets with little vases or figurines, confusing the eye, and making it impossible to enjoy any one thing out of the whole pimply lot.

Some persons may object to leaving books unprotected either by solid doors or by doors with panes of glass instead of panels. It is, of course, proper to protect gentlemen's libraries in this way, as they are rarely intended for use, but are only a part of the general upholstery and furnishing of the house, the same as the pictures and the bric-à-brac. The architect in planning the house put in a "library," as of course, and what is a library without "books"? The library was not made for the books, but the books were bought because there was a library. A library without books would be as unmeaning as a cellar without wine. There are many tricks played in the matter of wine; profound talk of "green seal" and "yellow seal" and other mysteries, and cobwebs and dust added to bottles that will not grow old as fast as our knowing-ones in wine can drink it up; but the wine, whether good or bad, whether really out of one's own cellar, or only "bought at our grocer's," cannot escape being tried. The books, on the other hand, in the so-called "library," may not be books at all, but only backs of books glued on to bits of wood— an artifice by no means uncommon. But, whether so, or only books never read because unreadable, or books in editions and bindings too costly to be used or lent, the book-case that holds them may as well be protected by doors, and locked up with a lost key. For lovers of books, however, a house without books is no house at all; and in a family where books make a great part of the pleasure of living, they must be where they can be got at without trouble, and, what is of more importance, where they can

Detail of No. 54.
Effect of Slots for Book-Shelves.
No. 55.

share in the life about them and receive some touches of the humanity they supply and feed. The little child plays up and down the room and runs his fingers across their backs, or pushes them in and out, or knows the one that has pictures in it, and pats it approvingly with his flattened palm. The young girl runs over them with her eye, and taps a little here and there with a rosy reflective finger-tip, then draws out one that promises, or one long-known, and saunters with it to the favorite reading-place. For all who enjoy them, use them, depend upon them, the books are there at hand; not shut up, like clothes in a wardrobe, or silver in a chest, but free to the hand like the basket of apples or the pitcher of water on the sideboard.

There are "practical" objections in plenty against the use of doors for book-cases. They stick; the key is always lost; they hide the site of some of the books when the door is of glass, and when they are solid how is one to know that the case holds books at all? Then, when the doors are opened they are awkwardly in the way, and if there are children or young people in the house, they are sure to be left open, and to be run against. But, after all, my chief objection to doors on book-cases is, that they are inhospitable, and hinder close acquaintance. To have to ask for a key, or even to open a door unlocked before we can put our hand on a book, or look the shelves over to find one that suits us, is as bad as having to tug off a glove to seize a friend's hand. And what is more like a true friend than a book-case filled with real books?

"Dust!" says Martha, as she reads this. "What a place for dust such a book-case as yours must be!" It is true that dust does collect, but not much, if reasonable care be taken, and if the books are often used, and, at any rate, I maintain that dust, or the danger of it, is, of the two evils, rather to be chosen than the danger of not using the books at all; of having the family grow up without the habit of reading books, consulting them, seeking refuge in them. These habits, early and naturally formed, have more to do with culture than might be thought. The young people go to school or college, and hear lectures on English literature, or study books on the subject, and they come away with few ideas and little knowledge. Then, as they go out into the world, they come, perhaps, to think they would like to know something more, or perhaps they feel the need of knowing more, and so attend lectures, or listen to readings, to get in a hurry what they need. But knowledge got in a hurry is as poor stuff as leather tanned the new way, or kiln-dried timber, or bread made with baking-powders, or any of the modern substitutes for the old-time methods of time and patience. The only way really to know anything about English literature, or any other literature, is to grow up with it, to summer and winter with it, to eat it, drink it, and sleep with it, and this can never be if the book-case that holds the books in the house we grow up in has doors that lock.

If we must cover our books, for fear of dust, a curtain is all that can be allowed, and a curtain is little less troublesome than a door. I am not sure that a curtain is not more troublesome than any door. To be as little in the way as possible, it should be of some thin silk, and should slide with metal rings on a metal rod as lightly and easily as can be contrived, and, after all this trouble, the amount of dust kept out will be found to be but small. Besides, a curtain hides the books from sight, and one might as well hope to be warmed by a fire he could n't see as to get their full service out of books shut up behind doors or curtains. Glass doors have this to say for themselves, that they do give some glimpse of what is behind them, and show a little hospitality.

Some years ago, in an exhibition of furniture held in London, there was a book-case, designed, I believe, by Mr. Burges, the architect, which was closed by a curtain; but this piece was a small affair, and so not liable to the objections that would hold against closing a book-case such as is shown in cut No. 54, page 165, with curtains running along the whole front, or even along each of the four divisions.

This was only, in fact, a square box with shelves, set up on a table, and with a curtain hung across its front. The curtain was of plush, if I remember; but that was not a good material, and all the effect obtained might have been got as well by using silk. It hung by rings from a wire that was stretched across the *outside* of the upper edge of the box, so that when it was drawn it showed the *whole* of all the shelves and all the books. The book-case was made of plain wood, and painted with some good decoration on a red ground, and the curtain was of a gold-yellow cut on a red ground. In the upper left-hand corner of this square of plush there was embroidered a bee-hive, and the bees were flying back and forth in a straggling line between their hive and the lower right-hand corner. In the upper right-hand corner might have been written some motto—a line from Milton:

" They at their flowery work do sing,"

or the like. This was a pretty piece of furniture to hold a hundred books or so,—small copies of favorite authors that one likes to have at hand,—and, being meant for a parlor-piece, a little more elegance was admissible than would have been fitting for a work-a-day book-case.

We feel a little pity sometimes, for the Roman bookish people who had no books, properly speaking, but only scrolls. And to our modern hands, scrolls are unmanageable things. But there's much in habit, and the Japanese to-day, who make great use of scrolls (though they also have books in plenty), know how to use them, unrolling them and rolling them at the same time, as they read them or study their pictures. But there was one advantage in the Roman scrolls,—they were not heavy, and when they moved about they put them into a box like a bandbox, setting them up on end, so that a considerable number of volumes could be carried about on their journeys without adding inconveniently to their baggage. Our books, however, are too heavy for any such arrangement, and a very few add seriously to the weight of a trunk. This is sometimes an inconvenience: when one is taking a long journey, it is pleasant to have books, and they are the one thing not to be had. Cicero, our school-boy readers will remember,—if we are fortunate enough to have them,—when he is praising books, praises them, among other things, because they can go into the country with us. If he had not been too "swell" for such a condescension, he might have carried a small library with him in his hand, as one of us might carry a hat-box.

This, by the way. My point is, that the books in a house—the books the family is to be fed on—ought to be made as accessible as possible. There will often be a few books—rare editions in costly bindings—that are to be locked up, and not to be exposed to promiscuous handling; but these are really not books—they are bric-à-brac, curios, and no true lover of books would care to have many of them in his possession.

Cut No. 56 is a pretty little book-case in a house which the taste of its owner has transformed from a commonplace cottage into a home where simplicity, elegance and comfort have come and settled down for life. This is just an improvised shelf for books one likes to have in a bedroom or sewing-room. The side-pieces are partly supported by the chair-rail, and are cut well away below, so as not to interfere with the furniture.

Cut No. 57 shows a book-case fitted into the space between the mantel-piece and the window of a small room, the problem to be solved having been, to accommodate both the book-shelves and a large working-table against the same wall space. This was partly for the sake of convenience, that the owner might have his books of reference within easy reach, and partly from necessity, since the room was not large enough, or the wall space not skillfully enough divided, to permit the book-case to be in one

Books within reach.
No. 56.

place, and the table in another. The table was about five feet long, the space between the chimney-pier and the wall a little short of six feet, and it was desired to get all the good possible out of this space.

I may note, in passing, that the artist who has made
the drawing of this subject has placed the window at the
student's right hand instead of at his left hand, so that the

"Of Studie toke he moste Cure and Hede."
No. 57.

light comes wrong. Of course, in reading or in writing,
as well as in drawing, the light should come from the
left hand, both for the sake of the eyes and for comfort,
and our student would never have taken the pains he
did to rig up this corner, unless he could have started

with the necessary condition of "light from the left hand" fulfilled.

Against the chimney-breast, then, and against the wall at the window end of the space to be filled, uprights were planted,—solid planks of pine,—chamfered on their front edges, and projecting three inches farther in the lower part than in the upper. This was partly for more stability, and partly because deeper shelving was needed below for bigger books. These uprights were not fastened either to the chimney-pier or to the wall. They were held in their places by the shelving. But, as six feet is too wide a space for a shelf that is to support books to span, a third upright was placed at a point that permitted the table to be set against the wall between it and the one that was placed against the chimney. The narrower space thus inclosed was filled with shelves that went down to the floor,—five shelves in all,—adjustable by grooves in the upright at various heights to suit, and useful for diction-aries and folios. Over the table are three shelves (and the table itself, pushed well back against the wall, makes a fourth shelf), and these, having a span of five feet, and dividing between them a height of about three feet, accom-modate a goodly number of books, such as are in constant use by the owner for reference in his tasks. It may be added, that these shelves are made thicker than would commonly be thought necessary (the lower one is of two-inch stuff, and the upper one of inch and a quarter); but a shelf that sags with its load of books is a disagreeable, and even a dangerous, thing, and it was thought best to err on the side of safety. Besides, by molding the front edges of the shelves they lose any offensive look of too great stoutness.

The room in which these shelves are placed is a low one, but yet there is space between the ceiling and the top of the case for casts of the "Night" and "Morning" of Michael Angelo, but Mr. Lathrop remembered, perhaps, that these casts had been introduced into another book-case arrangement figured further on (cut No. 58), and so made our student a fencer, and gave him foils and masks and gloves for his book-case. For the sake of picturesqueness, too, he has half emptied the well-filled shelves.

Before leaving this drawing, I would say a word or two about the table. It is made on a good plan, and, after twenty years of constant service, is no whit the worse for wear. The supports are two thick planks with the edges cut and chamfered (inartistically done, in the owner's salad days) and stayed by four braces—two below which make an excellent rest for large books, and two above which give a solid rest for the thick table-top. In case of need, this table comes to pieces; the top is lifted off, and the braces are drawn out from the supports. When put together, it is as steady a table as can be desired. In the hands of a good designer, such a table can be made handsome as well as useful.

The design for the book-case, cut No. 54, has had so brilliant a success,—the original having been visited, measured and copied, until the plain, straightforward pine shelves would have blushed, if wood once shellacked could

A Screen of Books.
No. 58.

ever turn color,—that I fear the one I now bring forward,
in cut No. 58, may suffer in the comparison. But it is so
different and so excellent in its own way, I think it can

hardly fail to make friends. Such a design, besides, may be used where the other one could not at all be made room for. These book-shelves were designed for his own use by a gentleman of this city, and the drawing was made from the original by Miss Maria R. Oakey, and engraved by Mr. Marsh. The room in which the shelves are set up is rather a small one, narrow in proportion to its length, and having a fire-place in the middle of one side, a door-way opposite, a window at one end, and a door-way in the other. Accordingly, space has been saved, and the shape of the room bettered by the present device of building a book-case against the end opposite the window, and leaving the door-way, but substituting a *portière* for the door. The top of the case is designed to accommodate the casts of Michael Angelo's "Night" and "Morning"; and over the middle of this pediment was found to be a good place to hang and to rest a large circular dish of *faience*. The lower portions of the book-case, on either side the door, are ingeniously contrived for holding prints, photographs, architectural drawings, and the like; they are closed by a flap like the flap of a portfolio; this opens down, and the contents of the case are kept in their places, as in the portfolios of a print-seller, by pieces of thick card-board. A contrivance like this needs no particular description,—it explains itself, and recommends itself. It answers its owner's needs perfectly, and adds greatly to the appearance of the room, giving the distinction that always comes from means well employed and made to serve the utilities and the graces at the same time.

Cut No. 59 is a drawing of one end of the room described on page 151. If any one shall be led by it to think it a good notion to divide a large room up by screens and curtains instead of always by formal and permanent partitions, the little picture will be doing a part of its duty. To many people a large room is a great pleasure.

"And one describes a charming Indian screen."
No. 59.

Indeed, I think, most people like to have plenty of space in which to move about, but as we all like privacy sometimes, and seclusion from the doings of others, if for no other end than to have the temptation to talk and to look about us removed, it is good to have easy ways of attaining our object. The long, narrow parlors that are such an affliction to New-York housekeepers are much more elegantly divided by screens, which may be made as rich

or as plain as we choose, or by curtains, than by the
ordinary partition and sliding-door.   For comfort and for
coziness they often need to be divided, and yet they often
need also, when company comes, to be left free from end
to end.   But, more of this by and by.   The window and
curtain in cut No. 60 are at the other end of the room.

" But soft! what light through yonder window breaks!"
No. 60.

In our formal way of hanging curtains from a so-called
cornice, we lose the freedom and artistic movement of a
piece of stuff such as this curtain is made of; it becomes a
mere piece of machinery, and calls the dumb-waiter brother,
and the furnace-register sister.   But, hung by rings and
hooks to a brass rod, and moved back and forth at pleasure, it becomes another creature, and is second cousin at
least to the pictures and casts.   From being a pesky,

troublesome, dust-collecting member of the family, it is now a docile, cheerful, neat-handed minister of sunlight and cool shade, no trouble to anybody, and only pleasant to live with.

And, while I am speaking of screens, I may ask the reader to look back at cut No. 11, page 56, for a drawing of a very pretty Italian fire-screen, which I found in a house full of beautiful things. This consists of three frames, inclosing panels covered with some dark cloth or plush, on which peacocks' feathers are laid, and the whole protected by glass. The frames are loosely united to one another, which gives a pleasantly familiar air to the screen, as if it were standing at ease on its own hearth with its hands under its coat-tail. It is the only fire-screen I ever saw that one could forgive for shutting out the fire.

Cut No. 61 is a good hint for a screen, out of a Japanese picture-book; the stand is framed together and decorated with a painted pattern, and the screen itself is

Screen, from a Japanese Picture-book.
No. 61.

made of breadths of some prettily patterned material hanging loose by rings from the topmost rail. These strips are sewed together at the top, but near the bottom they are allowed to part, and the decorated framing of the screen shows between the openings.

Cuts Nos. 62 and 63 are intended to hint at ways of grouping simple objects in a picturesque and yet natural way, so as to get something out of them besides their individual elegance or interestingness.   Cut No. 62 is made

"We met by chance."
No. 62

up of a chair, well shaped and comfortable for a chair not intended for lounging, covered with old needle-work tapestry; a Chinese table of · simply carved teak-wood with a marble slab let into the top; and a Japanese scroll hanging upon the wall. The other cut, No. 63, shows one of the old-fashioned card-tables so commonly met with in old-

A Surprise Party.
No. 63.

fashioned homes, and now much sought after. It supports
one of the useful Japanese cabinets of lackered wood, and
on this is one of the Japanese tray-stands, which, in its
turn, supports a jar with flowers, whose gleam is reflected

in a deep-framed mirror with its beveled glass. In arranging these objects, the artist's intention was to show how a dark corner may be lighted up, and, perhaps, also how things which, beautiful or handsome or curious in themselves, lose something of their value by isolation, and are also sometimes in the way, and apt to find themselves thrust into closets and corners, may be made pleasing to their owners and just to themselves. Everybody must have noticed how corners seem to be, in nine cases out of ten, mistakes; how seldom is it that any good is got out of them. There is, to be sure, the corner-cupboard, a delightful invention, of which the reader has already been shown some pretty examples in these pages; but they are more at home in the dining-room,—for no reason, to be sure, except a traditional one. Corners, however, are fond of a bust occasionally, and, as things go, this may be allowed the best thing to do with a bust, seeing how small our rooms are apt to be, and how difficult of solution the pedestal question is. The corner chosen, too, is to be a matter of consideration; one of those on either side the window is the fittest, the effects of light and shade being the most telling there. Our way of muffling up our windows with heavy upholstery stuffs, however, makes these corners almost useless for any such delicate light as is needed for the refinement of sculpture. Meantime, much pleasure for the eyes can be procured by putting together some such group as this, composed of a few rich-looking (in this case inexpensive) things, with subdued color, as in the porcelain vase on the edge of the table, and in the one that holds the flowers, with sober, rich reflection all through the trophy, brought to a ripe accord in the gleaming mirror.

———

A change is coming over the spirit of our time, which has its origin partly, no doubt, in the memorial epoch through which we are passing, but which is also a proof that our taste is getting a root in a healthier and more native soil. All this resuscitation of "old furniture" and revival of old simplicity (more marked, perhaps, in the east than here in New-York) is in reality much more sensible than it seems to be to those who look upon it as only another phase of the "centennial" mania. It is a fashion, so far as it is a fashion, that has been for twenty years working its way down from a circle of rich, cultivated people, to a wider circle of people who are educated, who have natural good taste, but who have not so much money as they could wish. We go to the rich people's houses, and see in their parlors, bedrooms, and dining-rooms, beautiful pieces of furniture of the old time, made when there was a class of men who looked with pride upon their trade of cabinet-making, and wrote books about it, in which they talked with as much gravity and affectation of learning, about perspective and proportion, as if their theme had been the solution of the sphere, or the elixir of life. In one house we find a corner-cupboard like cut No. 34, an exquisite piece of inlaid work, with its ormolu mountings (not mere rough castings, left as they came from the mold, and not meant to be examined closely, but finished

with as much artistic care by the *ciseleur* as if they had
been mountings for plate), and with its door-panel gracefully painted by the hand of Angelica Kauffman herself.
We see hundreds of pieces,—for we are getting to be rich
in this country in these beautiful, handsome, curious pieces,—
and we come away with a conviction that the furniture
of a particular period can reflect the delicacy of feeling,
refinement of manners, and all that goes to make that sub-
tile quality of the mind which we call taste, as well as
some of the productions of man's skill which we are fond of
thinking of more importance than chairs and tables.   And
we find on looking about us, that the furniture of the Revolutionary period is evidently the outcome of a refined and
cultured time.   It would not require to strain a point, nor
to deal in paradoxes, to prove that the people who designed,
bought, used and enjoyed such furniture as we see to-day
displacing the French and German miracles of ugliness
that have been our only wear of late years, must have
been a delicate-minded, cultured, and sensible race, with
a very lively sense of the limitations of decoration as
applied to things in daily use.   We are all of us growing
to like these qualities, to enjoy them, to try to make them
our own, and to communicate them, if we can, to our
children and those about us.   There is beside, I suppose,
the pleasant knowledge that this furniture, if not all of it
made in America, was all of it made for Americans, or
bought by them; and there is a feeling that in going back
to its use, in collecting it, and saving it from dishonor, and
putting it in safe-keeping, we are bringing ourselves a little

nearer in spirit to the old time. Of course, this is but superficial,—no need to say it,—but we live in a world where even superficial influences have weight.

There is one comfort in the Revolutionary furniture—it is seldom we come across a piece to which the words ugly or awkward will apply. Certainly, they will never apply to

Things New and Old.
No. 64.

the pieces that belonged to well-to-do people. There was a "style" in those days, and in colonial days, and the rich people had the best pieces, of course, and the not-so-rich and the well-off followed the style as closely as they could; but even in pieces that belonged to poor people, we see the excellence of the model. I have seen a great many fine specimens of this old furniture, but I never saw a

piece that I would not willingly own, if I needed it and
had room for it. There is always merit of some kind. It
is well-shaped, it is useful, it is made of handsome wood,
it has excellent moldings and rich turnings, or picturesque
carving—and its individuality is not the least of its recommendations; there are never two pieces exactly alike.
There was no one in those days, apparently, who made
things "for the trade."

Cut No. 64 is a "restoration" effected in an old house
at Newport, by Mr. McKim, one of the foremost of our
young architects, who has shown an uncommon sort of skill
in finding out what there is left in an old house to build
upon for modern comfort and elegance. Here was the old
kitchen of a sea-side house, with its big fire-place and its
wainscoted wall, and the architect has, by a simple enough
treatment, turned it into a handsome parlor. The whole
house has been conserved with the same judgment—the
old kept wherever it was sound enough, and suited to a
new lease of life, and whatever new was added kept true
to the spirit of the old time, though without any antiqua-
rian slavishness.

––––––

The vignette on the title-page is a bit of old iron-
work,—a double candlestick, picked up at a Christmas booth
in Paris streets, and since, for many a day, found a most
useful table companion to one who always works at night
by candle-light. It lifts easily by the strong projecting
handle, and is not to be upset.

Before leaving the living-room, I must allow myself the pleasure of a tilt against pianos as we make them in this the present year of grace—"bow-legged megatheriums," as somebody has hit them off, the ugliest pieces of furniture which we of this generation, fertile in ugliness, have as yet succeeded in inventing. The first pianos were prettier than any that have been made since, but they were too spindle-legged for real beauty, and owed too much to the color of the wood they were made of, with its pretty inlayings and marquetry, and painted panels above the key-board—too little to the excellence of their form. A handsome piano, one that an artist could enjoy the sight of, does not exist to-day out of museums, nor is made by any one of the legion of manufacturers. But a piano, even a "square" or a "grand," might be made a stately ornament to our drawing-rooms, and even the "uprights," which try to be as ugly as their four-footed and hooved brethren, but cannot wholly succeed, might be made much better than they are, in artistic hands. Some time ago there was on exhibition at Goupil's rooms, in New-York, a water-color drawing by one of the new school of Italian artists, Rossi, in which a lady was seated at a piano, in the style of Louis XIV., very ornate with flourishing, carving and gilding not exactly to be recommended, and having painted on the inside of the lid a dance of Cupids, or some sacred mystery of that sort. Why can't some of our young artists induce some one of the young piano-makers with his fortune to make, to combine with some clever designer, and devise a case for them to paint? The result might be delightful, and even if the

first go-off were not wholly successful, it would show the
way. It would be good to see a herd of the heavy-
footed antediluvians that stretch their huge bulks about
our drawing-rooms, turned out of their luxurious quarters,
to give place to something that should seem more like an
instrument of music. As it is, the loveliest woman that sits
down to play at a modern piano is a little dimmed; the
instrument, instead of setting off her beauty, seems to be
doing its best to disparage it.

Attempts have been made by English designers to
improve the shape of the modern piano-forte, but, thus far,
they have only succeeded in adding to clumsiness of shape
clumsiness of ornament. I wish some one would try the
experiment of a perfectly plain case, and let it be decorated with color simply, after the fashion of the clavichord
in cut No. 10. This rests upon a stand, and the raised
lid has a pastoral landscape with figures painted on the
inside. This drawing was made on the block by Mr.
Lathrop, from an etching by W. Unger, after a picture by
Gonzales Coques, which is in the Gallery at Cassel. I had
the drawing made mainly for this clavichord, but it will be
of use to us in relation to other matters. The low-studded
room is hung with tapestry or brocaded stuff up to about
six feet; above this are hung pictures, and the large window-frame is divided into a number of small lights. How
much more in keeping with such an instrument as this in
a room so furnished, than with the handsomest of our
modern pianos in the most fashionable of our parlors,
sound these lines of Leigh Hunt:

THE LOVER OF MUSIC TO HIS PIANO-FORTE.

Dear friend, whom, glad or grave, we seek —
　　Heaven-holding shrine!
I ope thee, touch thee, hear thee speak;
　　And joy is mine.
No fairy casket filled with bliss
　　Outvalues thee!
Love, only, wakened with a kiss,
　　More dear may be.

To thee when our full hearts o'erflow
　　In griefs or joys,
Unspeakable emotions owe
　　A fitting voice.
Mirth flies to thee, and Love's unrest,
　　And Memory dear,
And Sorrow with his tightened breast
　　Comes for a tear.

Oh, since few joys of human mold
　　Thus wait us still,
Thrice blest be thine, thou gentle fold,
　　Of peace at will!
No change, no sorrow, no deceit,
　　In thee we find;
Thy saddest voice is ever sweet,
　　Thine answer kind.

INVITING A FRIEND TO SUPPER.

TO-NIGHT, grave sir, both my poor house and I
Do equally desire your company;
Not that we think us worthy such a guest,
But that your worth will dignify our feast,
With those that come; whose grace may make that seem
Something, which else could hope for no esteem.
It is the fair acceptance, sir, creates
The entertainment perfect, not the cates.
Yet shall you have, to rectify your palate,
An olive, capers, or some bitter salad
Ushering the mutton; with a short-legged hen,
If we can get her, full of eggs, and then
Lemons and wine for sauce: to these, a coney
Is not to be despaired of for our money;
And though fowl now be scarce, yet there are clerks,
The sky not falling, think we may have larks.
I 'll tell you of more, and lie, so you will come:
Of partridge, pheasant, woodcock, of which some
May yet be there; and godwit if we can;
Knat, rail, and ruff, too. Howsoe'er, my man
Shall read a piece of Virgil, Tacitus,
Livy, or of some better book to us,
Of which we 'll speak our minds, amidst our meat;
And I 'll profess no verses to repeat:
To this if aught appear, which I not know of,
That will the pastry, not my paper, show of.
Digestive cheese, and fruit there sure will be;
But that which most doth take my muse and me,
Is a pure cup of rich Canary wine,
Which is the Mermaid's now, but shall be mine:
Of which had Horace or Anacreon tasted
Their lives, as do their lines, till now had lasted.
Tobacco, Nectar, or the Thespian spring,
Are all but Luther's beer, to this I sing.
Of this we will sup free, but moderately,
And we will have no Pooly or Parrot by;
Nor shall our cups make any guilty men,
But at our parting, we will be as when
We innocently met. No simple word
That shall be uttered at our mirthful board
Shall make us sad next morning; or affright
The liberty that we 'll enjoy to-night.

BEN JONSON.

CHAPTER III.

THE DINING-ROOM.

THE suggestion made early in these pages, that, in general, there is no need for a separate parlor, but that one room, the living-room, may be easily and comfortably made to serve all the social needs of the family,—a place of meeting for themselves, and a place in which to receive the visits of their friends,—was not meant to include the dining-room. There ought always, if possible, to be a separate room for meals, though I have known cases in plenty where there was no distinction between the dining-room and the living-room. But in all these cases the living-room was an exceptionally large apartment, and no confusion resulted, as is apt to be the case where the experiment is tried, from the appearance of Betty at the door with the announcement, "Please ma'am, I want to set the table, ma'am." As a rule, our rooms, especially in our cities, are too small to make this double employment possible, or at least convenient, and, as provision is almost always made for a separate dining-room in our houses, we may as well accept the arrangement as being, on the whole, the better one, considering the complicated ways of modern life. I wish we had not twisted and bound ourselves up so inextricably in these complicated ways. More than we think, or are willing to allow, of the difficulty that surrounds housekeeping in America,—the trouble with servants

"Unless the kettle boiling be."
No. 65.

that makes such a mean tragedy in so many women's lives,—comes from the labor imposed upon the servants and upon the employers by the unnecessary fuss we make about living. The root of the difficulty is in the separation between our two lives, the domestic one and the social one, and the social one has been allowed to become so formal, ostentatious, and exacting, that in too many families it is by far the more important of the two—it regulates and controls the domestic life. It is hardly possible to dispute the proposition: that if the domestic life were made the leading one in any family, that is, if the whole household order, and all the arrangement and furnishing of the house, were made to accommodate and develop the family life,—the social element being obliged to suit itself to the family arrangement, and take them just as it found them,— life would be tenfold easier and tenfold happier than it is in America, where there is less domestic life and less domestic happiness than in any other country. This is the only land known to geographers where the greater part of the population lives to please its neighbors, and to earn their approval by coming up to their social standard. We all do it, rich and poor, merchants and mechanics, poets and politicians. Mr. Elliott's book shows that all like to have interiors, and to have their interiors known of men.

I have told the story before—but 't is a good illustration of my meaning, and will bear repeating—of the poet who had built himself a house in the country, and who consulted his worldly friend on the question of mantel-pieces. This was a quarter of a century ago or so, and it was almost unheard of for any one to have wooden mantel-pieces; but the poet had a mind for them, and asked Mr. Worldly-wise what he thought about it. " Mr. Nightingale," said the man of affairs to the poet, very solemnly, and with a warning finger, " marble mantel-pieces will be expected of you!" I wish I could add that people did n't get of Mr. Nightingale what they expected; but, unfortunately, they did, and the pity of it is that, after we have cut off our tails to please the foxes that have lost theirs, we get nothing for our pains. Nobody ever thanks us for cutting off our tails. They tease us till we do it, and when we have disfigured ourselves, then they cry out on the baseness of conforming with fashion. People say that the world loves conformity, and to have all coats cut one way. A certain conformity is unavoidable and good, nor is it ever worth while to break bounds for the sake of being singular. A wise woman said to a young boy who insisted on wearing his hair long, and bore with martyr-like conceit the sniffs and sneers of the other boys in the college: "You had better short your hair like other folks, Lawrence; there'll be enough, and more than enough, serious things worth fighting for in the world, and you had better keep your pluck to defend your principles."

Oak Dining-Table, Louis XIV.—Room for Four.
No. 66.

This was good advice, and if the illustration shall be turned against me for advising people not to conform to fashion in their ways of furnishing their houses and of living in them, I must answer that these very things have much in common with principles, and bear such relations to the essentials of life (as I understand life) that we have a right to think of them, not as mere mint and cummin, but as the weightier matters of the law of living. The world does love conformity in generals, but she takes a lively interest in a refusal to conform in particulars. She likes the sky, as a rule, to be blue; but she has no objection to an occasional mile or so of apple-green between the horizon hills and the swarthy band of upper cloud on a winter afternoon; nor has she

ever objected to the poet's crowding simile on simile in
praise of the sunset's purple and gold. A friend told me
that at the close of a lecture he had been delivering on
Titian, when all the pleasant things and grateful things
had been said about his hero, it was like a tonic, when a
bright face looked up in answer to his question, "And I
hope you, too, were pleased, Miss Bella?" "Oh, no, I
hate Titian and all the rest of them!" I suppose he would
n't have liked to have his whole audience of the young
lady's mind, nor to have had it expose itself so bluntly;
but he insisted that he liked that unexpected dash of hostility, it was the vinegar that gave the salad its savor.

No person with a good natural eye for color, with
hospitable thoughts, with a love of comfort, and with common sense, ever departed from the conventional way of
furnishing a house, for the sake of suiting his house to his
own character and likings, without being rewarded by the
world's cheerful acceptance of the innovation. Ten to one,
the independent suiter-of-himself will find his innovation
accepted by fashion, or by the good sense of the world,
and, incorporated into its own system, made a new law of
the Medes and Persians.

So, if any one chooses to have his living-room and his
dining-room in one, he has only to make up his mind to
it, and then look about to see how it may be done without first showing elegance and comfort to the door,—two
inmates who ought to have their permanent seats at every
fireside. I should say the only absolute requisites for such
an arrangement are a large room and convenient nearness

to the kitchen and pantry. There must be room enough to leave the field clear for Betty when she comes to set the table, and this there will never be if there is room for only one table which must serve the family for all its needs. Such is the unconscious perversity of human nature, that, so sure as there is but one table, the children will get their books or their toys on it, or the husband will get out his writing, or spread out a map for reference as near as possible to the dinner-hour, and Betty, who always knows her rights, and knowing, dares maintain, will have to face disappointed children and a disgusted man. A lady once told the writer that when the dinner-bell rang, all her daughters put on their bonnets and went out for a walk; and it is the same with most of us in our dealings with times and seasons, and the bars and barriers of daily life. Here would be the triumph of the settle-table on which I have so often harped, and of which I have shown at least two illustrations. Of course, somebody would be sitting on the sofa when Betty came in and wished to turn it into a table. The children would have just that minute begun to make a house or a fortress of it, or papa would have seated himself there just to glance at the "Evening Post" before dinner. But one seat is easily changed for another, whereas a table has to be cleared off, woman's work put away, books and maps or writing materials got rid of,—and this is no slight trouble.

I am, then, either for a table reserved exclusively for eating from, or else for a table that is only a table while it is wanted.

I know a private house where there is a table twelve
feet long, at least,—fifteen, perhaps,—which is a spacious
field for the deploying of all the household forces. It is a
noble table, after a Jacobean model, and the cloth is often
laid at one end of it, and dinner served without obliging
those who have been working along its generous length to
strike their tents and retreat with bag and baggage, or
scrip and scrippage. This, however, would not be good to
do as an every-day thing. One advantage in having a
dining-room separate from the living-room is, that we get
variety, and unbend the too stiff-stretched cord of daily
work. This change of scene is almost a necessity to those
who have been housed all day. But in this particular case,
it was only a possibility that a part of the table might
have been in use before the dinner, and that the worker's
implements remained undisturbed during the meal. The
big room in which the table stood was little used during
the day, and it was only at night that it became the
great center of the family gathering. And, certainly, it was
a pleasant rallying-ground, and the scene of much hospitable
intercourse and cheer. Our hostess knew the liking most
people have for a cozy seclusion, and, if there were but
few of us, she made a screen of ivy, against which brighter
hues of leaf or flower were relieved, and so fenced off the
"howling wilderness," as B. once called the rest of the
table, until dessert came, which, after a turn about the
room to inspect M.'s cabinet of *curios*, or a stroll in the
garden, we came back to find, perhaps, served at the other
end of the table.

We have such a treacherous climate in our northern states that it is useless to recommend a steady dining out-of-doors in summer-time, as is so often practiced in Middle France and in Southern Europe. Still I have known a family to keep a table standing on the broad veranda of their country house, where they breakfasted, dined, and took supper every day in the summer-time that the weather permitted; and it was a very cheerful custom. I think all the freedom we can get in our eating and drinking is desirable—all, I mean, that is consistent with comfort. I wish even punctuality were not so much insisted on. There ought to be a fixed hour, and then I would have all who are on hand sit down; but it ought not to be counted the mortal sin it is to come a quarter of an hour late, and it would n't be such a sin, if we did not make such formal affairs of our dinners. There is one pleasant table around which as good company gathers as at any in the land, and there is form and ceremony enough to keep the wheels oiled; but if a straggler comes late, he neither gets cold soup nor the cold shoulder, but his excuse is accepted without too much examination, and perhaps he finds comfort in the fact that somebody else for whom he has a great liking is very apt to turn up even later than he. It may cheer up some people who are made melancholy by thinking what delightfully disorderly times they seem fated to have at their own table, while at other people's houses everything is so quiet and respectable, to read the account Allan Cunningham quotes of the way things went on at Sir Joshua Reynolds's dinner-table:

"There was something singular in the style and economy
of his table that contributed to pleasantry and good humor—
a coarse, inelegant plenty, without any regard to order or
arrangement. A table prepared for seven or eight often
compelled to contain fifteen or sixteen. When this pressing
difficulty was got over, a deficiency of knives and forks,
plates and glasses, succeeded. The attendance was in the
same style; and it was absolutely necessary to call instantly
for beer, bread, or wine, that you might be supplied before
the first course was over. He was once prevailed on to
furnish the table with decanters and glasses for dinner, to
save time and prevent the tardy maneuvers of two or three
occasional, undisciplined domestics. As these accelerating
utensils were demolished in the course of service, Sir Joshua
could never be persuaded to replace them. But these trifling embarrassments only served to enhance the hilarity
and singular pleasure of the entertainment. The wine,
cookery, and dishes were but little attended to, nor was the
fish or venison ever talked of or recommended. Amid this
convivial, animated bustle among his guests, our host sat
perfectly composed, always attentive to what was said,
never minding what was eat or drank, but left every one
at perfect liberty to scramble for himself. Temporal and
spiritual peers, physicians, lawyers, actors and musicians
composed the motley group, and played their parts without
dissonance or discord. At five o'clock, precisely, dinner was
served, whether all the invited guests were arrived or not.
Sir Joshua was never so fashionably ill-bred as to wait an
hour, perhaps, for two or three persons of rank or title,

and put the rest of the company out of humor by this invidious distinction."

Perhaps it may be admitted that Sir Joshua's table was a trifle too free and easy. He was never married, and the accounts we have of his sister, Miss Reynolds, who kept his house, represent her as little less careless than her brother. Still, though it would have been no doubt an advantage to have had more order and neatness at the table, yet it was of more importance to have good company, and it is mere commonplace to say that with Burke and Johnson, Goldsmith, Garrick, and Mrs. Thrale at table, it would n't have been in human nature to think about the dishes.

But, whether the living-room be used for meals, or there be a separate room for eating, there ought to be room enough for the waiter to get easily around,—ample room and verge enough. Personally, I dislike a small dining-room, but then I dislike small rooms in general. True luxury of living seems to me to demand spacious rooms. Nothing gave me such a generous notion of the old Italians as the big rooms they left behind them. You find these big rooms even in the inns, and in other houses where you would least expect them. Still, in a country where big rooms are the exception, and hardly to be found at all, except in the hotels, it is of no use to insist upon this point. Our houses are getting smaller and smaller, and the rooms more and more cut up,—so we must take what we can find.

One comfortable thing about our dining-rooms in general we may be glad of—that they have so little furniture

The "Last Sweet Thing" in Corners.
No. 67.

in them! The dining-table, the chairs and a sideboard are all the pieces we must have, and with these the room must be a small one if it is uncomfortably crowded.

Small or large, however, the dining-room ought to be a cheerful, bright-looking room. The east is a good aspect for it; a south-east aspect, if possible, because it is particularly pleasant to have the morning sun at breakfast, and then the southern sun makes the room cheerful all day, and plants will flourish too, and they are a happy addition to a dining-room, both for health and beauty. At dinner-time, if the dinner-hour be a late one, the aspect of the room will be of less importance, because the lamps will be lighted; but I think we shall find our account in having the morning sun strike across our breakfast-table.

The breakfast-table, however, as we have established it, following the English, I suppose, is an institution I wish were upset. Most people, if they would speak out their honest minds, would, I am sure, agree with me in thinking the American breakfast a mistake in our social economy. To force all the members of a family to get up and be dressed at a certain hour is not sensible, and yet a worse feature is, that they are all to sit down together at a common table, most of them in a very unregenerate state of mind, and not at all themselves, and in a condition far from suited to make social intercourse easy. The whole household is tormented to produce this unsatisfactory result. The servants have to get up at unnatural hours, and, in consequence, they are in a ticklish state of temper, ready for explosion on the most delicate expostulation. Nothing is ever well cooked, but this matters the less because nobody has any appetite. The business man—I mean the ideal business man—is occupied at breakfast-table with trying to do three things at once—to bolt his food, to bolt his newspaper, and to keep a steady eye on the clock. The only one of the three he succeeds in accomplishing is the last; he knows at every mouthful what time it is to a second, and he prances away from the table to catch his horse-car, steam-car, or ferry, every morning with the regularity of a planet. The servants have been routed out of bed; the wife, which is of vastly more importance, has been robbed of her morning rest; the children have been made uncomfortable,—all for no better end than to comply with a cast-iron system that never had any reason in it. Suppose the early breakfast-table were abolished, and let the separate members of the family take what light snack they wanted, when and where they would, those at home meeting later in the day,—say at noon,—for a regular breakfast, and the husbands and sons looking out for themselves at restaurants and cafés near their places of business. In Paris, gentlemen come home to breakfast, business people (the city being so built that it radiates from a center out) living as near to their shops and offices as they can contrive, so that the breakfast is generally a family meeting, and a very happy and cheerful one too. The various members of the family have got well shaken up by eleven or twelve o'clock, something has been accomplished, life has gone on more smoothly and equably, and parents and children are in a less critical and exasperating mood.

I don't mean to advocate a wild license in the matter of lying a-bed, or getting up when you please. But early rising, or rising when it is time to rise,—for there never

"The pippins and cheese have come."
No. 68.

was a greater humbug than the doctrine of early rising for its own sake,—is one thing, and early breakfasting for the family in common is another. Nobody needs (except day laborers) much solid food immediately on rising, or after being dressed. A cup of coffee, a roll and butter, possibly an egg—this would be enough and plenty for the average of people who live by their brains to work on till twelve o'clock. As I have said, this is all that any one can get well cooked in his own house at the early hour of seven or eight in winter, and all that most people have any appetite for, both which facts prove beyond dispute (unless somebody undertakes to deny them) that Providence does not favor early family breakfasts.

Extension-tables are so common nowadays, that it is rare to see in a dining-room a table that cannot be enlarged at pleasure. But if a small table is wanted that will yet seat four, or even six, comfortably, cut No. 66 shows a design that has been found very useful in actual service. It is an accurate copy made from a French model of the time of Louis XIII., a period when the furniture united elegance and solidity in a very satisfactory way. It was bought originally for a dining-table, and it is as picturesque and serviceable an affair as need be. It is made of oak, and, as will be seen, it has two leaves, which are supported by drawing out one of the legs.

Another cut, No. 68, represents a more elaborate table,—more elaborate in its mechanism, though the design is every bit as simple. This table has an extension top, but the support of the top—the four legs and the frame-work—is solid. The top draws apart, and either a broad or a narrow leaf is inserted in the opening, according to the room wanted. At its largest, it will seat eight people comfortably,—one at each end, and three on each side,—and this is as large a company as people who do not give dinner-parties are apt to invite. This table was made by Mr. Matthias Miller from drawings by Mr. John F. Miller, architect. The top is of mahogany, and the supporting frame of black walnut. It is a piece of work which it is a perpetual pleasure to look at, and time has added to the art of it the charm that only time can give, by bringing out the richest glow in the mahogany and turning the black walnut into bronze. Of course, the wood has never been varnished, the only treatment it has received being a frequent rubbing with a flannel rag just moistened with linseed oil. It takes but a short time to call out all the wonders of a table's face with such simple means.

I have never seen an extension-table that was well designed, though they are very often well enough contrived for their purpose. Indeed, nowadays, they may be said to have reached perfection; but this perfection is no more interesting than the perfection of the last steam-engine, or the last sewing-machine. They all belong together, and it would be as absurd not to have extension-tables that open and shut without friction as it would be to have steam-engines and sewing-machines that should get out of gear every five minutes. What is important to us in our present quest is, that we should have extension-tables that are shapely pieces of furniture,—the design representing the structure, not trying to conceal it. The extension-table and the piano-forte are the two puzzles the designers have been beating their brains over for the last fifty years, and they must own, if they are candid, that success has not attended their efforts. This of mine was designed for a special purpose. The dining-room it was wanted for was a very small one, and the points to be made in the design were three: to keep it small, to have the top well supported and look as if it were, and to make it handsome. The result was entirely satisfactory; between the designer and the maker, a really handsome, practicable, and well-made piece of furniture has been produced, and it is probably—to speak modestly, and not to tread on anybody's corns—the prettiest dining-table in the world. The materials are black walnut for the frame, and mahogany for the top. I should like to have had it made all of mahogany, but it would have made it cost too much, so I contented myself with a piece of old San Domingo for the top, and now I don't know that I should care to have it different from what it is. The posts, or legs, are turned, the caps being slightly enriched with carving (though the drawing does not show this), and there is a little carving at the ends of the four pieces which unite the frame at the top. The lower edges of these frames are molded, and the cross-pieces that unite the legs below are also molded. But all the ornamentation is kept as simple as possible, and the beauty of the piece is in its form, and in the color of the wood. As for the working of the top, it is as perfect as everything that comes from Matt. Miller's hands, and slides as if it were oiled. In the thirteen years it has been in steady use, it has never once refused to do its duty, and has never caused a single ejaculation to escape the fence of the teeth of one of the myriad handmaidens who have had the pulling of it open and shut. In fact, such a compliant piece of furniture is rather an incentive to calm and pious thought than to the angry passions, and, when one considers how much bad manners have been born of bureau drawers that stick, and book-shelves that wont gee, and doors that refuse to open or shut, it will be seen that there is a moral side to well-made furniture, which we are too apt to forget.

It does not appear whence the tradition came—nor do I know that it prevails at present—that dining-rooms ought to be somber in their general color and decoration, in opposition to drawing-rooms, which ought to be light and cheerful. We were taught that dining-rooms ought to be fitted up with dark hangings and furniture, dark paper, dark stuffs, and the rest. The reasonable view would seem to be that a dining-room should be as cheerful a room as it can be made. Its decoration may be sober and rich, but it ought not to be somber. One reason against its being so is, that dark walls and hangings eat up a ruinous quantity of light, and the principal meal of the day is almost always nowadays served at a time when we must employ artificial light. I believe there have been given some physiological reasons for darkish dining-rooms; but they are such as apply not to dining-rooms so much as to feeding-places, and such as would recommend themselves to the breeders and stuffers of Strasburg geese. The pundits said digestion went on better in the dark, and in silence,—which latter may be the reason why little children are not allowed to talk at table! Surely, we have nothing with this answer; these words are none of ours, and so long as the question is of dining,—an occupation as much intellectual as gastronomic,—we will counsel that the dining-room shall be so decorated and furnished as to encourage the most cheerful and festive trains of thought, and the sunniest good-nature. Of course, if the dinner is an early one, and the room fronts the south or west, the light may have to be tempered by the decoration of the room; but this can be done without diminishing its cheerful look. A very pretty dining-room which we have seen had a wainscot of black walnut, with panels of white pine oiled and shellacked. In a few weeks, these had become by this treatment a rich golden yellow, that harmonized perfectly with the walnut. They would also have looked well stained (not painted) with Venetian red, and then shellacked. Between the wainscot and the cornice, the wall was papered with a pale lemon-yellow paper, on which was a figure containing dark green and red. It gave force to the otherwise weak effect of the paper, and did not look spotty, but kept the wall-effect a unit. The room was a small one, and the low ceiling was laid with a blue-gray paper, well covered with a set pattern, in a darker shade of the ground; and the cornice—which was a wooden molding, only about three inches on the wall and two on the ceiling—was painted black and red, and had a narrow molding of gold, less than a half-inch wide, running along directly under it. The effect of this room was equally pleasant by daylight or lamp-light, and there was always such good cheer on the table, and so many pleasant people about it, that I never heard the dining-room gave anybody an indigestion.

In cut No. 53, on page 157, was shown a piece of Chinese furniture in use in a dining-room, which will recommend itself by its simplicity,—the only ornament upon it being the lacquer on the drawers and the pretty handles. For purposes of every-day use, it was thought best to take out the sliding panels, eight in number, which ran in grooves before the two main divisions. These panels are ornamented with figures of birds and flowers cut out of soap-stone, which are stuck by some futile kind of Chinese glue on to the polished wood, from which they were all the time falling and getting themselves broken. These being taken out and laid aside, there remains a square box with shelves and two handy drawers, the lacquered cranes and shrubs on these drawers giving just enough ornament to relieve the plainness of the cabinet. For the present, this cabinet rests upon the table which has just been shown to the reader in cut No. 66. But the cabinet and the table are not altogether harmonious, and it would be better to have a plain stand, or even a cupboard, made to support it; as it is, it might be copied in a way to get all its advantages,—which have been found in practice to be many,—and the cost could not be serious. Suppose a carpenter with some feeling for his business were asked to make just such a case, arranging the shelves as they are in the original,—one dividing the space into two equal parts, and the lower half divided by a shelf at one side. The drawing shows this shelf a little too high up; it divides its half of the lower division exactly into halves, and it also does not come out to a line with the front of the cabinet, but only half way, so that a tall-necked cruet or a drinking-glass can stand in front of it. This way of arranging shelves is peculiar to these Orientals,—Chinese and Japanese alike,—and if looked into it will be found to

"In tea-cup time of hood and hoop."
No. 69.

be grounded in common sense, as are many of their ways. So far as appearances go, it takes off from the formal look of shelves all alike running from side to side,—as it is the universal European custom to make them,—and, for accommodation, it allows us to give the small things perches to their mind, as well as to provide that the large things shall have ample room and verge enough to stand at ease.

How to light our dining-tables is often a puzzle, especially in the country.   It seems to me that, as a general
thing, our gas-fixtures are too heavy-looking, they pretend
to be too much.   I know none of them are really as heavy
or as solid as they look, but that does not make the matter better.   If they are not as heavy as they seem, there
is no use in their seeming heavier than they are!   If we

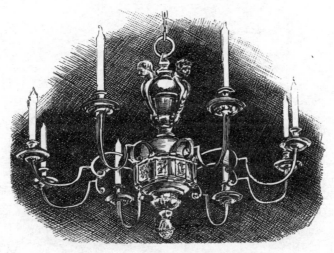

"Sweetness and Light."   Electrotype copy of a Silver Chandelier from Knole.
No. 70.

think about it, we shall perceive that there is no reason to
be given for a chandelier or a gaselier either being or
looking heavy or very solid.   Light is not heavy in itself,
nor are candles very heavy, while gas is, of course, a synonym for lightness.

The chandeliers and branches of old times were, as
everybody knows, models of delicacy and grace.   The aim
seemed to be to make the supports and holders of the

candles as harmonious with their whiteness and slenderness, and with the spiritual beauty of the light they were to give, as was possible. The slender arms that held the candles were wreathed and twisted into strong but graceful scrolls, and the main stem was made as slim as was consistent with the weight it had to bear—the base alone was loaded to prevent upsetting. It was a great deprivation when we were obliged to give up candles for illuminating. Nothing could be prettier than the effect of a room prepared for an evening party, decorated with flowers and lighted with wax candles. Candle-light is the only artificial light by which beauty shows all its beauty—it even makes the plain less plain. I do not know why it was that when gas came into use it was thought necessary to make all the chandeliers and branches clumsy and mechanical. Perhaps there was an unconscious connection in the manufacturers' minds between these instruments of illumination and the ponderous machinery and manipulation by which the gas is produced.

But, in reality, though nothing that may be devised for lighting our rooms can ever be so pretty to look at as candles, yet gas has also its poetry, and, as its use is established, we are bound to think how it may be used gracefully. There is no doubt that we Americans are unreasonably in love with machinery and contrivance, and that the makers of gas-fixtures have played upon our love of ingenuity until they have made us accept the most monstrous and complicated gas-machines for the decoration of our rooms. I live in the blessed hope that gas will one day be superseded by something better. It is unhealthy, it is troublesome, it is expensive, it tarnishes our silver, our picture-frames and our wall-papers, and how can it do this without injuring those who breathe it? But such as it is, we need not make it more disagreeable to the eyes and mind by bringing it into the parlor through a clumsy machine made up of wire tackle, hoisters, chains, weights and bronze frame-work. No more do we want statuettes or intricate ornaments upon our gaseliers. Beauty and utility are served best by a combination in shining metal (not in dull bronze) of carved and twisted branches through which the fluent gas shall really make its way, and that shall look as if the designer had taken into consideration the nature of the substance that was to pass through his pipes. At present, nearly all the designs for gas-fixtures appear directly to contradict the use they are to be put to, and instead of flowing, graceful lines, all the lines employed are angular and hard.

The best gas that is made nowadays is so poor, and so much trouble with the eyes is ascribed to its action (I wish the doctors would pound away as vigorously against gas and furnaces as it is their fashion to do against bad sewerage), that many people have learned to use either the German student-lamp or the French moderator, while some, more radical still, have frankly gone back to candles, and work only by them. With one· of their lights and a soft coal fire, it is still possible to make one's parlor look as if it were a living-room and not a dying-room. Even if it be urged that a gas chandelier is the best means of illuminating a dining or supper table, because it permits all the people to see one another, I still demur that if elegance or picturesqueness is aimed at, the old silver-plated branches for candles are our only wear. Or such a chandelier as is shown in cut No. 70,—one of the pieces of a suite of bedroom furniture, toilet-table, mirror-frame, etc., etc., made out of solid silver, and still existing at Knole. Copies of this chandelier can be purchased. One of them was at Philadelphia, exhibited by Elkington. The expense of candles is an item hardly worth considering (it was not their dearness, but the troublesomeness of them that sent them out of use), and every woman knows that no light sets off her complexion, her dress, her ornaments, like the soft light of candles. The diamond, for example, is a dull stone by gas-light; its prismatic sparkle is only seen by candle-light.

Another modern tendency that seems to have nearly run the length of its tether is toward what is generally spoken of as *massive* furniture. We have been making our furniture so heavy of late, that the amount of solid wood in it added to the carving, inlaying, and veneering with different woods, has made it very expensive. Of course, the Bowery and Canal street have followed Broadway and the Fifth avenue, and we can hardly tell cheap furniture from dear, by the price. The so-called "Eastlake" furniture has had much to do with keeping up the tendency we speak of. The one thing the designers of it seem to be after is to make it look "solid," and the one thing they seem in "mortal" dread of is that it shall be graceful or elegant. Some of the productions of the mills that turn out this uncomfortable lumber are wonderful to behold. Most of it would look clumsy in an Italian palace. In our American parlors and bedrooms it is not at home. Many persons, however, who do not like it in a parlor think it is just the thing for a dining-room. Why we should consider that the furniture of the dining-room ought to be so much heavier than that of the parlor, I do not know. Probably we got it from the English, who, a few years ago, had that notion, though they did not always have it, as may be seen by cut No. 69. This is copied from a sideboard now in this country, and which many of my readers will recognize as belonging to a style of which many examples—some as elegant no doubt as this, some very plain and inferior to it in design—are still to be found in old houses. In making this furniture, our ancestors were aiming at lightness of form, economy of space and delicacy of execution. All the best pieces are finished with extreme care, and they are so well put together—so skillfully and so conscientiously—as in many cases to have defied the wear and tear of nearly a century. Some chairs which had, no doubt, been made by one of the best English makers of the last century were recently bought from the kitchen of a dismantled house (to which room they had descended from the parlor, in the course of the gradual ruin of the family), and though they had been put by the beggarly inmates to the roughest use, and had lost their seats, sacking, stuffing, covering and all, they needed nothing but to have this lack supplied, and to be well cleaned and polished, to be as good as ever they were. It needs little examination to be assured that much of the solidest-looking "Eastlake" furniture (I mean that made in

The Children's Quarter of an Hour.
No. 71.

this country) would have succumbed under the ungentle treatment received by these chairs.

The "Eastlake" furniture must not, however, be judged by what is made in this country, and sold under that name. I have seen very few pieces of this that were either well designed or well made. None of the cheaper sort is ever

either.   Mr. Herter has had some pieces made which were
both well designed and thoroughly well made, as all his
furniture is, however we may sometimes quarrel with his
over-ornamentation; and Mr. Marcotte has also shown us
some good examples in this style.   But these are not to be
referred to as examples of cheapness, which was one of the
recommendations of the "Eastlake" furniture.   They are
only referred to as doing the style (if it be a style) more
justice than the lumps of things we see in certain shops,
though, in truth, these lumps are a good deal more like
the things recommended in Mr. Eastlake's book than the
stylish, elegant pieces designed by Messrs. Herter and
Marcotte.

   The sideboard shown in cut No. 71, made by Cottier &
Co. from their own designs, is one of the best modern
sideboards I have seen, and well deserves to be recommended as a model.   It is made of hard wood, stained
black and then polished.   The drawers and doors have
key-plates and handles of brass, of that fine gold-color
which is now given to it, but, with only this exception,
there is nothing added to relieve the black of the wood-
work.   It will be observed that there is no carving, and
scarcely any molding on this piece; but no one would
think anything wanting who should see it with even so
little upon it as a dish of fruit, a few glasses and water-
bottles, and on the shelf some blue plates, not put there
for show, but in daily use.   Much less would the eruptive
carving, and the stuck-on ornaments, and the coarse moldings that are considered indispensable to a "stylish" side-

board, be missed from this one on a feast day, when fruit and flowers, and glass, and silver, are busy "making reflections" on the gleaming surface for the benefit of those who have eyes!

The old-fashioned sideboards are often desirable pieces to have, but I do not believe in copying them, however skillfully it may be done. I would not hesitate, if I were in want of a sideboard, to buy a good example of the style shown in cut No. 69, if I could find a genuine old piece in first-rate condition, like some Mr. Sypher has recently picked up, and which are in his show-room. They are not such perfect specimens as the one which Mr. Lathrop has drawn, but they are of the better class, and one of them is an uncommon one to be on sale.

But unless I could get an old one, and a good one too, I should much prefer having one made after a design of my own time, to having a copy made of something old-fashioned. We make pretty things nowadays, or can make them, and the difficulty of getting things simple and unpretending in design is not half so great as we pretend to believe. The trouble, half the time, is with ourselves. We don't want things simple and unpretending; I mean, very few of us do. We are not strong enough in our own taste to be able to relish plain surfaces without panels, edges without moldings, and a pleasingness, generally, that depends wholly on good proportions and nice finish. Ornament is a thing to be desired, but to be desired it must be good, and it must be in its place. If the reader be a young married couple, let him look up from this page with candid eyes at the set of "Eastlake" furniture which she has just bought with the money he has been saving up for a year or two for that especial purpose, and ask herself how much of the ornament that is stuck upon it or gouged out of it, regardless of cheapness, is good. And, ten to one, if he can find a bit of it that is good, it will be put on in the wrong place,—that is, where it cannot be seen, or where it can be easily knocked, or knocked off, or where it will easily knock its owner.

N. B.—Of course it will be of ash, the coldest, most unsympathetic, most inartistic of woods; and most likely it will have some cold blue tiles let into its surface—tiles, things that, except for actual utility, have no right to be used in connection with wood. A table-top may be covered with tiles if it is to be often in danger of a wetting. Such a table makes the best stand for plants. Or a wash-stand may be covered with them, or a fire-place surrounded by them, but, used with wood as ornament alone, they are always out of sorts; they feel their own incongruity and make you feel it too.

Cut No. 72 is a more homespun sideboard, but a useful one, and far from ill-looking. It is a genuine old Puritan piece, one of those alluded to awhile ago—page 162—as having been found in a barn-yard, where it had for many years been given over to the hens. From having cold chicken on its top, it had come to have warm chicken inside, and it was no easy matter to remove the traces of the hens' housekeeping. But solid oak, well pinned together and mortised, is proof against much ill-usage and bad weather, and this sideboard showed that it had not lived so many years in a Puritan family for nothing, and been humbled and put to base uses for another life-time without profiting by its experience. After careful cleansing and a good polishing, it turned out much handsomer than it had been in the good old times of which it had, no

De Profundis.
No. 72.

doubt, often thought sorrowfully, and it now makes an envied ornament in one of the prettiest and happiest homes of young Boston.

It so often happens that our dining-rooms are too narrow for comfort that I have asked Mr. Lathrop to make a drawing of a certain wall which was to be kept as flat as possible, since the room was very thin in the flanks, and had to be humored. I think the reader will admit that the result (cut No. 73) is picturesque without being odd, and that it looks as if some comfort might be had around such a fireside. I must mention that the pier was of greater width than usual, that the fire-place was small, and that there was no mantel-piece other than the shelf the reader sees in the wood-cut. The occupant of the room took things just as he found them, and, without proposing any violent changes, used the material he had as a basis for his improvements. One of the English grates, first brought to us by Cottier & Co., was set, and about it, to use them up, a lot of old Dutch tiles which had been bought at a bargain and as good things to have in the house. These tiles were inclosed—to hold them to the wall—by a molding of wood, stained black and polished. As the top row of tiles was found to extend a little over the two side rows, the molding was simply given a jog (instead of cutting the top row to make it even), and the result was so happy that it almost looked like design. If the border had gone up straight at the sides, it certainly would not have looked so well as it does with the little jog at the upper corner. We shall find it a very good working-rule in life—in these matters at least—to take what we have, and see how much we can accomplish by working upon that as a base, not thinking it necessary to turn, and turn, and overturn, in order to get the whole completely to our mind.

All around the room which contained this fire-place and mantel-shelf there was carried a chair-rail—the dark strip of wood that is seen below the brackets. The position of the brackets was allowed to regulate the placing of this strip; the height chosen for it was that which would bring it where it would look best in relation to them, and then it was carried around the remaining wall spaces at that height. The base-board was left as it was found, but the angles of the pier were covered with wood, because the plaster was pretty sure to be chipped if left unguarded. There was a small hearth of tiles, not extending further to either side than was needed for safety. And I should have said that the Dutch tiles were an odd lot,—some with the old Bible stories, some with landscapes, and others with conventional patterns; but they were allowed to take care of themselves and to choose their own mates, so that when they were in place they had an accidental look that was pleasant enough to the eye. The base-board, the shelf and its brackets, and the chair-rail were painted a dead black, and the black border around the tiles (which, though there were a few purple ones among them, were nearly all blue) was polished. The wall between the chair-rail and base-board was washed with water-color of a sort of brown, and the rest of the wall was washed with Venetian red. A shining brass fender with its brass-handled fire-irons, a generous copper coal-scuttle, and the objects on the shelf, gave color enough and brightness upon this background. The broom that hangs upon the chair-rail is one of those Japanese brooms made of the fiber of the cocoa-nut, with handles of bamboo. They come with longer handles than the one shown in the drawing, but this was bought for a light hearth-brush. They are serviceable for easy work, the fiber being fine and soft, and they are much prettier to look at than any brushes we can buy here. I may note

" He can do little who can't do this."
No. 73.

in passing, the pedestal on which the bust of Clytie stands, and which would be a good design for some one to work out in better materials than this unfortunately is made of.

It was bought for its looks, and after twenty years' wear and movings innumerable it still lives, and will be good, I suppose, for another twenty years. Now that everything made of metal is copyable by the electrotype, why should not some one copy real antique tripods for us—they were often made to serve as supports—and so give us one solution at least of the question, "Where shall we find a good pedestal?"

These English grates are certainly very pretty and convenient. The ornament on this particular grate consists of a slender vine filling up narrow parallel grooves on the face. They are " stopped" against a border running around the opening of the fire-place. On this border the pattern consists of small wheels, like snail-shells cut across, which change with the direction of the light. The bars are given a slight double curve, and are ornamented a little on the face; but all the ornament is delicate and unobtrusive: it owes not a little of its attractiveness to the sharpness of the casting. The Japanese tea-kettle—and their bronze (or is it copper?) tea-kettles are useful affairs—rests on a trivet of iron that belongs to the grate, but which can be removed at pleasure. The trivet is round, with one slender leg which passes through holes in the two uppermost bars. This enables it to be swung over the fire, or to be turned so that the kettle can simmer at pleasure. One of these kettles is shown in cut No. 65, where it is seen on the table, boiling (but not boiling over) with zeal to make a good cup of tea. For those whose happiness does not depend on their having a silver, or even a silver-plated tea-kettle on their tables, these Japanese kettles may be recommended, but not, of course, if they are to have rough usage. Though they are well made, the metal is kept rather thin, and dents are not so easily smoothed out of them as they are out of silver.

As somebody may, perhaps, puzzle for a moment over the title of cut No. 73,—"He can do little who can't do this,"—I may as well explain that it hints at the small cost incurred in the arrangement of this fireside. Brass fenders, copper coal-scuttles and brass-handled fire-irons do, indeed, cost a great deal of money, if one goes to the fashionable shops; but they are all the time being "picked up" for very little money. There are thousands of these things still in the hands of the original owners all over the country, and we know of ladies who, by a little general-ship with junk-men, have got hold of treasures of fender and fire-irons worth taking much more trouble for than a few words across the garden-fence can give. Still, even in the shops, these brass and copper things do not cost so much as modern fashionable things that go as far in looks; and our talk is now of "looks,"—not of what we can get along with or without.

The grate, too, cost, brought to this country, a great deal more than it did in England, where it is produced in answer to a wish for cheap grates. But for this we have to thank our customs duties; and there are, besides, to be taken into account, the expenses of packing, cartage, and commission. I mean that when these grates, and grates in this same spirit, come to be made here, they will be as cheap as the cheapest, and they are certainly far prettier.

For the rest,—the tiles were picked up and cost, at auction, say, ten cents apiece. But in the shops they are dearer, though there, of course, they are in perfect condition; those in the picture are chipped, and they are what dealers call "an assorted lot," which means, there are no two alike. The mantel-piece is pine-wood painted black, and so is all the wood-work shown, except what holds the tiles, which is of hard wood and polished. The walls are washed with water-color. There is nothing here which fashionable rich people would not laugh at, and yet the owner and his friends think it quite jolly, and, in the slang of the time, "vote it a success."

In a small dining-room, tables like the one shown in cut No. 27, page 78, will be found useful. They can be used as a side-table for the bread and water and dessert-plates, or for a dumb-waiter, which was the word applied to a stand of this sort before we began to apply it to the lift. It was for this that they were made to revolve, as by this contrivance any object the table contained could be brought under the hand of the person at whose side it stood.

At the same period, dumb-waiters were made in stages revolving around a central shaft, the lower stage three feet perhaps in diameter, and the two upper ones decreasing in a graceful proportion. I believe only the lower stage revolved, as a rule. On the upper stages were put the dishes of fruit which nowadays it is the fashion to arrange in the middle of the table. The French, to-day, **have** these dumb-waiters in use. They are small, square, in **two** stories, and with four legs, and the top is generally of marble—the gray marble of which the French make so

Coffee-Table, à la Turque.
No. 74.

much use. However shaped, they are extremely convenient, and by putting at least the bread and water within our reach, they enable us to be rid a little while of the servant.

Cut No. 74 is another of these small tables, designed by Mr. Frank Lathrop on a Turkish theme, and drawn by him also.

Some time ago, a comically despairing letter was received by the writer of these pages, from a lady who expressed, in good set terms, her dislike of white china for the table, but did not see how she was to help herself. I fully sympathize with my correspondent, and confess to having never been able to understand the liking of my country-women for plain white china. The only place where I am content to see it is on the table of a hotel or restaurant, because there I want ware which tells me at a glance if it has been properly washed. But in my friend's house, or in my own, I wish to take the proprieties for granted, and to have my eyes play the epicure, not the pedagogue. And they can never be pleased with the look of a table that has no color in its decoration. I have elsewhere complained of our American love of white,—white walls and ceilings, and white houses,—of white marble if possible; if not, then of wood painted white and set off with green blinds.* This, it is to be hoped, will gradually cure itself; the signs are neither few nor discouraging; and as the white walls and white ceilings go, the white china will go along with them. To tell truth, those of us who did not like white china had for a long time much trouble in finding any good decorated china to take its place. And the white china, being all French, was really so very pretty in its shapes, and so fine in quality, that it seemed as if shape and surface might almost compensate for the cold, unthink-

---

* A white house may be endured when it is not white, and then only. This happens when the trees about it tone it down with their shadows to bluish-gray. The blinds, too, get mixed up with the foliage, and so lose a little of their obtrusive individuality.

ing white, that could not be brought into sympathy with anything about it.   It took the yellow out of the butter, made the milk look blue, cast suspicion on the tea, took all the sparkle out of the sugar, and, in short, made it impossible for the breakfast to do itself justice.   At dinner it was the same, only the vegetables and meats, being of coarser fiber, did not so much mind it; but the way white china behaved at dessert was really shocking.   Fruit does not know how to behave itself when it is put into white china dishes, and eaten off white china plates.   I am not sure but some dreadful results might have been spared us if the serpent had only offered Eve the fatal apple on a white china dessert-plate, with a white doily for her fingers. He knew better.   He showed it to her on the tree, and when she saw its red cheek shining out from among the green leaves, and with a bit of blue sky between the branches, she succumbed at once.

Still, as I had said, after all our complaints of the whiteness of white china, it looked up with its shining morning face, pert, but impassive, and said: "Well, what are you going to do about it?"   And what we were to do was the puzzle.   This was in the time of those of us who are just beginning to feel the iron enter our souls by hearing the children (other people's children) call us in irreverent moments, "old" this or that.   It was in the time when this portion of the present population was young, that French china began to be freely imported; and the white undecorated porcelain was then, as now, the most frequently seen.   The French shapes were always the prettiest and the most practical, and even the whiteness, which seems to many people nowadays a serious defect,—the one imperfection in so much perfection,—was not thought a blemish in those colorless days. As I have already remarked, the extreme delicacy of the French porcelain, its fine polish, the uniformity of its texture, the serviceableness of its shapes and its lightness, were real recommendations to those who had only known English earthenware for table use. And people who liked white "hard-finish" walls,—these also an invention of the same period,—and white ceilings, and white-painted wood-work, and white houses, and white tombstones, would have been inconsistent to have complained of the whiteness of their porcelain.

But, just before the introduction of French porcelain into common use among us, there was a time when the English were making very good shapes in a fine earthenware, and decorating it with excellent taste. Indeed, the very reverse of what we have been saying about the French porcelain will apply to the English ware of the late last century, and of the early years of this century. The gracefulness of the shapes, and, in some cases the elegance, in others the richness, of the decoration made amends for the indifferent quality of the ware itself, and for its want of lightness. Much of the early Worcester and Wedgwood ware was very handsome, and so was much of the ware now known from the name of its maker as "Spode." But, services of these English manufactures were only brought here as "best" services by those who could not afford Sèvres or Dresden; and as the inclination in this country was always for French things, as soon as the French began to establish other porcelain factories than the Royal, and to export a cheaper sort of ware, we all bought it with avidity and with reason, for it had much to recommend it.

We are better off to-day, and I do not think anybody can complain with reason that white china is our only ware.

To begin with, I don't know why we should insist on having all the pieces of porcelain or earthenware on our table—at breakfast, dinner or supper—alike. Why have everything in sets? We already allow ourselves some freedom at dessert and at tea; why not, ladies, make a heroinic strike for freedom the table round? There never were "sets" known till modern manufacturers began to take a trade view of life in all its phases. Of course, there must be harmony, but harmony does not mean uniformity. And if the general color of our service is blue, or red, or yellow, a bit of either of the other colors may come in with the one, and no harm done. Now and then at sales, on the breaking up of old households, pieces of old Worcester, or Wedgwood, or Spode, or Devonshire, may be met with, and if they are in good condition—neither nicked, nor chipped, nor cracked—they should be bought, always provided they are pretty, and they will make a good foundation to work upon. It does not do, however, in china, any more than in pictures, to go by names. Go by what is pretty, or rich, or effective, and if on turning up your tea-cup or its saucer you should find a famous potter's name written on it, thank the gods that they made you poetical, and gave you a pair of eyes of your own for what is pretty.

But it is not at all necessary to go out into the high-ways and by-ways searching for china for our tables. Of course, it stands to reason that decorated ware must cost more than plain ware; but there are all grades of cost, and very pretty services of English earthenware, French earthenware (dignified by being called *"faience"*), and Dresden porcelain can be had nowadays at very reasonable prices. The manufacture of each of these countries has its own peculiarities. The English has undoubtedly a more domestic look, and though it would be hard to say why, yet I think it is really true that a table set with English earthenware has an air more in accordance with American notions of comfort and home than the French *faience* can give. The French *faience* has a more elegant and "know-ing" look; and in tone it is always superior to the English ware made to-day, which cannot, it would seem, escape a certain rawness. But neither is the French *faience* equally good. There was an alcove full of it exhibited by some one at the Centennial Exhibition, and I looked in vain through it for ware as good in tone as I bought in Paris in 1869. This of mine was cheap ware, too; but then, in our Exhibition, the French manufacturers of pottery and porcelain did themselves scant justice. A New-York firm, the Messrs. Haviland, long known for the excellence and the good taste of their importation, made a most interesting display of costly Limoges *faience;* but the only show of *faience* of the cheaper sort—of which so much is now made in France—was the one I have spoken of, and though the articles had much merit, there are many firms in France that do much better. The English have been striving of late to introduce new designs into their manufactories of pottery, but, with few exceptions, they have not been successful. They are riding the Japanese and Chinese hobby to death, and breaking their necks in the race for what is *bizarre* and monstrous. The English are only good when they are simple and sincere. Simplicity and sincerity are their strong points; and everything they have ever done that has been good, has been good because it had these qualities. Just now both the French and the English potters are following the same road. Each is engaged in copying its own manufactures of past days; the English are a little later than the French in seeing the advisability of this course in an age so uninventive as ours; but they are doing very good work with the disadvantage that their models are neither so various nor so artistic as the French. The French reproductions of their old wares of Rouen, of Nevers, Lisle and Strasbourg, especially of the first two, are very popular at home, and interesting even to outsiders; we are already becoming familiar with them here, and easily learn to like the plates and dishes, which thus far are pretty much all we get for table use. The most of the articles manufactured after old patterns in France are ornaments useful, or only make-believe useful,—clock-cases and candlesticks, mantel-vases, wall-baskets, match-safes, and so on. But for the table, one finds dessert-plates, fruit-baskets and dishes, salad-bowls, cruet-stands with their cruets, and things of this sort. These are the more common; but whole services are made. Some of my readers may have observed at the Fair, at the stand I have mentioned, a group of little custard-cups, the youngest of a family of dinner-dishes of which a portly, yet shapely, soup-tureen might have been the mother. They were too pretty to live, however, and were early marked by some relentless buyer and snatched away in beauty's bloom.

The Dresden china is porcelain to begin with, and it is of course dearer on that account. But it is not dear if one reckons it in comparison with Sèvres or fine Worcester. There is a handsome blue obtained by the Dresden works, much of which has lately been imported into this country, and I believe Collamore has sets of it on sale almost all the time. If one does not feel like buying a whole dinner-service of this or any other ware, it will be well to get, say, a soup-tureen and soup plates; or, a fruit-basket, four dessert-dishes for nuts and cakes, with dessert-plates; or, a flat bowl for ice-cream or whatever sweet messes the neat-handed Phillis dresses—and divide the rest of the dishes between other sorts of china or of earthen-ware. The Worcester people have lately been making an extremely pretty dessert-service, after one of their old patterns. There are plates, as many as you will, and then four different dishes for fruit, nuts, cake and other trifles. These dishes are leaf-shaped, round, or of diamond shape, but with the sides fluted, which causes the edges to have a scolloped look. The colors are a pretty red and gold, and the effect of them on a table is altogether lovely. Everybody knows by this time what can be done with Chinese and Japanese china for tea and dessert; these wares have the recommendation of being hard too, and the objection some persons make that they do not come in sets, seems to me no real objection, but rather a recommendation.

The most serviceable ware for every-day use is the blue India china. It is an article of regular manufacture, and that produced to-day does not, so far as I can see, differ in the least from that which was made fifty or a hundred years ago. I believe, however, that one or two of the varieties of it are not made any longer—there is one kind, a dull soft blue on a bluish ground (the self-color of the porcelain) with the edges gilded, which may still be manufactured; but, certainly, is not imported any longer. Mr. Sypher has, at the time of writing, the larger portion of a set of this sort; but this is not the only kind that has gone out of trade. There is still another, more delicate, and thinner than the variety in Mr. Sypher's possession. I mention these merely because pieces of these different kinds of Indian blue china are all the time turning up, and those of my readers who are interested in the matter may be helped in finding what they want, if they know what to expect. The blue china I am recommending for daily use is the common variety which is now kept in stock as an article of ordinary commerce by certain houses in the china trade,—by Collamore, of New-York, and Briggs, of Boston, to name two places where people may

always go with the certainty of finding pretty much everything that is going in the way of pottery and porcelain.
This ware used to be very commonly met with in Boston,
brought into use, I believe, in the time when the great
India and China houses of that city were in their pride of
place. Speaking mildly, there must be tons of it in the
good city and its suburbs to-day, though I dare say much
of it is stowed away in garrets, and cellars, and warehouses; for it is no longer in such general use, nor any
longer what it once was,—an external sign that you
belonged to the elect, and were of the *sangre azul*. But
it can never go out of fashion entirely, for its pleasingness
is something substantial, not a mere skin-deep good look;
but good color, good form, though without the least flourish
in the world, and a solidity that is almost proof against
that pest of housekeepers—the maid, who, in spite of
threats, remonstrances and tears, will put all her china into
the dish-pan at once and rattle it around with the mop.

No doubt many persons will be a little repelled by the
first-blush coarseness of the ordinary blue India china.
But let them remember first, that this coarseness troubles
them more than it would if they had not been used to the
impeccable smoothness of the French porcelain, and then
that it really is not the porcelain that is coarse, but the
decoration,—the china itself having a very fine grain.
And as for the decoration, let our reader who is looking
for a substitute for white china boldly try the experiment
of a few pieces of this blue, and see if she does not soon
find its homely markings more attractive than the smooth

regular bands and lines of color which is the general decoration of French porcelain, or even than the finely painted flowers and fruits that are put upon the more expensive services. There will always be people who will have a liking for these displays of dexterity, which do not deserve to be liked except as curiosities, and then only when they are done with exceptional skill. Even then, to my mind, they are worst when they are best, and I would give all I ever saw, if I owned them, for a few pieces of ordinarily good Oriental porcelain,—Indian, Japanese, or Chinese,—or even for some good old earthenware of Worcester, or Wedgwood, or Rouen, or Nevers, or Strasbourg. And I am not afraid but that anybody with a good eye, and a sense of the fitness of things, would agree with me that these designers knew what design is, while the decorators of Sèvres know very little, if anything, about it. The best fruits and flowers I ever saw painted on china—I mean "natural," not conventional, fruits and flowers—are some of those painted at the time when Martolini was director of the works at Meissen, and when, as we are told by the authorities, the art was on the decline. Martolini's flowers and fruits are not conventional, and they are not natural; but they are enough like the flowers they stand for to recall them, and they are laid about the surface of the piece in a careless, irregular way that is very effective.

It is surprising what a character a little well-decorated china will give to a table; and yet not surprising either,— it is as natural as the superiority of a well-papered wall.

or a well-covered carpet over even that "sweet ashes-of-roses" or "delicate pearl-gray" that people have been so long almost compelled to take refuge in.

If you don't like white china, just vow you wont have it, and stick to your purpose like a man, or rather—a surer dependence—like a woman, and you will find your way clear enough, especially in these days. Reform might begin with a good India or Dresden or Worcester cup, saucer and plate for "papa," and the indifference of "the better sex" (Lord Bacon's word—none of mine, ladies!) to such trifles as china and to "nonsense" in general, would be quickly shown by the playfully concealed jealousy and mild snappishness of the owner, if any one else should happen to get his cup by mistake. Mamma might then hint to the children that she would like to have just such another as papa's "if she could afford it," and if the children had had any training to speak of, they would not long let mamma pine for such a small matter. And the two ends of the table thus beautified, it would be easy to go on and make the table harmonious throughout.

It is an objection to blue china with many, that the cups have no handles, and the vegetable-dishes and soup-tureens, handles that one cannot easily get hold of. The latter count in the indictment I don't think very formidable. The hand soon gets used to the little pig's head, or lion, or pomegranate that serves for a handle; and a servant who knows that she will disgrace herself before the whole company if she lets a cover fall, will find a way to avoid doing so. No servant who has a feeling for her business ever breaks china *before folks.* If she were once known positively to have broken a piece, she could never safely deny the responsibility for the fragments discovered from time to time in the ash-barrel, or revealed on the grass-plot in the back yard with the melting of the snow in the spring. The covers of the vegetable-dishes are therefore reasonably safe so long as they are on the table, and the chances of breakage afterward are less for them than for other pieces.

The absence of handles to the cups is a thing to be considered in discussing the blue India ware. I believe no cups of Eastern make for Eastern use ever have handles— at any rate, it is not the custom. The coffee and sherbet drinking Orientals set their cups in little metal stands of filigree-work,—a device which our soda-water sellers have adopted,—and such stands might at once settle the no-handle difficulty and be a pretty ornament to our breakfast and tea tables. Chinese and Japanese cups with handles are common enough, but the handles have been put on for the accommodation of Europeans. India china is less frequently so provided, and this is a pity, because, being thinner (I speak now of the wares of commerce, not of exceptional pieces), and the cups brought to a more delicate and lip-pleasing edge, the ware is preferable to any other porcelain of the same price. The purchaser must therefore consider for himself whether he and his family are likely to find the want of handles a serious trouble; and if he think it will be one, he must find cups of another ware to match his India plates and dishes as well as may be.

Cut No. 75 is a group of pieces of furniture, all of **it** belonging to Old Colony times, drawn by Mr. Lathrop for Bryant & Gay's "History of the United States." The

Old Colony Days.
No. 75.

cupboard at the left belongs to the same class, and I think to the same time, as the one which was figured on page 227, cut No. 72. These pieces were made of oak, and are fastened together by wooden pins. The carving, though rude, is effective. There is not much of it, but it is put

where it does the most good. A desire to get something
of the effect of carving in relieving plain surfaces, without
at the same time incurring much expense, explains the
device of pieces of turned-work, cut in halves, and fastened
by the flat side to certain parts of the piece, as at the
ends of the division between the upper and lower baluster
columns, and between the lower baluster and the foot on
which the piece rests. These are best seen at the left-
hand side. Similar pieces of turned-work, cut in two, are
made to serve as pilasters, one at each side of the door,
with a round-arched panel in the upper of the two stories
into which the cupboard is divided. There is no waste
room in this cupboard. Besides the six cupboards* proper,
there are drawers in the three other divisions,—in that
which answers to the frieze, in the base, and in the
part between the upper and lower range of closets. The
height of the whole is such that the top can easily be
reached with the hand, and it is thus equivalent to a
shelf. In this old piece, as in all of the same style that
I have seen, color has been employed as a further ornament. The baluster columns were painted black, or red
picked out with black, and the other turned ornaments
as well, while the panels were occasionally decorated with
ciphers in a flourish of heraldic foliage, or with birds
and flowers in a half-conventional, half-natural style. But

* How the word cupboard has changed its meaning! From standing for a
set of shelves (boards) on which plate could be displayed, it has come to be
applied to a closet in which things can be shut up. Some of the old cupboards,
like the sideboards in vogue to-day, had closets below them, and these have
gradually usurped the name of what was once the superior portion.

these painted decorations have been in almost all cases effaced,—whether intentionally, or merely by hard usage, cannot be told. I wish they had been left, for I should like some examples of homely, but effective, color decoration to survive, and point the way to something better in the art of decorating furniture than prevails at present. I have already touched on this subject, but at that time I did not know that there was any one here who was likely to help us in getting the sort of decoration needed. The house-painters cannot help us, though there are men among them who could if they were made to see the profit of it; and our artists (being so superior, as they are to Giotto, Delli, Gentile da Fabrino, Paolo Uccello, and the rest of the early Italians, who all painted furniture, door-panels, bridal chests, trays, shields,* whenever they could get a chance)—our artists are, for the most part, above any such degradation of their profession, and it is only in England that we see a return to the charming old fashion. There it is, nowadays, getting to be common to call upon artists to do this work, and some interesting results have been produced. In the Philadelphia Exhibition there was a piece of furniture with panels painted by Mr. Murray. It was exhibited by Messrs. Collinson & Lock. The reason why we do not see more of these pieces painted by the

---

* We have several specimens of this work in our country: panels taken from these Italian chests in the Jarves collection in Yale College, and a fine example of a chest with its panels still in place in the Boston Museum of Fine Arts, with three or four trays in the Jarves collection, and in the little-known and neglected but most precious Bryan collection of pictures—early Italian and others—in our own city in the possession of the Historical Society.

old Italians is, that the panels have been cut out and framed as pictures, in the greed of amateurs and owners in the last hundred years. Some day, no doubt, the same fate will overtake this fine cabinet decorated by Mr. Murray. On page 105, cut No. 39, there was shown a cabinet made by Cottier & Co., for which Mr. Lathrop painted two most beautiful panels. And Mr. H. M. Lawrence, of Albany, beside having decorated a number of pieces of china in a very interesting way, has also painted several panels with flower-decoration that seem to me to show much promise. I wish somebody had venturesomeness enough to design a cupboard, or wardrobe, or book-closet for Mr. Lawrence or Mr. Lathrop to decorate; but in these matters, there seems nowadays not only to be no venturesomeness, but no desire to get out of the comfortable ruts we are all jogging along in.

Yet, all the time people are doing things to please themselves, and striking out in the experiment some good ideas. Thus a gentleman told me the other day that, wishing to fit up his kitchen in a substantial way, he seized the opportunity offered by the sale at a bargain of a considerable number of paneled outside shutters taken from an old house, and still in good condition, from having been made of hard wood, and in a time when carpenters knew what a panel meant; and with these he wainscoted his kitchen, paneling the walls at small expense, and making a stylish room of it. If people really loved their houses,—loved them as we *can* love material things from their association with what is nearest and dearest to us,—

and if they did love them, they would n't be so willing to give them up and change for new ones, as they are with us,—they would find many devices to improve them, not in the mere "dumb-waiter," "permanent wash-tub" sense of the word, but in the sense that makes them homes for home-loving, cultured families,—devices that, while they

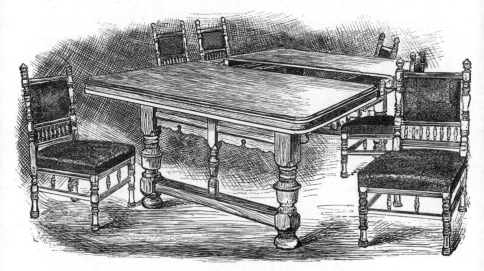

Extension Dining-Table and Chairs.
No. 76.

would add much to their attractiveness, would make small demands upon the purse.

The difficulty of getting a dining-table that shall be both good-looking and serviceable has already been descanted upon in these pages, but, I fear, to little purpose. I give here a few illustrations that may help some of my readers to a solution. Cut No. 76 shows a table recently made by Cottier & Co., with its accompanying chairs. Cut No. 77 is a variation on the design for the end support of this same table. This particular table was made of oak, and with regular and systematic rubbing—five minutes or so each day, before the cloth is laid—it will acquire a mirror-like smoothness and polish. Now, a dining-table, as a rule, is seen only when it is in use, and then only the top of it; so that it may be made of two kinds of wood, one less expensive than the other, as was done in the case of the table shown in cut No. 68, page 210. As for costliness, the hard woods are all about the same, barring mahogany, which was dear before it came to be the fashion, and is dearer since, of course. But the pleasure that a good mahogany top to one's dining-table will give, as the years go by, is worth straining a point for; particularly as mahogany is a first-rate wood for wear, and literally, with good treatment, proves better and better as life wears away. The best combinations would be walnut and mahogany, or ash and oak; but the top ought, by rights, to be of one or the other of these two handsome hard woods,—oak or mahogany,—so that it may bear the taking the cloth off at dessert. Then, the rest of the table might be of some cheap wood. In cut No. 76, the frame of the table is shown to be very heavy and strong There is no need of this, unless the table is a large one, and meant to stretch out on occasion to a great length, as was the case with this one. In such a table, all the folding-rack that supports the additional leaves has to be accommodated by sliding back under the ends, and the table must be solidly built to bear the weight and strain. Cut No. 77 shows a lighter structure: in the drawing, the size of the balls turned on the legs is a trifle exaggerated; they are, besides, rather egg-shaped than round. The bottom rail will be found a convenience, and not in the way. It will be noticed, too, that in both these tables the top projects well

Design for End Support of Dining-Table.
No. 77.

over the frame, so that there is no danger of knocking one's knees against the table-leg in sitting down. This should always be carefully looked out for in constructing a dining-table; to knock one's knees in sitting down to din-ner is one of the minor miseries of life.

I have already spoken of the desirableness of intro-ducing the fashion of decorating furniture with painting. I have recalled to my readers the commonness of painted decoration in early Italian times, when cabinets, sideboards, wardrobes and trays were painted with figure subjects,— religious, historical, mythological,—often by artists who afterward became famous. The peasant-furniture of Europe, particularly in Germany, Switzerland, the Tyrol, and Holland, is decorated, and often with pretty effect, with a mixture of a primitive arabesque design and flowers. And now and then one sees at Castle Garden an immigrant's wooden chest that, with its bright colors, shines among the shabby trunks and boxes of the rest of the company like a peacock among the barn-door fowl. In the Exhibition, too, we had an opportunity of seeing some of the coarsely painted but effective furniture from Tunis,—among the rest, some of the hanging shelves like the one on page 30, cut No. 3. All these shelves were early bespoke, and late in the Exhibition it was impossible to buy one, for people who could n't think such coarse carpentry and rough painting good enough for their parlors, saw that they would look very well in the half-light of their entries; and certainly few hat-racks and hall-mirrors at the fashionable shops are half so pretty as these rude articles.

Cut No. 78 is a copy of an engraving in M. Rodolphe Pfnor's "Ornamentation Usuelle," Paris, 1866–7, where it is described as manufactured at Toelz, Tyrol, Bavaria. The material is of pine, perhaps, and the decoration is painted,— flowers and their leaves, with borders, bands, and ornaments in lively colors on a yellow ground. The back of the chair, which is in the same style, is pierced at one point in a heart-shape, but the remaining surface is covered with a painted decoration. The tops of these tables are often a slab of slate. A continuous foot-rail runs around the four sides, so near to the floor that the foot easily slides upon it without much thinking; and, although the legs have a strong outward slant, the top projects so well that they are not in the way. A drawer slides in grooved pieces fastened to the under side of the table-top, and is handy for holding the table-cloth and napkins. A few

Table and Chair from Tyrol, Bavaria.
No. 78.

years ago, Messrs. Kimbel & Cabus made several tables after a design similar to this, but they were decorated with carving rather than painting, and this made them more costly. I remember, however, that they were very pretty, and seemed all the prettier for breaking up the monotony of New-York furniture shops with something altogether new on this side the water.

Cut No. 79 is copied from a photograph of a picture by Mr. E. L. Henry, which is engraved for the sake of the corner cupboard,—a good specimen of its kind, more

"Why, this is Spode!" (From a Painting by E. L. Henry.)
No. 79.

picturesque than the one figured on page 104, cut No. 38. That one, however, was a fixture, while this is movable, though always to be placed in a corner. In justice to Mr. Henry, I am bound to say that the engraver has not given the vivacity to his copy that the artist has put into this really clever picture. In the original, the expression of the old gentleman who is looking for the "mark" on the bottom of the tea-cup, and the action of the old lady who is reaching up for one of her pet pieces, are very truly given, and the soft sparkle of the glass and porcelain on the shelves could not be bettered. However, it was not hoped to give these things; the form of the cupboard was all we could reasonably aim for.

I may take this place to say a word about the home decoration of porcelain, which is at last getting started after having been for years discouraged by the indifference or mild hostility of the dealers. It has long been plain that it was idle to hope for help from the importers and decorators of porcelain and earthenware, because they could not be made to see that their interest lay in getting to be independent of the foreign workmen. The decorative arts are in rather a despairing state in this country, because the dealers in wall-papers, china, furniture and printed and woven stuffs find it cheaper to "convey" foreign designs than to employ men who could invent fresh designs and patterns. The only way, apparently, in which these arts can be given an American impulse is by people outside these decorative trades making their own designs and getting them executed. Perhaps the easiest of these arts to make a beginning with will be the decoration of porcelain; and, as one of the main difficulties, the getting it baked, namely, is now put out of the way, there is no reason why everybody who has any liking for dabbling in colors should not buy a few earthenware plates and some colors and begin to decorate china. Of course, many of those who make the experiment will fail and give up trying, and many of those who fail at first will up and at it again, and will succeed at last. But if the occupation can be fairly set on foot, and enough people can be induced to give up working in worsteds and painting wall-mottoes, and to try their hands at decorating china for their friends or for the public, a beginning may be made of waking up the dealers to some interest in supplying the home market with home work. How much better it would be if the girls' schools, instead of spending so much time as they do in teaching their pupils to "draw pictures," to copy "drawing-cards," and "studies," "*études à deux crayons*," and the rest of the feeble tribe, would make up a class for painting china, furnishing the scholars with a few good models, taking them now and then by way of object to their usually objectless daily walk, to the Avery, and Prime, and Castellani collection of pottery and porcelain in the Metropolitan Museum,—thus improving their taste and exciting a healthy interest in the study of the art.

There is so much lay talent always latent in societies, that if this one were stimulated and brought out into active competition with the professional market, that in its turn would have to save itself and supply—as in most cases it easily might—a better answer than any amateur could to the popular demand. In this way, or in some other, must be met the want of American productions in this or in the other decorative arts. After all, the imported things, beautiful as they sometimes, perhaps often, are, do not satisfy the people at large. They want something that has a home flavor; but it looks at present as if they must supply this want themselves.

Miss Maria R. Oakey has drawn for me a handsome chair of carved oak (see cut No. 80), such as is occasionally to be found on the other side the water, and when found ought, by all means, to be purchased if possible. These chairs have the double advantage that they are both handsome and comfortable; and that they are well made is proved by the way they have stood their century or two of wear-and-tear. When we are looking at this Jacobean furniture, or at the earlier French furniture of the time of Louis XIII. or of Henri II. of France,—which compensated for inferior richness by its stately elegance and its artistic reserve,—we debate a little with ourselves whether our furniture of to-day does not err a little on the side of austerity, or whether when sumptuous, as of course it often is, it does not owe its sumptuousness too much to stuffs and extrinsic ornaments, too little to its design. The study of the work of former times, so much in vogue to-day, whatever it may be doing for our higher art (and its usefulness in this regard may reasonably be questioned) is putting off indefinitely the day when we shall have originality in our own manufactures. The furniture designed to-day, where it reproduces the forms of the last two hundred years,—such forms at least in which carving did not play an important part,—is often very handsome, but when the designer is thrown upon his own resources he rarely

A Jacobean Chair.
No. 80.

comes out well. You may go through one furniture establishment after another and not find a sideboard, a bookcase, a bedstead, a writing-desk, that is well designed, hardly one that is designed at all. I am speaking now of the ordinary places into which we all of us go when we want to economize. I am not thinking of the Marcottes, the Herters, the Cottiers—because in these places we do often see pieces the design of which has been carefully thought out, and which shows some independence; though even in these places there is far less individuality to be found than there would be if the society their proprietors cater for were not so fond of walking in ruts. But, besides that, we have to admit in the face of all the evidence, that the designing faculty is not very active in this age; we weaken what we have of designing faculty by perpetually and persistently copying the designs of those who have gone before us. Those earlier times were as profuse in design as ours are poor, and we go on robbing them without in the least diminishing the supply. In France, in Germany and in Italy, the workmen have attained great skill in reproducing the design of the Renaissance time, but this is mere copyism; when they attempt to originate, they are, artistically, little above London or New-York.

We have, therefore, in our poverty of the artistic faculty, thrown ourselves on bareness or simplicity, as we like to call it, and, in default of the power to carve and to produce luxuriant forms, we have covered up our nakedness with a world of bric-à-brac. For closed cabinets, rich in architectural forms and sculptures, caryatides and panels, we have *étagères,*—mere assemblages of shelves, with no beauty in themselves, and meant to pass unnoticed in the beauty or curiousness of the multitude of objects that fill them. We make no more tapestry, and we try to persuade our-

selves that wall-paper can take the place of that mode of
decoration with its entertaining individuality. We have but
little art in our day that would have been called art in the
great days; and, in our own country, hardly any art at all
that is reckoned such outside of our own boundaries. At
any rate, if the statement be quarreled with, we must
admit that we have no painting or sculpture that can fairly
be called "decorative," and we never shall have until our
artists get down from their high-horses and condescend
("condescend!"—hear the word, spirits of Giotto and
Raphael, of Veronese, and Titian, and Tintoret!) to paint
our walls for us, nor think it enough to sell us their little
squares of paint at killing prices—the frames not included!

Drawer Handle and Half of Key-plate of French Bureau.

"A BED is certainly the most precious and most favorable asylum here below. In fact, when I look at it, and when I think how, when I step into it, I am suddenly, as if by enchantment, rid of fatigue, cold, wind, dust, rain, importunate visitors, tedious conversations, common-place remarks, pompous assertions, bragging, putting forth headstrong opinions, contradictions, travelers' stories, confidential readings of a poem, or even of a whole tragedy, and that in place of all these, one has pictures, thoughts, memories to be called up, that he is in the midst of a chosen society of phantoms and visions just to his mind — when I think of all this, as I look at a bed, I know not what words to make use of to express my enthusiasm and veneration."

CHAPTER IV.

THE BEDROOM.

"BLESSINGS," said Sancho, "on the man who invented sleep!
It wraps a man all about like a blanket!"

SO FAR as possible, all the rooms in this ideal house of ours
front the sun, or are visited by the sun for an hour or
two every day.   I hold this almost essential to a bedroom,—
that it should have, not merely light and air, but the direct
rays of the sun, and that there should be no furniture nor
hangings in the room that are likely to be injured by the
sun.   It is not always possible in New-York City to obtain
this southern exposure.   Owing to her position, and to the
direction which as a consequence of that position has been
given to her streets, it so happens that, with the exception
of those which are built upon the avenues, all the houses
have one side always in shade, and the other always in sun.
And as the lots present their ends, not their breadth, to the
street, the bedrooms have to be divided, so that one half
have a northern, and the other half a southern exposure.
The houses on the avenues facing east and west get the

sun in the morning and afternoon, but none during the day; so that we are all about in the same box. But everybody who has had any experience of a New-York

A Duchesse.
No. 81.

winter knows that the sunny rooms are the pleasantest, and I think we all have a feeling that they are the healthiest.

Everybody who has lived in Paris, or anywhere in Europe, knows the prejudice that exists there against admitting the night air into bedrooms. The German horror of fresh air inside the house at any time, whether by night or day, is well known, and has been harped on by travelers—English and American—for many a long year; but,

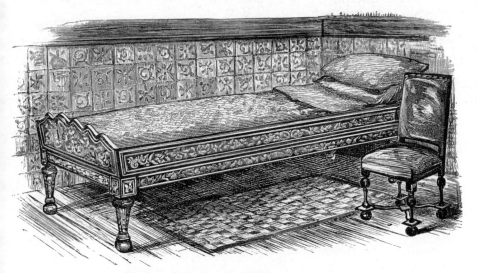

Dutch Bedstead.
No. 82.

in France and Italy, the prejudice is chiefly directed against fresh air at night. In Paris, educated people will gravely tell you that you will become blind if you leave your windows open at night; and if, after a year of the deadly practice, you ask them how they account for your eyes being still unimpaired, they only shrug their shoulders and insist that Americans and English are not like other human beings. For my part, I like as much sun and air as I can

get, and should never be able to sleep at all if I must
have my window shut at night, while, at the same time,
I admit that the Germans, French and Italians are as
healthy as any other people, and get along famously under
a system that I am persuaded would soon make an end
of me.

The doctrine I am now stating, then, so far as it is
doctrine at all, is to be considered as only my own affair,
and to have no authority behind it except myself and a
few hundred physicians, English and American, who would
confess, I dare say, if put upon their honor, that plenty of
sunlight, fresh air,—night and day,—open fires, the absence
of furnaces, and also of drain-pipes and gas, would make
their own skill little necessary in the preservation of health,
and diminish greatly the amount of disease to be cured.

But whether or not we can get all these advantages
extended over the whole house, I am sure it would be a
good thing to secure them for our bedrooms.   Besides
exposure to the sun during the day, there should be some
means of letting in the outside air at night.   If people
object to bluntly opening a window, then some one of
those ventilators that are attached to the window-frame
may be used; or, better, it may be ventilated by a good
open fire-place, which ought to be the only means of heating a bedroom, as indeed it is the cheerfulest and most
attractive.   Now that soft coal is so abundant, of many
sorts, from the English cannel to the American kinds, and
that grates for burning it are common enough, there is no
excuse for using anthracite, either in a grate or in a

stove. Of course, wood, if one can afford it, is better than the best coal, giving out equal heat, more beautiful to look at in burning, and cleaner in the using; but wood is getting dearer and dearer, and only rich people can afford to burn it. Soft coal answers all purposes, and what epicure could ask for a greater pleasure than to open his eyes in a winter or autumnal morning upon the soft sunshine streaming in at his window, and to listen, during the few moments that he allows himself for argument as to the precise time when he shall get up, to the light crackling, sizzling and whispering of the newly lighted coal in the grate! Getting up and dressing under such circumstances is a luxury; no matter what cares the day may have in store for us, here is an hour of serene enjoyment, and no need to envy the man who has a room on the north side of his house and who lets in a little burnt air from the cellar through a dismal hole-in-the-wall, and knows that the rest of the day in Wall street will be well matched with this beginning! In fact, such a beginning would go near to spoil a man's wedding-day.

With sunshine and an open fire, there is only one other customary enemy to be got rid of in the bedroom, and that is the fixed wash-stand. This machine is useful enough in public places, in hotels and restaurants, but ought to be banished, both for sanitary and æsthetic reasons, from our domestic life. Leaving out of view the expense of plumbing arrangements,—their liability to get out of order, the frequency with which they get stopped up, the freezing in winter, and all the evils water and drain

A Corner Fire-place.
No. 83.

pipes are heir to,—I believe it is now admitted that the drain-pipes are the source of a great deal of the disease of our cities and even of our country towns. Convinced of this, and seeing no certain way to prevent the evil so long as drain-pipes are allowed in bedrooms, many people nowa-days are giving up fixed wash-stands altogether, and sub-stituting the old-fashioned arrangement of a movable piece of furniture with movable apparatus,—the water brought in pitchers, and the slops carried bodily away in their native slop-jars.

Whether healthier or not, I think there can be no doubt that the old way is the more comfortable by far. The new fashion was introduced here in a stress of weather, when the Irish Sea was much disturbed, and everything in the shape of domestic comfort was sacrificed to the needs, or rather to the demands, of the crew. Before the invasion of the Biddy tribe from the bogs of Ireland, the labor of the house was looked upon as a part of the price paid for domestic enjoyment. But the Irish naturally cared nothing for the domestic enjoyment of the people who hired them, and bluntly refused to do the work required even if they were paid for it. Their brute ignorance, their carelessness, their slovenliness and their conceit made it impossible to continue certain ways of living that were pleasant to all of us, because they called for intelligence, conscience, neat-ness and teachableness in those who were to keep them up. It was laborious to fetch and carry coal, to clean out grates, to watch and replenish fires, and so we were obliged to give up fires all over the house and be content with one big fire in the cellar. It was laborious to fill lamps with oil, and so laborious to keep them neat and trimmed, that no servant that respected herself was ever known to do it. So we gave up lamps, and contented ourselves with one big gas-tank in the middle of the town, from which our little pipes were fed with ophthalmia and granulated eyelids; and oculists, hitherto rare birds, became as plenty as sparrows.   Carrying water and emptying slops was the worst labor of all, and washing-day was the worst part of it; so the stationary wash-tub went into every kitchen, and the stationary wash-stand into every bedroom; and now the heart of ould Ireland was satisfied, and she would have shut up in measureless content if only she could have made the whole family sleep in one mechanical bed, that should slam itself down ready-made at night, and slam itself up ready-made in the morning, and if the principle involved in stuffing sausages and bottling ale could have been applied to the population (the Protestant American population, I mean), *en masse*, so that we could have been filled with meat and drink, and the labor of washing dishes and setting the table also got rid of.

I prove that I am not of the *sangre azul* by declaring that I am bored by servants; can never eat if one is behind my chair, and would always rather do anything myself than have a servant do it for me.   But, I am ready to admit that, so far as the desire to be rid of labor is concerned, our servants are only doing what everybody does, and there can be no doubt that our Irish invaders found the Americans only too happy to live by machinery, and tickled as children with a new toy at every device that destroyed the domesticity of their homes, and turned them into hotels and manufactories.   A man need n't be afraid of being martyred for saying to-day that a person

sitting with his feet over a hole in the floor and reading
by a gas-burner the doctor's bill for attending his family in
their attacks of illness caused by the entrance of sewage-
gas into his house through his drain-pipes, is an edifying
spectacle. For a good many people are thinking the same
thing, and, in spite of the additional labor involved, are
determined to come back to simpler and more enjoyable
ways of living. Thanks to the good gift of petroleum oil,
and thanks to the inventor of the student-lamp, there is no
longer any excuse for one's hurting his eyes by reading
at night; and thousands of people who a few years ago
were lauding gas to the skies are now consigning it to its
proper place,—in halls, and offices, and streets,—refusing to
allow it in their parlors and bedrooms, and replacing the
gas-fixtures with lamps for burning kerosene. The same
spirit of common sense, and a desire to break up our present mechanical way of living, are driving the fixed water-
basins out of our bedrooms, and bringing the open fires
into all the living-rooms, leaving the poor furnace out in
the cold of the halls and entry-ways. A few more years
and we shall be restored again to some of the cheerful
comfort our forefathers had in this world, which nothing
but man's restless perversity makes it so hard to live in.

Cut No. 84 is a washing arrangement that has been in
use for a year or more in a friend's room, and has been
found convenient. A piece of India matting, of a finer
sort than would be generally used for the floor, is fastened
to the wall by the brass hooks which come for hanging
small articles from, and which serve the same purpose here,

the mat being fixed by the sharpened end of the hook to the "chair-rail" which runs around the room about four feet from the floor, and the hook end being used, as will be seen, for suspending a whisk broom and a duster.

The mat, beside having a very neat appearance, is useful to keep the wall from being spattered. The stand

Chinese Stand—South American Water-Jar— Russian Bowl.
No. 84.

itself is one of those Chinese teak-wood tables with a marble slab let into the top, which are always to be seen at Mr. Sypher's. Some of these stands are a good height for pedestals, others are low enough for stools; the present wash-stand is a middle size, and just right for the purpose. These tables and stands are strongly made, and the wood is well seasoned and stands our climate, and, what is more

trying, our houses, very well. They are among the most useful of the things imported from China, besides being really handsome. The bowl supported by this stand is a lacquered wooden bowl, from Russia,—such a one as is often seen of a small size, and not at all difficult to find as large as this one. It is lacquered with red and gold, the decoration being coarse in execution, but first-rate in effectiveness. The water-jar at the side is from South

America, made of a fine red clay. The arrangement of these articles thus accidentally brought together is far from being unpleasing, and Mr. Marsh has not often done a better piece of engraving than this.

Cuts Nos. 82, 85 and 86 are bedsteads which, however pretty the reader may allow them, I fear he will criticise

"You have waked me too soon, I must slumber again."
No. 85.

as not being very hospitable. But so long as the reader can get a notion of how a bedstead may be simply treated and look pretty, the size of the example is of no importance.

Cut No. 85 was designed by Mr. John Miller, and was made by Mr. Matthias Miller. It is made of oak. The side-rails pass through the corner-posts, and are held by the wooden pins, the ends of which are seen projecting

from the sides of the posts which are in shadow. The
three rails of the ends—one at the top below the carved
finials, and the two others near the bottom—also pass

"A bed is the most delightful retreat known to man."
No. 86.

through the corner-posts. The upright pieces that make
the upper division of the foot-board are cut out in a pattern where the edges come together. The answering pieces
in the head-board are left plain with closed joints; but the
top of each piece is cut into a pattern, and the assemblage

of them makes a very pretty cresting. Mr. Sandier made this drawing, and Mr. Marsh has engraved it.

Cut No. 82, page 267, is a Dutch bedstead, drawn by Mr. Lathrop from an example in Mr. Sypher's warerooms. Both the head-board and the foot-board sloped slightly outward. The wood was inlaid in a way with which we are now familiar enough, and the upper cap of the foot-board was cut in curves, so that the bedstead, rather austere in form, became, by its agreeable color and these few incidents of form, a comfortable-looking bed. Somebody thought so at any rate, for it was bought and carried off almost before Mr. Lathrop could get his drawing finished.

Cut No. 86 is a bedstead designed and drawn for me by Mr. Sandier, by Mr. Herter's kind permission. It does not need any description, I think. The problem was to get as much elegance as possible by the simplest means, and this bedstead ought to be much copied if many of my readers like it as much as I do.

———

What pleasant places our mothers' bedrooms used to be! In the old-time American formal and pretentious way of living,—with the dining-room in the basement, and on the principal floor the grave-yard parlor, in which none of the ornaments could be touched, nor the chairs and sofas sat upon,—it was good that there was one room in the house where domestic feeling was allowed a chance to root itself at ease; where the sun had leave to enter and stretch himself upon the carpet; where the seats were comfortable, and lolling with a book delightful—a room where the soft-blooming fragrant flowers of the homely motherwort took the place of the testy "touch-me-not" that grew so prim and profuse in the handsome room below.

Up to this room, that with its open fire and slipshod neatness seemed always sunny even on dull days, ran the children "home from school" and stormed the maternal citadel for luncheon. Then out came the precious tin box, much dearer to the hungry children than any "safe" with its metaphorical tin, and whose crisp inscription, "CAKE," has been improved by a youthful adept at acrostics, into "Can a kitten eat?" and the mildly delicious seed-cake it contained having been dealt out in generous hunks (oh, expressive vocabulary of childhood!), the pleasant, do-nothing, noon-day hour was slipped along the rosary of time. No parlor, however free to let its luxuries or simple elegance be enjoyed; no nursery, even, made to play in and sensibly kept rid of things that might be hurt; no living-room, with its furniture and fittings meant to be used,—can take the place, I think, of the "mother's bed-room," which still exists, I hope, as of old, in many and many a home. It would be a pity such an "old shoe" of a room should ever be given up, for, in our undomestic American life, unless the mother consents to make an early Christian of herself, and have, for a few hours of the day at least, "all things in common," she will find herself knowing as little of her children as their father does; and in America, it is a common experience that it is a very wise child indeed who has more than a speaking acquaintance with his own father.   To be a really tempting place, however, the "mother's room" should have an open fire in it and look toward the sun.   Its free-and-easiness, moreover, should keep within the bounds of elegance, which need never be divorced from fitness and comfortableness.   For the children's eye is forever being educated, and ugly things ought not to be brought superfluously before them.   I do not believe in surrounding children with luxuries; on the contrary, their lives ought to be made as simple as possible, and the fortunate ones are they whose youth makes them acquainted with some hardship; but, what they do see ought to be of a character to refine the taste, accustom the eye to harmonies of color and form, and insensibly help it to form standards of judgment.

Nowadays, there is positively no excuse for having ugly things about.   A few years ago, the carpets were almost all highly reprehensible.   To say that they were barbarous would be to pay them a compliment, for no barbarous people ever made such crudities of line and color as the old "Brussels" and "ingrain" carpets showed us; though the "ingrain" designs were often better than those of the more expensive kinds.   This was because fewer tricks were played with warp and woof in the cheap carpet, and the designs were more evidently structural.   The objection to all the carpets of the former time—cheap and dear alike—was, that the patterns were too defined; whether "set" or "flowing," they could not be made to blend with what was placed upon them, but pushed themselves so impertinently to the fore, that the carpet became the chief thing in the room, instead of being, as it should be, only a background for the rest. Of late years, there has been a great improvement in the designs of all carpets, from the most expensive Wilton to the cheapest ingrain. In the richer sorts, dark,

"And all Arabia breathes from yonder box."
No. 87.

soft tones with patterns—if patterns they can be called— of spots and stains, that now appear, now hide, but are never in the way, are to be bought in many of the shops. Some of the best English carpets are as thick and soft as the best of Persian make, and the designs, when they are not too daring, or when the makers are content with copying the quieter Eastern patterns, are a great improvement on the older manufactures. But one may as well spend his money for an Eastern carpet outright as buy one of these English carpets. There would be the certainty of getting a design that had no taint of South Kensington in it, and that would be sure not to be the same through any square foot of its space. For one thing, Eastern art is valuable to us: it rebukes at every turn our scientific love of precision and symmetry, shows us the charm of irregularity, and teaches us how to make two sides of a thing alike while keeping them quite different. Whether we shall ever get this into our blood, I don't know. It is an essential principle of all the best decorative art; and necessarily so, because all such design is as far removed as possible from mechanical assistance, and has no other rule or measure than the eye acting through the hand. No two Ionic capitals of Greek workmanship, even in the same temple, are alike in anything except general size and character. No more are any two Doric caps alike, nor any two moldings of any style, nor any two successive feet of any Greek ornament. The notion instilled into our minds that the Greek architecture is all monotony and repetition is of English or German origin.

There needs to-day to be a protest made by some one against the mechanical character of our decoration, for, with an unexampled demand for decoration in our furniture, our furnishing, our jewelry, our porcelain, there come an unexampled supply, and the manufacturers, of course, bring all the labor-saving appliances they can contrive to supply this demand.   Immense furniture-mills are set up, and to such perfection has machinery attained, that the logs go in at one door, and come out at another fash-

"When clothes are taken from a chest of sweets."
No. 88.

ioned in that remarkable style known here as " Eastlake," and which has become so much the fashion that grace and elegance are in danger of being *taboo* before long.   Then " rugs" being all the rage, and the beautiful ones being, as they always must be, expensive, the manufacturers are turning out cheap rugs by the acre, which are no whit better—nay, are much worse—than the carpets of thirty or forty years ago. So with pottery and porcelain,—our china-shops are filled with things whose only recommendation to our novelty-loving people is their novelty and their loudness. And all these things—the furniture, the rugs, the pottery—are so cheap, that everybody gets them, and, of the smaller decorative things, gets so many that our homes are overrun with things, encumbered with useless ugliness, and made to look more like museums or ware-rooms than like homes of thinking people and people of taste.

I dare say, however, that all this superabundance—superabundance in the supply and superabundance in the buying—is necessary, and that not only good to trade and to manufacture, but good to art and taste, will come out of it. The way of it will be something like this: Exclusiveness being natural to human beings (it comes simply and excusably enough from our dislike of monotony and of repetition), people will demand more than they do now things that show some individuality in design, that are not made "in quantities to suit purchasers,"—that are not even to be had in pairs. Then we shall find the makers of furniture producing single pieces or single sets, into which the workman has put some special design which he does not copy in the next piece, even if he keep the general form. Design, and finish, and serviceableness, will be most considered, and cheap display—the bane of almost all our fashionable furniture nowadays—will be avoided. When a few rich people, who have an educated taste besides, will encourage the production of furniture that is worth admiring and keeping for its own sake, not merely because it is in the fashion, we shall see the turn of the tide. At present, there is hardly anything at all of this done even by the richest people (I mean, little that I hear of); and as for the general run of us, we don't so much as think of doing it. People naturally and reasonably count the cost, and when they find that it not only costs a good deal of money but a good deal of time and study to get a piece of furniture well designed, they just wont try to do it, and fare as well as they can without.

At present, then, we are in this strait. The things we see for sale in the shops are all either good or bad or indifferent copies of old-fashioned things, or of Oriental things of to-day. Hardly anything with the stamp of our own time and country is to be had. What, then, are the young people to do who want to furnish their houses, and have comparatively little, or really little, money to do it with? I say in the first place, that there is no excuse nowadays for anybody having ugly things. If they have them, they are themselves to blame, for they must have chosen ugliness and rejected, if not beauty and elegance, then simplicity. "Wedding presents," I hear some reader whisper. Yes, I know. But wedding presents are almost always of silver, or ornaments, or small things that after a year's display where they can catch the giver's eye on reception days and "calls," can be stowed away. Few people are cruel enough to send in furniture; for that the young housekeepers are responsible, and if they will take the advice of those who have been through the mill, they would begin with only what is absolutely necessary, and make up their minds that, though they want but little here below, yet they want that little long; they want to grow up with it, to use it, enjoy it, and make it a part of their domestic

French Bureau, with Fine Brass Mounts.
No. 89.

history. The main reason why people cannot go to an architect or a designer and get their furniture made for them in special, is that they think they want much more furniture than they do, and there is not money enough to supply all their needs. At least one or two things might be so procured, and, for the rest, a steady search kept up until the needful pieces are found, at once useful and handsome. Here in New-York, people go to the houses which supply the needs and cater to the whims of the rich—houses where you are told plainly that they cannot afford, and do not propose, to sell cheap things. Then there is complaint and disgust, and those who have prof- fered their advice on the subject of furnishing are taxed with ministering to luxury and expense. But it may safely be said that many more people might become the owners of the things they admire, and justly too, at Herter's or Cottier's, if they would be content with one thing or two; but they want all, or want everything "in keeping," as the phrase is,—a thing not necessary at all. If people will have anything, let them be content to earn it. I am not writing, nor ever have been, for people who can go to Cottier's, Marcotte's, or Herter's, and buy what they want. Nor do I see why anybody should think it necessary to spend a cent of money or a minute of time on furnishing his house with chairs and tables if he does n't wish to. An angry gentleman writes from Texas to complain that the prettily designed, delicately made sofa, of which a cut was given on page 65, is not suited to his needs. "Where would such a sofa be," he cries, "after four or five romping boys had played circus on it some rainy day?" Where, to be sure? But my Texan critic must reflect that he cannot have his cake and eat it too. If he has four or five romping boys who have no barn or nursery or shed to play circus in on rainy days, he must be content with furniture that will stand being run over rough-shod. And I, for one, should never think of insisting that, such being his plight, he should make misery for himself by having everything handsome about him.* It is not for such as this gentleman I am writing, nor for the rich who can do as they will; but for those who have a desire to make their homes agreeable to the eye as well as comfortable, and yet who have to consider the cost at every step.

If carpets are not desirable in the living-rooms of the house, much less are they desirable in the bedrooms. The French lay a strip of carpet or a rug at the bedside, which they call a *"descente du lit,"* and in many houses this is all the concession made to comfort, but in our climate this is insufficient; we must have more than this for "looks," even if we do not need it for "comfort." A good rug at either side the bed, and one of the long narrow rugs stretched at the foot of the bed between it and the fire-place, and reaching from one side of the room to the other, will cover the floor generously, and will not hinder the thorough sweeping and cleaning of the room.

The extreme plainness of cut No. 87 is lightened and relieved by the shelf at the top, supported at the front by

* As this gentleman's note was intended for publication, I make no excuse for quoting a sentence of it. "The furniture of 1776 is nice for those who like odd things, and have a mania for such collections; but, for actual use, I don't like them. Most of them are square, angular, and 'spindling,' looking as if they would not last—not solid enough." Now, considering that this furniture of 1776 has been in constant use since it was made, and is in these times of revival of old fashions starting on a new lease of life—what becomes of the doubts as to its solidity? The truth is, it is almost all of it first-rate furniture; well designed for use and good looks, and it is no mania for collecting that makes people snap it up wherever they see it for sale, but good sense and good taste.

turned pieces, and at the back by a solid pane which may
be filled in with marquetry, or better by a mirror. It has
four long drawers and two short ones, and, as will be seen,
while taking up but little room, is a convenient and com-
modious piece of furniture.

Cut No. 88 is an old-fashioned bureau, with a mirror
in a frame of the same date. There are four drawers;
the fronts of the three lower ones being cut out of the
solid wood so that the ends project and the middle retreats,
the same curve being given' to the base of the bureau and
to the upper drawer, which is carved with three shell-like
patterns that adapt themselves to the shapes of the lower
drawers. The handles and key-plates are of brass, and
thus, by a very economical use of material, a good deal of
variety in shadow and reflection is obtained.

Cut No. 90 is a Japanese affair, and in ten years' use
has proved itself a good friend. It would be at home, I
suppose, a common enough thing; but that has nothing to
do with its substantial merits. In its own land, it was at
once traveling-trunk and bureau; and it is a good type of
the article which in Japan serves both these needs, and
which is, I believe, in effect, the only piece of furniture
they can be said to have. Sometimes the affair is modified, and enriched with lacquer inlays and enamels until it
becomes a splendid cabinet; but it almost always retains,

"In all its weal and in its moste pride,"

the symbols of its vagabond nature in the poles by which,
when need is, it is borne from place to place on the

shoulders of coolies. In the richer cabinets, these poles are elegantly made and richly ornamented, to sort with the rest of the piece; but I suppose that when these humbler bureau-trunks are to be carried about, the coolies use poles of their own for the purpose.

The present example is in two parts, one of which stands on the other; though there is no reason for their being placed so, except for the convenience of the owner. The arrangement of the irons at the ends indicates that the lower one rightly belongs above. For while either can be lifted and carried off separately, yet it may sometimes be desirable to carry both off together. In this case, put the upper of the two boxes below the lower, and turning up the end handle, suspend it from the two projecting knobs; then pull up the other handles, one at each end, and slip the pole through, hoist to shoulder, and away! The adjustment of these handles is an illustration of simple common-sense Japanese contrivance. The handle of the box that is to go on top when the two are to be carried off together is pulled up vertically, slipping up and down in its iron staples. But the handle of the lower one turns out, and then up, because only so can it be passed over the two iron knobs. When its American owner has occasion to move, each part is easily lifted by its handles like a trunk. Everybody knows how unmanageable a monster a well-filled four-story bureau is.

My friend's reason for putting the lower part of his bureau above was to get the shallow drawer, where hand-kerchiefs and collars, gloves, etc., are most easily kept,

nearest the hand, and also to have the closet and the deep
drawer for shirts where they can be most easily reached.
No one but a man knows what a blessing this shirt-drawer
is.   It will hold the week's wash of shirts without tumbling
or crowding, and nothing else need be allowed to usurp a

Grand Combination Trunk Line.
No. 90.

place in it.   In these four drawers is room for all one
man's linen; and in the little closet, which contains three
drawers and a hiding-place for money besides (which the
owner did not discover until after a year's possession),
there is room for all his trinkets and valuables.   When the
two boxes are placed together, the whole measures three

feet one inch in length by three feet four high, and one foot five deep.

This chest of drawers is made of a very soft and light wood, and it is, I think, only for protection against rough usage that it is so bound about with iron. This iron, however, is thin, and adds but little to the weight of the boxes. The handles are much heavier than they need be, but they are well shaped for the hand. Each drawer is provided with a lock, and one key opens all but the closet, which has its own. Taking only the body of this Japanese contrivance, and rejecting all the iron-work, why does not some one of my readers who wants a good bureau have one made on this model, either of walnut, mahogany, or oak, and furnished with brass handles and key-plates, the door hung by brass strap hinges? These brass handles and key-plates are made now in England very commonly, and the Household Art Company of Boston used to keep them on sale; but there are plenty of ways of getting them. It is to be noticed that the boxes are made with absolute plainness; there is not a molding nor a chamfer to be seen, much less any tiles let in, or any rosettes stuck on. When it is done, and set up in its polished plainness (oiled and rubbed, not varnished), with its mild-shining brasses, my lady shall devise for the top a covering of plush or velvet hanging over a little at each end, and over this a strip of linen with fringed or embroidered ends; and then, with the swing-glass in its place and the needful nothings of the toilet in theirs, the result ought to commend itself alike to the mind and the eye.

The French piece (cut No. 89) is redeemed from commonplace by the fine brasses with which it is ornamented; the general form is good, and many years' use has proved the bureau a comfortable one; not too high nor taking up too much room on the floor. The ornaments are of that fine brass in which the French of the early part of this century worked with so much elegance of taste and fineness of finish, and which we see very coarsely imitated in our own time. The handles of the drawers of this bureau are designed as the necks and heads of swans issuing from a wreath of leaves. They are good, serviceable handles that cannot break nor come off, and they are besides elegant in form. Very little of this early nineteenth century French furniture is met with in this country, nor is it often offered for sale even in Paris. But it is occasionally seen, and as it only gets to our second-hand shops after much domestic tribulation,—the ruin and decay of families, or a forty years' wandering in the boarding-house desert, in places where neither quails nor manners are to be had,— it often presents a doubtful appearance to the rummaging eye. But if it prove to be a genuine piece, and if on close inspection the brass is seen to be as purely chased and sculptured as if it were gold or silver—buy it, by all means ('t is sure to cost but little), and when it has been polished up and set in its place, "I will warrant it to give satisfaction." For, all the French furniture of the old time was well made, and their cheap furniture of to-day is much better made than ours, so long as it is kept at home. When it is brought to this country, however, it does not stand fire at all. Nor, for that matter, does even the foreign furniture that has been made a hundred years resist the furnace-heat of our houses. No sooner does winter

A Love of a Bonnet-Box.
No. 91.

come than the French furniture—and the English too—begins to gape and yawn and stretch out its arms for home.

Cut No. 91 is another combination lock-up; an antique this time, but with some serviceable modern points about it. It has three drawers on the lower half, which is furnished, as every such piece of furniture ought to be, with strong handles by which it can be drawn out from the wall on sweeping-days; and the upper half has a flap which closes its whole front, and which opens down, stopped at the right angle by a horse-hinge, or some one of the common contrivances for that purpose. A lady would find this a good place for her hats and furs (if there were not too many of them); or, if she were of a literary or financial turn of mind, here is the place for her account-books and her papers.

Our people do not generally believe in pine, but I think that either of these chests (Nos. 90 and 91) would look very pretty made of pine and stained a good red, or a good black, or simply left the self-color of the pine, and shellacked. I was the other day in one of Mr. McKim's houses, in which all the interior fittings were designed by him to be executed in common pine, and it is long since I have been in so cheerful and comfortable-looking a house. The wood-work was not skimped, there was enough of it to make you aware of its presence, and to aid the liberally welcomed sunshine in giving a warm and hospitable look to the rooms. I think of this house just now because the owner had employed the village carpenter to make some pieces of furniture of pine wood, and they had proved more fortunate than such ventures often do. But it is greatly to be wished that more people would risk the experiment. It is the only way I see to get cheap furniture that shall be well made. In this case some picture in a book or journal was shown to the carpenter, and he was asked to come as near it as he could, and, being a workman with some taste and sense of proportion, he managed to solve his problem with considerable success. The work is often in these cases done with thoroughness: the trouble begins when the thing is to be ornamented. Then the fatal facility of machine-work, scroll-sawing, knobs and rosettes, stuck on, comes in to spoil what might otherwise have proved a sensible piece.

Why would it not be a good plan for three or four or half a dozen people living in a country place, to club together, and, taking some one of the pictures in these pages which they all agree to think well of, to ask some architect—Mr. McKim, Mr. Babb, or any other man of taste and sense—to make the necessary working-drawings for the village carpenter? Each contributor could then order his piece made of the wood he might prefer, and no two of the pieces need be exactly alike. This plan, I think, would give better results in most cases than trusting to any carpenter, however clever, to translate one of these drawings into *his* vernacular.

Cut No. 92 is a South American pitcher, members of whose family may be seen at china shops in this city, and which ought to find a readier sale than they do. They are made of red clay like that used for flower-pots; the cover is removable and can be used or not, and for once I am able to say, with a cheerful heart and a clear conscience, that here is something that may fairly be called cheap. "Cheap, call I it, for to define true cheapness, what is it but to be nothing else but your money's worth?" This pitcher cost a dollar and a half, there or thereabout, "a little more than one, and less than two;" but it may be that no one of my readers who shall go to look for one will like it when he finds it. The ware is too coarse to suit many; ladies especially will object that it is not as agreeable to handle as the smooth French porcelain.

I recommended this particular pitcher the other day to a lady who wanted a water-holder to go with one of the

painted and lacquered wooden bowls of which there was mention and a cut a little way back, on page 274. There is a good deal of South American and Spanish, Italian and Portuguese peasant-pottery that would be very useful to us in this country, where nothing but French and English wares are to be had. I wonder some traveler with time and money (not much of the latter is needed), and wanting employment, does not go about Europe and collect a ship-

South American Water-Pitcher.
No. 92.

load of the jolly water-vessels that are made by the hundred thousand in all the Mediterranean lands, and which we know would have a great popularity here, because every scrap that was sent to Philadelphia was caught up before the distracted owners had learned to translate *maravedis* into dollars.

I am glad to be able to add the wooden bowls which I have just spoken of to my small but hopeful list of cheap utilities and prettinesses. They are so handsome and so useful that I think many of my readers will thank me for letting them know about them. There are eighteen sizes of these bowls imported, and they are sold by the diameter— at so much an inch. The largest size sells for three dollars, but these are rather unwieldy. A useful set of four, the largest fourteen inches across, costs $6.62. Their decoration is in red and black on a dull gold ground. No two are alike in design; the work is coarse but effective. These bowls are very light to handle, and they will stand boiling water; but too much soap injures them. At present they are to be had only in Boston.*

As for the rest of the toilet furniture, there need be no difficulty, surely, in supplying one's needs nowadays, for pretty and useful trays and small dishes may be found anywhere,— at Collamore's, at Vantine's, at Drake's, at Hawkins's,— that is, provided the searcher does not insist upon having his soap-dish, his brush-tray, his bowl and pitcher, all blood relations.

Cut No. 93 will be recognized by many of the readers of these pages as an indispensable part of the furniture of the bedroom in old-time days. These bedside chairs, with their great ears, and their ample breadth, and depth, and height, were a sort of half-way house between the bed just left, or just about to be entered, and the world of active work. You slid out of bed into this hospitable lap, and

---

* The address of the Boston dealer who has the Russian bowls for sale is Frank B. Norris, successor to E. C. Dyer, 56 Summer street, corner of Arch street, Room No. 8.

having just put Satan behind you, with his multiform and
multitudinous arguments against getting up in general, you
now proceed to meet a second series of objections to putting on your stockings.   If my readers shall object to this

A Half-way House.
No. 93.

chair as an encourager of laziness, I will change my com-
mendation and speak of it as an excellent resting-place
when one is tired, or convalescent.   Having persuaded
them to let me smuggle it into their rooms on this plea,

I am sure they will end by agreeing with me as to the desirableness of having such a chair in the house. As for the making of it,—I doubt if one could get such a thing made nowadays. It is not elegant enough. But there are plenty of them to be bought out of old houses in New England; and once restuffed and covered with a flowered chintz, they are ready to serve a new generation as they served the last. It is worth while having a slight attack of the measles just for the pleasure of getting well and eating a baked apple out of an "old blue" saucer in front of a sea-coal fire, sitting in this chair.

"For wash-stands," as Lord Bacon would say, "they are better open than closed," I think cupboards and shut-up places are to be avoided. The best for a wash-stand is a table, of a size appropriate to your room, with a drawer and a shelf below. Cut No. 94 is a good type of a wash-stand,—a French example,—with perhaps more of a look of English comfortableness and enjoyment of the water-privilege than one associates with the French. In Paris, a large wash-basin is called an English basin, and certainly the basins provided for the French market by the manufacturers are of singular smallness. But I am not intending to join the sniffers at French cleanliness. I found them every whit as neat as ourselves, or as their neighbors, the English, with their enormous appliances for "cleaning themselves," and "tubbing,"—two odious phrases which they are fond of, and with which they make washing and bathing seem very vulgar employment. Paris is abundantly provided with baths, none of them free, I believe, but all very cheap, and they are much frequented. A French lady was once asked why the wash-basins in general use in Paris are so small. Her explanation was, that French

French Wash-Stand.—Japanese Towel-Rack.
No. 94.

ladies are always washed before they get up by their maids, and that little bowls are more handy than big ones, and can be often emptied and filled.

At the time when this French wash-stand was made, English fashions were all the *mode* in Paris, and ever since they have rather gained than lost in favor. This wash-stand is an example more elegant than is commonly met with, of a style much used in Paris, and very little known here. The towel-rack at the side of this stand is a Japanese affair, made of wood stained black and lacquered, and mounted with brass.

In Paris they have great furniture establishments, on the same principle as our "Stewart's," where one can go with whatever purse, and find what he needs. Here are the most modest outfits, and, in the fashion of the day, the most expensive; and here one can order made what he fancies. We have one vast establishment for the manufacture of furniture in this city, but it is only for the making of costly (or seeming costly) articles. No poor student, no young couple starting off in life with a purse that has a bottom, no people settling in the great city for a winter's social enjoyment, need go to this place to get their wants supplied. It is a pity there were not such a place; but in New-York at least, if not in America, you are well enough off if you are miserably poor, and well enough off if you are comfortably rich; but if you are neither one nor the other, Heaven help you! Agar was not a New-Yorker; had he been, he never would have prayed as he did. He would have said: "Give me *either* poverty or riches;" and pert Nerissa, had she been born in Gotham instead of in Venice, would never have uttered her lady-in-waiting wisdom: "It is no mean happiness, therefore, to be seated in the mean." In New-York, alas, it is very mean happiness indeed. Still, in this, as in many things, we are learning from the Old World.

In these great warehouses of the Faubourg St. Antoine, then, you find the jolliest little wash-stands, the lower half a chest of drawers, and on top, a marble slab with holes cut in it for the different vessels,—the basin, the water-carafe, the tumblers, the soap-cup and brush-tray,—over all which apparatus shuts down a cover, that, when opened and

A Place for Everything.
No. 95.

standing upright, bears a mirror, of no particular use that I could ever see, since it is not, of course, high enough to reflect one's face; but the French are plainly of the mind that a mirror can never come amiss. In order to allow of this cover shutting down over the whole apparatus of the wash-stand, the pitcher is made of the most amusing *flatness*. It often looks as if it had been sat upon before it was baked. But it does its duty like a man for all that. Another Yankee contrivance in these wash-stands is to have the top slide out bodily, so that it will project two or three inches from the face of the drawers below. This is in order to prevent the front of the piece from being spattered when we are washing our face o' mornings.

Such a wash-stand as this was once brought home to America, and had its marble slab broken (of course) in being carried a short distance from New-York on the rail-road. To do the company justice, they paid damages; but instead of attempting to replace the pretty French marble, its owner made a slab of tiles take its place. The tiles were small,—an inch and a half square,—and were laid in putty. The slab, when finished, was thicker than the marble one had been, for the French can cut their marble very thin, and I think the tiles alone were thicker than the original top. The wooden flooring on which from necessity they were placed, and the putty on which they were laid, made the whole thicker and heavier. But it cost a little less than to have replaced the marble, and the look of it when done was more attractive; and then, the tiles will not stain with water, and are far less liable than marble to resent the bangs that patient furniture of the unwary servant takes.

Cuts Nos. 95 and 96 are only hints of simple picturesqueness. The three corner shelves,—the longest at the top instead of at the bottom,—and the corner stand, with its rounded top shelf supporting a water-cistern, and its rect-angular lower stories, may please some people by their unexpectedness as well as by their usefulness. Mr. Lathrop devised as well as drew them.

Shelves for a Corner.
No. 96.

This cut, No. 97, is a French piece of about Louis Philippe's time. It is made, I believe, of mahogany, with fine brass mounts—on the corner columns, the edges of the panels, of the sides, and of the drawers, and about the mirror. The mirror is set in the door, and

Old-time Elegance.
No. 97.

easily reflects the whole figure. Below are two drawers
made to appear like four.

For myself, I have such a dislike to almost the whole of what are called in housekeeping "modern improvements" (being a disbeliever in the benefits of gas, plumbing, and heating apparatus, except where, as in hotels and factories, they are necessary on a grand scale), that I naturally prefer a contrivance like the "cistern," cut No. 95,—convenient, pretty to look at, and in no danger of becoming a diphtheria-trap,—to one of our fixed basins. Another, the reader may remember, was shown on page 40. However, I am well aware that there is a sufficient reason for our American wholesale adoption of mechanical contrivances in the miserably inefficient character of our servants. In nine cases out of ten, we use gas, furnaces and plumbing instead of lamps or candles, open fires and movable washing-apparatus, because it saves immensely in the labor and expense necessary to carry on a household. But, nowadays, when better servants are to be had, and "service" is getting to be more and more a profession, we may reasonably plead for a more domestic, and a less hotel and steam-boaty, way of living, knowing that in doing so we are pleading also for healthier ways of living, and not merely for picturesqueness. Besides, it may cheer up the weaker brethren who are made uncomfortable by doing differently from their neighbors, to know that a great many people are on the side of reform in this matter, and that it may almost be said to be "the fashion" (magical word!) nowadays to work by a "student-lamp," or a "moderator,"—the perfection of light-givers,—with an open fire of soft coal in the grate, and no pestilent, life-destroying furnace within

the four walls; while, upstairs, the plumbing is confined to
the bath-room, the movable wash-stand with its china and
glass and "comforts" generally, being restored to its old
supremacy,— taken out of its closet prison, and set in
light and air.

Bedside Table.
No. 98.

We will waste no words
with people who go through
England, with its absolute
perfection in the art of domestic living, and whose good
inns everywhere, in town or
country, make our bare, dreary
barracks more desolate in
the remembering—and sigh
for what they call the "modern improvements" they have
left behind them. To some
people, a great ingredient in
the charm of Europe is, that
they are rid of the very
things that others are all
the time sighing for.

A friend writes: "I shall
never forget, when remem-
bering the minor pleasures of my visit to England, my
first experience of an 'inn.'

"We went directly to Chester, and, to the disgust of the
porters, declined to go where, being evidently 'gentry,' we
should have gone by instinct—to the elegant spic-and-

span, bran-new 'Grosvenor,' but insisted on being carried to one of the old-fashioned inns. We found a large house with its traditional 'landlady' in the bar, and were shown into a waiting-room while our parlor was made ready. This proved to be a large apartment, furnished in a comfortable, home-like way, with the same sort of furniture that would have been found in an ordinary English house—I mean, there was nothing in the room that suggested it had been furnished 'on contract.' When dinner-time came, we found the table laid in our own parlor, the waiter and his boy in black coats, white neck-cloths, and white cotton gloves, and the table set like one's own and different in no respect, not even in the quality of the furniture, from what one often saw afterward in England at the tables of very good people. We had ordered our dinner beforehand, the landlady having come up and asked us what we would like, very civilly, and kindly helping us to choose, so that when we sat down, the tiresome waiter we had left three thousand miles away, with his skipping alternations from freezing neglect to pushing obsequiousness, and his 'bill-er-fare' with its chaos come again, and its damnable iteration, were a forgotten nightmare, and the dinner was a foretaste of Paradise. I remember that after dinner when the dessert was set,—the cloth being actually removed and the old mahogany revealed,—the waiter, in putting on the table some handsome old Worcester plates (made in the days when there was a Worcester that had something better to do than making bad copies of Japanese perfections), whispered that 'Mrs. ——, thinking we might like, as Americans, to see some old china, had sent these up,' and how was it possible after that to feel that we were in a hotel? The surprise was reserved, however, for bed-time, when, on going to our chamber, we found a small fire flickering cheerfully in the grate, the candles lighted, the curtains of the four-post bedstead drawn and the clothes turned down, while at one side of the room, placed upon a cloth of its own and with its own towel-stand supplied with bath-towels, was the welcome hat-bath, an English gift to the world worth all the sewing-machines and steam-engines that were ever invented. Here was a comfortable lap of fortune to have fallen into, and we hummed with Dr. Johnson those lines of Shenstone that no home-staying American (at least, since the good old days of 'Bunkers!') can ever understand the sense of:

> 'Whoe'er has traveled life's dull round,
>   Where'er his stages may have been,
> May sigh to think he still has found
>   The warmest welcome at an inn!'

"Among my reminiscences of travel, I do not know of any sharper contrast than between this comfortable inn at Chester and the hotel we went to on arriving in New-York—one of the three or four 'first-class' hotels; for, whereas in Europe no one who is merely after comfort, and not after a showy way of spending money, ever goes in a city to the first-class hotels, here at home it is never safe to go to any other. At this hotel we were shown into a big bare room, containing just what was necessary for decent living—a carpet, a bed, a bureau, a looking-glass, a table and four chairs, with the inevitable furnace-hole in the wall, the gas-burner where no one could use it in dressing, and the wash-basin in the narrow closet—a scientific desolation (your room being exactly like every other in the caravansary) which we Americans have carried to perfection. At dinner, we sat in the well-lighted, hand-somely proportioned dining-hall, and 'fed'* with the multi-tude—the gentleman in front of us enjoying his ice-cream, water-melons, peaches and coffee all at once—he at the tail of the *carte* while we were at the head. Yet for all this bare and bleak discomfort, we paid far more than for the English hospitality."

The lady's dressing-table, cut No. 99, also designed by Mr. Sandier, was engraved in Paris by M. Guillaumot. The table is low and long, and of good breadth, and has two drawers. The glass is large, and I believe does not swing. The shelves at the sides, supported on slender columns, are rather intended for lights than for the flower-glass and

---

*With what instinct in the choice of a word Shakspere makes Lady Macbeth betray her scorn for the people who flocked to her solemn supper. "*Feed*," she said, "*Feed*, and regard him not!" If she had been thinking of them as human beings, she would have said "Eat!" but she thought of them as swine, and her word fitted her thought. This remarkable woman, whose lady-like instincts make us the more regret her indiscretions, and more willing to excuse them on account of that neglected education which somebody beside ourselves has de-plored, shows, in another passage of the same scene, that she had a genius for hospitality:

> "My royal lord,
> You do not give the cheer: the feast is sold
> That is not often vouch'd, while 't is a making,
> 'T is given with welcome: To *feed* were best at home;
> From thence, the sauce to meat is ceremony;
> Meeting were bare without it."—MACBETH, Act III, Scene 4.

"And now confessed the toilet stands displayed."
No. 99.

knickknacks the reader sees. This seems to me a good design, and one that might be easily copied. I think it will look best in wood stained black and polished.

"We were now returning from the long walk. We had reached the middle of a clean Faubourg, where the houses were small, but looked pleasant. It was before the white door-step of a very neat abode that M. Paul had halted.

"'I call here,' said he.

"He did not knock, but taking from his pocket a key, he opened and entered at once. Ushering me in, he shut the door behind us. No servant appeared. The vestibule was small, like the house, but freshly and tastefully painted: its vista closed in a French window with vines trained about the panes, tendrils and green leaves kissing the glass. Silence reigned in this dwelling.

"Opening an inner door, M. Paul disclosed a parlor, or salon—very tiny, but I thought very pretty. Its delicate walls were tinged like a blush; its floor was waxed; a square of brilliant carpet covered its center; its small round table shone like the mirror over its hearth; there was a little couch, a little chiffonnière, the half-open, crimson silk door of which showed porcelain on the shelves; there was a French clock, a lamp; there were ornaments in biscuit china; the recess of the simple, ample window was filled with a green stand, bearing three green flower-pots, each filled with a fine plant glowing in bloom; in one corner appeared a guéridon with a marble top, and upon it a work-box and a glass filled with violets in water. The lattice of this room was open; the outer air breathing through gave freshness, the sweet violets lent fragrance.

"'Pretty, pretty place!' said I. M. Paul smiled to see me so pleased."—
Villette, Chapter XLI.

" * * The dimity curtains dropped before a French bed bounded my view.

"I lifted them; I looked out. My eye, prepared to take in the range of a long, large and whitewashed chamber, blinked, baffled on encountering the limited area of a small cabinet with sea-green walls; also, instead of five wide and naked windows, there was one high lattice shaded with muslin festoons; instead of two dozen little stands of painted wood, each holding a basin and an ewer, there was a toilet-table dressed like a lady for a ball, in a white robe over a pink skirt; a polished and large glass crowned, and a pretty pin-cushion frilled with lace adorned it. This toilet, together with a small, low, green-and-white chintz arm-chair, a wash-stand topped with a marble slab, and supplied with utensils of pale-green ware, sufficiently furnished the tiny chamber. * * * * * I knew—I was obliged to know—the green chintz of that little chair; the little snug chair itself; the carved, shining-black, foli-ated frame of that glass; the smooth, milky-green of the china vessels on the stand; the very stand, too, with its top of gray marble, splintered on one corner;—all these I was compelled to recognize and to hail."—Villette, Chapter XVI.

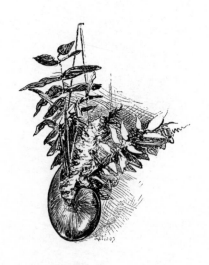

CHAPTER V.

WORDS HERE AND THERE.

A WEEK or two ago, at a prettily furnished table,

> "In after dinner talk
> Across the walnuts and the wine,"

chance brought up the name of a poet-philosopher very dear to some Americans who were young thirty years ago, never thought of without a stirring of the heart, mingled of reverence and affection. It seems that in his old age this man, like many another whose work has been a force to help lift his generation up to a higher plane, is not so rich in this world's goods as he would be if all the grateful thoughts that spring up at the mention of his name were coined into gold and poured into his lap. He lives in a plain, good house in the country, the windows of which look out upon a modest acre or two of his own; he eats plain fare, and is pleased with what he eats, and cares, no more than the most homespun of his neighbors, for luxuries, or for the things that go for show. His luxuries are the liberal sunshine that streams in at his windows, the Æolian harping of the pine-tree grove that shelters his house, and the peace that dwells within its walls. It happened that some well-to-do people from the city had been visiting the poet's family, and they brought back to town a melancholy report of the condition of things they found there. Would Peek-in street believe it! The poet's table was set out with plain white china (Heaven grant that a closer view might not have found it only earthenware!), and some of it was chipped, and the tumblers were not mates, and the wine-glasses were in such a way that they actually had to be supported by the tumblers! It matters not that to this plain house, and to its frugal New England table, came the picked society of the world, or that the best people in the land think it an added pleasure to their lives to be of the company. These fine city people (one wonders how they came there!) saw nothing but the plain living, and found no compensation in the high thinking.

An incident like this might make one ashamed of the time he has given to thinking and writing about "things," if he could not comfort himself with the assurance that there has been nothing in his treatment of the subject, or in the advice he has given, inconsistent with good sense or with right ways of living. It has been taken for granted that all his readers knew how little furniture, and decorations, and equipage, have to do with happiness or with true largeness of life. Almost all the great men of this world have lived in an absolute independence of things. The shining lights of our own time especially have been remarkable in a luxurious society, for the Spartan simplicity of their surroundings.

We all know of Wordsworth's abstemiousness, and though this were excessive, yet it is of a piece with English habits; and Shelley and Keats, Hunt and Godwin, knew how to be happy and to make others happy, without a parade of "things." It is true, that though the list of great men, and of men not great, but who live in the immortality of our affections, who have known "how to do without," is a long one, yet there are others who make a love of "things" respectable, to say the least: Solomon, Plato, Julius Cæsar, Thomas à Becket, Lord Bacon ("a queer list," I think I hear the reader laugh!), will befriend with their example— lovers of luxury, every man of them!—whoever wants an excuse for having two gowns and everything handsome about him, and does not wish to be written down an ass for the same!

What excuse, then, for writing all these pages to tell people how to do what so many good people get along very well without doing, without desiring to do? No excuse at all is needed, for these pages are not written for those who do not want advice, but for those who do, and though plenty of people are well content to go through life without spending money, thought, or time, upon superfluities, yet the number is far greater of those who are not content with this wholesale abstinence; who will round the edge of their rough work-a-day world with beauty, or, at least, with taste, and who want better fare than only "to drink the clear stream and nothing eat but pulse;" and we have wished, being of their party ourself, to give them a helping hand.

But now and again comes a letter or a spoken word that tells us the mark aimed at has not been always hit. Letters like that of the Texan gentleman, quoted in one of the earlier pages of this book, are not the kind we refer to: that was an unreasonable complaint, because the writer should have known we were not attempting to cater for persons in his case. Indeed it would have been easy to put his complaint in a humorous light. It was somewhat as if a writer had made an essay on "Flower Gardens," and after giving some hints as to the ordering of them, and adding some pictures of the flowers it would be well to have if you could get them, he should receive a letter saying that the writer did n't like the essay, nor did his neighbor either; for they could n't see how their cows could get enough to eat in these lily and violet beds, while the thorns of the rose-bushes would infallibly prick their noses. But, along with many letters which the writer of these pages received thanking him for what he was trying to do, and asking for advice in sundry plans and difficulties, came one, evidently written by a person of culture and refinement, complaining very amiably but very decidedly that to people of small means the author's suggestions with the objects pictured were of hardly any use. "I wish that some one," the letter went on to say, "would write for people with small incomes, telling them how to get pretty furniture and furnish their houses with taste for little money."

Now, we can assure this well-meaning correspondent that no one, however desirous to do what is wanted of him, can accomplish the task—not for want of literary skill, nor for want of sympathy with people of small means, but because all the conditions of the furnishing market are against us. People may dress on a little money, and may set a good table on a little money; but unless they give a great deal more time to it than they ought to be able to afford, they cannot, here in America, furnish their houses elegantly and individually on a little money. Now and then one can find in an old country house, or at auction, a piece of furniture—a chair, a table, a sideboard—which he gets at a bargain; but, to get a roomful, a houseful, of good furniture, and get it for a song, so rarely happens that the hope of it need not be entertained. I know of one house which is almost entirely furnished with old American (or English) and old Dutch furniture, but it is one house picked out of ten thousand. It belongs to a deservedly prosperous artist, and the collecting this furniture has been the amusement of stray hours for many a year. The old Dutch furniture, remarkable for its richness and for its condition, was bought in Holland while its owner was a student there; and, handsome as it is, cost but little money, partly because at that time nobody cared for such pieces, and partly because it was bought from poor people who did not know its artistic value. The owner told me that one of the largest and handsomest of his cabinets belonged to a poor family living in a room with no floor but the earth. The cabinet was probably the last relic of their better days, or was a fixture of the old house itself,—all that was left of a houseful of such furniture; but to those who owned it now it was

only a big cupboard, much too large for anything they had
to put in it, and so they gladly saw it changed into a
handful of hard cash.   As our student was going to Italy
in a few days, however, he was obliged to leave his cabinet
behind him, and when he returned he found it waiting for
him where it had stood for many a long year (perhaps
ever since it was first made), and he then transported it to
New-York with the other pieces he had collected.   To-day,
at Sypher's and at Pottier & Stymus's, there are six or
eight pieces of this same style of furniture, any one of
which costs more than all the pieces our young student
brought home with him put together.   The specimens of
American, or old English, furniture that he has in his town
house, and with which his country house is furnished
throughout, were all collected from the farm-houses of the
region around his country house, and they were all bought
for far less than must have been paid for ordinary modern
furniture such as is sold in the wholesale establishments of
Canal street and the Bowery.

The only use there is in citing such a case as this is
to show what has been done, and to suggest what may be
done by another.   But nothing can be done by any one
who does not care enough for the matter to take a good
deal of trouble to get what he wants; and to those who
insist so warmly that a house cannot be made pretty and
attractive without money, I venture to insist as warmly
that money is the least important element in the business!
Taste and contrivance are of far more importance than
money; and of all the attractive houses that it has been

my good fortune to see, by far the greater number have owed their attractiveness to the taste and to the ingenuity of their owners rather than to their long purses. A person with no need to think about the cost of anything, may go into Cottier's rooms and buy and order right and left, and give the house commission to decorate and furnish, and upholster, and fill his cabinets with "old blue," and never spare for cost, and when all is done, nobody who comes to visit him shall say, "How beautiful this is! How interesting! What taste you have!" but only, "Oh, then, I see Cottier has been with you!" There has simply been a transfer of goods from one show-place to another.

The truth is, we are depending too much in these days on furniture and bric-à-brac for the ornament of our houses, and not enough on things more permanently interesting. We ought to seek (at least so it seems to me) the individual expression of ourselves, of our own family life, our own ways of living, thinking, acting, more than the doing as other people are doing, more than the having what other people are having. I am not in for a tilt against fashion; fashionable people may do what they like; 't were vain to say them nay. They may buy embossed brass coal-scuttles, and put them in the middle of their parlor hearths in front of dummy fire-places, neither coal-scuttle nor fire-place ever having been intended to be used; they may put china cats nursing their kittens on their satin sofas, and enjoy their being taken for real ones by old beaus and maiden ladies; they may put artificial flowers in garden-boxes in their windows; they may do anything that comes into their nonsensical, pretty heads, and all we shall have to say about it is what old Mrs. G—— said after some stylish girls had been "going on" and "showing off" their new-fangled dress and airs: "How nice it is of 'em to do so, dear!"

So when people want to know how they can do as the rich, fashionable people do, and not pay for it what the rich, fashionable people pay, I am lost in wonder, and have no reply. If you have taste, perception, contrivance, and if you really enjoy having tasteful, pretty, beautiful things about you, you will somehow have them; but they will come out of yourself, and will look like you, and not like another. But if you only want to be in the fashion, and to have things that either come from Marcotte's, or Herter's, or Cottier's, or look as if they came from one of these places, you must be content either to pay the round price for the real things, or to put up with such second-rate copies of them as your small means will buy.

"Oh, yes!" says an objective case; "but you talk about Cottier's, and you publish the most provokingly pretty pictures of elegant and costly things, and you describe them and descant upon them, and *aggravate* us so ['t is a woman, and a young and pretty one, who is talking, else never that pet word of pretty, young American women—a meaningless vocable, their own invention]—*aggravate* us so, that we can't rest till we have tried to get things like them, and then we find they are far too dear; and then when we ask you how to get them cheap, you tell us it can't be done! What makes you show them to us if you know we can't get them? What's the use?"

To this tearful indictment, what can we reply? First, it is a fact that many of the things figured in these pages are inexpensive compared with things of the same general, decorative and elegant character that are to be found in the rich shops. Very many of them belong to people who are not at all rich in this world's goods; and in those that only exist in the drawings of Messrs. Babb, Inglis, and Sandier, the intention has been to make them as inexpensive as possible. I believe that where people have clubbed together and had four or five of any one of these pieces made by a country carpenter, they have found they got far more for their money than they could have got by going even to Canal street,—I mean that their handsome table or book-case has not cost them as much as a homely, ill-made travesty of the "style" would have cost them.

No doubt many of the designs are of costly pieces, far beyond the reach of any but long purses. But let the reader note that these pieces have always been selected by the writer on account of their elegance and good taste rather than for ornate richness and luxuriousness; and all through these pages the writer's aim has been to put before the reader what are believed to be good models, not with the expectation that they would be copied or imitated, nor often holding out the hope that their likes could be had again, but only with the hope that something might be accomplished in improving the general taste. Yet even of this the writer has said as little as possible, for it is no small presumption for any one to think he can help his fellows much, and he felt pretty sure that, before he got to the end of his task, he would find he needed help as much as any one.

There is a fortune in store for any one who to-day will supply the public with well-made, well-designed furniture— well-designed both for beauty and use—at cheap rates. It can be done by first getting from competent hands designs that have been thoroughly thought out, reduced to their simplest elements, and so planned that they can be made in quantities,—on the same principle that Canal street furniture is made, the difference being in the workmanship and in the design; for it is not only the fact that the Canal street stuff is made by the hundred dozen at a time that makes it cheap. It is because the wood is not seasoned, and because all the parts are put together in the least scientific, "good enough," way. Injustice is often done to what are called "expensive establishments" by our not knowing the cost of making their goods. A chair made by Herter or Marcotte is put together in such a way that only violence can break it; and it can be re-stuffed and re-covered for fifty years, and be as good as new. Now, almost all the furniture made by these houses is made to order; they keep very little material in stock, and even their chairs and sofas, of which they keep more ready-made than of the other regulation-pieces, have to be covered to suit individual tastes. Now, let the reader think what is implied in this "making to order." A staff of accomplished draughtsmen has to be employed, and an accomplished draughtsman, if he be a steady, facile workman, is always able to command a good salary. Then, the best workmen that are to be had are kept all the year round on good wages; and, lastly, only the best materials are used, and for covering and the like, the fashion must be not only kept pace with, but wealthy paying custom depends on its being also a little antedated. I do not speak now of rents and the salaries of employés, but merely of the necessary expenses of producing furniture. We must remember, too, that rich buyers do not want their orders repeated for other customers, nor do they want things that other people have; and to make one piece of furniture alone is more expensive than to make six pieces alike. Does a man whose shoes have to be made for him exclusively, so that every projecting joint shall live at ease on its own corner lot, expect to pay no more than the boy who can slip his well-shaped foot into the first shoe of his size that is presented?

Fault was often found, in the circle of readers who were interested in these papers when they first appeared in "Scribner's Monthly," with the expensiveness of many of the things recommended; and many good-natured jests, and criticisms more or less acid, were tossed about, on the want of consistency shown by the writer in preaching economy and simplicity, while, at the same time, he at once tempted and teased the people with short purses by showing them Mr. Lathrop's charming drawings of the prettiest and costliest furniture to be found. Now, while admitting that his critics had a show of reason in their charges, the writer pleads in extenuation that he is really misunderstood, and that he does not mean any harm! He stands by all he has said about economy and simplicity, and the possibility of making our houses attractive without, at the same time, making ourselves uncomfortable by spending more money than we can afford in furnishing and decorating. But when it comes to giving illustrations that will support his propositions, he is met by a difficulty. Many of the pieces of furniture that in design and purpose answer to his notions are, in fact, expensive pieces. He takes them where he finds them, and has them copied as faithfully as he can, and without any attempt to show them less elegant and costly than they really are. But whoever will be at the pains to look over the pictures in this book of his will admit that, whatever the money goes for, it does not go for carving, and flourish, and display for display's sake. Nor is it a fact that all the things shown are expensive, that is, compared with the prices that would be paid for fashionable pieces of furniture intended for the same uses. One may well despair of getting anything cheap when he finds that even chairs so ostentatiously bare and matter-of-fact as those made by the Shakers, or the Vienna bentwood chairs, cost as much as some to be found in the fashionable shops that make a good deal more show. People are slow to learn, women especially, it would seem, that the reverse of the rule which holds true of their dresses is true of most of the furniture called fashionable nowadays. In the case of their dresses, women know that the "trimming," the ornament, often costs more than the body of the dress, and the more elaborate the dress, the truer this proposition. But in our fashionable furniture the reverse is true. The main cost is in the wood and the labor; the ornament is almost always cheap.

There was a little while ago quite a rage for a certain style of furniture that made a great display of seeming steel hinges, key-plates, and handles, with inlaid tiles, carving of an ultra-Gothic type, and an appearance of the most ingenuous truth-telling in the construction. The chairs, tables and bedsteads looked as if they had been on the dissecting-table and flayed alive,—their joints and tendons displayed to an archæologic and unfeeling world. One particular firm introduced this style of furniture, and, for a time, had almost the monopoly of it. It had a great run, for the purchaser was made to feel that in buying it he got an immense deal more for his money than he could get in any other style of furniture. Perhaps in another shop he would have to pay as much for the same piece of furniture without the so-called ornament—as much, or more than he was asked to pay for the showy piece. And in nine cases out of ten the showy piece carried the day. The reason of the difference in cost would be found in the fact that the plain piece was well designed in the first place by an educated architect,—a man with notions of utility and with good taste,—and then was well made by a trained workman out of good material. The cost of the piece represented good stuff, and skill in designer and in maker, but it did not represent sham of any kind. The piece would last a life-time, would always be a good servant or friend, improving in looks with time and use. The showy piece, it would be found, had been designed, not for use, but to make a display, and all the ornament contrived, like a player-queen's regalia, to get as much glitter and look of cost as tinsel and frippery can give. Now, in the writer's experience, it is the people who are taken in by this sort of thing, and who, to tell the truth, like to be taken in by it, who complain of the cost of many of the things shown in the illustrations to these pages. They will have show and display if they can possibly get them; and if they cannot have real elegance, they will take sham elegance, and thank the gods there are places where people are not too nice to give it to them.

But, granted that many of the things pictured in these pages are costly, the reader is begged to notice that it is not their costliness that is brought to the fore by the writer, but the beauty of the design or the utility of the things themselves. Their costliness is always kept out of sight, not "tortuously," as has been politely said, but really because the cost of these particular pieces was not our concern. The design is our concern,—the usefulness of the object portrayed, its suitability to our needs. Take the table and chair figured on page 72 (cut No. 23), which one person singles out as being doubtless more expensive than they look. Why were these objects chosen as illustrations? Was it because they were costly? Most certainly not. The writer never asked what they cost, and does not know. But he does think them both extremely pretty, and he chose them to show his readers because he thought them so, and for no other reason. The chair cannot be more expensive than others of its now common family, and the table no more expensive than tables usually found in drawing-rooms. But, supposing them both to be as costly as the critic suggests, this consideration does not affect us, because their costliness is in their material,—in the wood the table is made of, in the stuff the chair is covered with. And it was not their material, but their forms, that was the subject of praise. If a person should take a fancy to either chair or table, and if he should find on inquiry that the cost, as the piece stands in the shop, was beyond his means, let him ·have the table made out of pine, and the chair covered with chintz; they will give a different pleasure from that they would have given in their original garment, but it will be a new pleasure as good as the old. The book-case which is shown in cut No. 54 would be very little handsomer than it is if, instead of being made of plain pine, it were made of black walnut, or mahogany, or ebony. Its owner thinks it a very agreeable piece of furniture to look at, and finds it very convenient, both as a case for books and as a shelf. But he could only afford to have it made of pine, and he gets as much pleasure out of it, he thinks, as if, instead of costing fifty dollars, it had cost five hundred dollars, as it might easily have been made to. So, if he were bent on having the chair and table (cut No. 23), and could not afford ebonized walnut, with mahogany top and sides, for the table, he would have it made of pine, and have the chairs covered with some one of the pretty chintzes or Algériennes that nowadays make us quite independent of stamped velvets and gilt leather.

After the publication of the first of the articles of which this book is made up, several letters, as might have been expected, came to the editor, all asking for more minute and particular directions on various points only touched upon: the cost of this, that, or the other piece of furniture; where one might hope to find some piece which looked inviting as pictured in these pages, but seemed as hopeless of ever being achieved in real life as the prize pansy of a seedsman's spring catalogue. But more questions were asked in these letters about carpets and rugs than about anything else; it really looks as if house-furnishing turned more upon this one item than upon all else besides; as if, to parody Poor Richard, the American housekeeper were persuaded if she would take care of the carpets, the chairs and tables would take care of themselves. Yet this writer has not had any new inspiration on the subject of carpets and rugs since he wrote his first screed on the subject. It goes to show how the matter of carpets weighs on the housekeeping mind, that even in the summer-time it set people to writing letters about how they were to cover their floors the coming winter. One thinks in these autumn days how pleasant 't would be if we could only settle the matter as easily as the model housewife Nature does. Here is the lawn, that has been mowed to a velvet nap—the ideal, the poetic carpet!—and raked clean of every slightest twig or stick; yet a light breeze stirs of an afternoon, or blows through the night, and the dark green is golden yellow with myriads of locust-leaves, that cover the drives as well, and huddle in a bordering fringe along its edges. Nature's continual, kindly lesson is, "Don't bother!" but we cannot learn it, and, in spite of her and ourselves, make our lives as troublesome as our wits can devise. The advice to use rugs instead of carpets was given, not as the result of an individual discovery, but as a return to first principles, which had been followed for hundreds of years by nations who are admitted, on all hands, to have successfully solved a great many of the problems of external living.

In England and America, carpets were used in the beginning to cover up badly made floors, and to promote warmth by keeping the air from coming through cracks. As floors have continued to be badly made in these countries, as a rule, ever since they began to have wooden floors at all, and as these floors are rarely, we may say never, solid, but simply planks resting on beams closed on the under side by the lath-and-plaster ceiling of the room below, carpets have been held indispensable these many years; and as great perfection has been reached in their manufacture—as they are thick and soft, and may be handsome—they will hold their own for a long while,— certainly, until the floors are so well made as to permit us to do without them.

Yet they ought to be discarded on several grounds. They are the source of by far the greater part of the dirt and dust that annoy housekeepers and endanger health. It only needs some person of a statistical and worrying turn of mind to save the contents of the dust-pan for a month or so, or to insist upon the presence, at Hankinson's, of the members of the family who stand up for carpets to the bitter end—when the roller brings their end of the acre of painted woolen under the tell-tale beaters—to prove to any doubtful persons what dirt-makers and dirt-holders carpets can be. Of course, rugs are dirt-makers and dirt-holders just the same; but the advantage is, that they can be easily moved and shaken whenever it is thought necessary, and without occasioning any extra labor to speak of, whereas taking up a carpet is so troublesome an affair that it is seldom done more than once a year.

Of course, we all want to look, as well as to be, comfortable, and many persons are persuaded that a room whose floor is only covered in one place, or in spots, by rugs, cannot look comfortable. And it is urged, too, that the expense is much greater, or, at any rate, that nothing is saved by substituting rugs for carpets. The rugs are dear, and it costs to put the floor in order for them. It is a great pity that good floors are not common here; it is to be hoped that the new way of living in "flats" will make it necessary to build the floors more solidly, making them one compact mass, unburnable, and impermeable to sound or air. This is found easy to do in countries where it is not usual for one family to occupy a whole house, and where there must therefore be a substantial barrier between the several floors. Our readers have been told on this subject all we know, earlier in these pages, and we need therefore only repeat, that the best thing of all is a well-laid floor of narrow boards of hard wood, properly deafened, and well waxed or oiled; but waxing is the better way. If the floor be already laid, and a poor one, then, if it can be afforded, an excellent way is to lay over it a wood carpet, choosing one of the plainest patterns—a "herring-bone," or something as unpretending and as easily laid; but if that cannot be, then staining a dark color and shel-lacking would be a very good resource.

One of these ways the end can be accomplished of making the floor tight and smooth, so that the rug once rolled over and out of the way, the sweeping can all be done with a hair broom, and as little dust raised as possi-ble. It is understood that, unless it be a table in the center of the room, no heavy piece of furniture is to rest upon the rug, but that it is to be free to get up and go out and shake itself whenever the house-maid whistles to it. All this has been said or hinted before; but there is one point that has not yet been touched—a point on which nearly all the letters that the writer received, in query or criticism on the first appearance of these pages, exhibit anxiety. This is the question of symmetry. We have several times been asked how to treat the floors of two rooms opening one into the other, the "front and back parlor" of so many New-York houses. But it ought to be understood that "symmetry"—or, to use a word that will apply to color as well as to form—and these inquiries are chiefly about color—not "symmetry," then, but "balance"— is a thing whose laws cannot be taught. At least, it is as difficult to teach them to one who does not perceive them by intuition as it is to teach an earless pupil to keep time in music, to teach a bad speller to spell correctly, or to teach an awkward boy of twenty to get out of a drawing-room when his call is ended.

There are parlors belonging to rich men who are the sons of rich men, who have been educated carefully, and who have traveled and seen all that there is to be seen of splendid and beautiful, and yet, though their rooms are full of the external evidences of wealth and travel, the things seem unhappy; the colors all "swear at one another," as the French artistic slang has it; the chairs and tables, like people too early at a country party, are waiting for an introduction; and the taste—if taste it may be called—in the pictures and bric-à-brac is so discordant, that if the owner really likes one half of them we cannot understand how he should be able to tolerate the other. Of course, it is not fair always to judge the owner of one of these multifarious drawing-rooms by what he puts forward as his own taste. In nine cases out of ten it is not his taste at all, but the taste of the town, and he has meekly put himself into the hands of the fashionable furnisher. We might as well lay the charge of the theatrical, vulgar paraphernàlia of a modern first-class funeral at the door of the dead man upon whose unresisting body all these hideous "floral emblems" are piled. The fashionable undertaker sits on him when dead, as the fashionable furnisher sat on him when alive. We cannot judge of his taste until he shows it,—until he takes his house into his own hands, and makes it to his mind. It is to persuade people to do this that these pages are written; but the writer is not very hopeful of persuading any but young people and those who have a natural independence. Rich people are for the most part so bullied by their money, they don't dare do what they would like. And people who are well on in life do not, as a rule, take enough interest in the subject. They find the old shoes easier to the feet.

But the young people can be asked to look at nature, or—if they can't get into the country—to take the next best thing, and study the Japanese decoration on books and trays and tea-pots, with a view to ridding their minds of the belief that things ought to be in *suites;* that a front parlor must be like a back one; that one side of a chimney-pier must just reflect the other; that there must always be a middle and sides, and so forth, and so on— laws which are Median and Persian laws to tradesmen and conservative, safe, respectable furnishers, but not laws with which we are concerned. Nature, who never makes two sides of a leaf alike, nor two sides of a flower, nor two sides of a face, will surely repay industrious study of her works by some hint of how not to do it, when we are bent on seeing our back parlor reflected in our front one like the sky in a mill-pond.

Each room ought to be considered by itself, no matter if it be only nominally separated from another by the piers on each side of a wide arch-way. Its floor, its walls, its ceilings, ought to be brought into harmony by a right arrangement of color—that is the first thing. They are only the background for the furniture, the pictures, and the people, but they must have unity among themselves. It is not of course meant that they should be like one another, or that any one of them should be all of one hue. But, the wall being first divided up horizontally into its natural parts, the wainscot or dado, the wall-paper, the frieze and the cornice,—all these must make an agreeable impression upon the eye; and if a person does not feel that his own knowledge or instinct is all he needs to help him bring the business to a happy ending, he must get help from some artist or architect, or from some professional deco- rator, who is a decorator by nature and training. We have plenty of good. guides—Mr. Russell Sturgis, Mr. George F. Babb, Mr. Alexander Sandier, Mr. James S. Inglis, Mr. John La Farge, Mr. Francis Lathrop; if a man were in doubt as "how to present wall," any one of these accom- plished architects and artists could solve his doubt, and make him glad he had had it.

The walls once settled to the owner's mind, the floor may almost be trusted to take care of itself, and yet, before thinking of it, the ceiling ought to be married to the wall by being papered or painted in harmony with it. Our ceilings have been getting into bad ways of late, though rather mending than otherwise from what they were five years or so ago. Then the plasterers had it all their own way, and a pretty mess they made of it. They evidently thought "there was nothing like plaster." They have been taught better, of late, than to put into our always small rooms cornices heavy enough for a Roman palace, with center-pieces as ponderous and outlandish as their wits

could devise. Since architects have come to be consulted
so much with regard to the furniture of the houses they
design, it has been getting more and more the custom to
put the whole interior decoration into their hands, and the
ceilings have shared this good fortune—for it often is good
fortune—with the rest. A white ceiling can only look well
when the room is white, and it ought to carry out the tone
of the room, whatever that may be. The difficulty has
been that coloring the ceiling has been thought to be
attended with considerable increase of expense; it must be
painted or frescoed, and accordingly it is but rarely colored
at all. There is no reason at all why a ceiling should not
be papered as well as a wall, and, in building houses, if
all plaster ornaments were omitted from the ceiling, and all
cornices also, and the walls and ceilings made pretty and
harmonious with paper, or washed with color, money could
be saved, and a much more agreeable result obtained. Of
course, the paper on the wall should not be repeated on
the ceiling, but one chosen that will harmonize with that,
and, as a rule of general application, one that is lighter
than the lightest part of the wall. If there is a cornice at
all it ought to be small; something merely to break the
ugly line where the wall and ceiling meet; a wooden
molding will often be all that is needed, and will be
cheaper than plaster.

"But," says one letter-writer, "all this is expensive, and
we are tired of spending money; besides, you told us in
the beginning you were going to show us how to make
our houses pretty on next to nothing." The complaining

writer is not quite fair with us.   Nothing worth having is to be had without expense either of time or money, but many of the best things in house decorating and furnishing are those that cost least.   What I object to is the measuring beautiful things by a money standard, or a standard of fashion; and what seems to me most needed just now is, that people should put their own taste into their houses and not depend so much on professional help.

A CATALOG OF SELECTED
DOVER BOOKS
IN ALL FIELDS OF INTEREST

A CATALOG OF SELECTED DOVER
BOOKS IN ALL FIELDS OF INTEREST

CONCERNING THE SPIRITUAL IN ART, Wassily Kandinsky. Pioneering work by father of abstract art. Thoughts on color theory, nature of art. Analysis of earlier masters. 12 illustrations. 80pp. of text. 5⅜ x 8½. 23411-8

ANIMALS: 1,419 Copyright-Free Illustrations of Mammals, Birds, Fish, Insects, etc., Jim Harter (ed.). Clear wood engravings present, in extremely lifelike poses, over 1,000 species of animals. One of the most extensive pictorial sourcebooks of its kind. Captions. Index. 284pp. 9 x 12. 23766-4

CELTIC ART: The Methods of Construction, George Bain. Simple geometric techniques for making Celtic interlacements, spirals, Kells-type initials, animals, humans, etc. Over 500 illustrations. 160pp. 9 x 12. (Available in U.S. only.) 22923-8

AN ATLAS OF ANATOMY FOR ARTISTS, Fritz Schider. Most thorough reference work on art anatomy in the world. Hundreds of illustrations, including selections from works by Vesalius, Leonardo, Goya, Ingres, Michelangelo, others. 593 illustrations. 192pp. 7⅛ x 10¼. 20241-0

CELTIC HAND STROKE-BY-STROKE (Irish Half-Uncial from "The Book of Kells"): An Arthur Baker Calligraphy Manual, Arthur Baker. Complete guide to creating each letter of the alphabet in distinctive Celtic manner. Covers hand position, strokes, pens, inks, paper, more. Illustrated. 48pp. 8¼ x 11. 24336-2

EASY ORIGAMI, John Montroll. Charming collection of 32 projects (hat, cup, pelican, piano, swan, many more) specially designed for the novice origami hobbyist. Clearly illustrated easy-to-follow instructions insure that even beginning papercrafters will achieve successful results. 48pp. 8¼ x 11. 27298-2

THE COMPLETE BOOK OF BIRDHOUSE CONSTRUCTION FOR WOOD-WORKERS, Scott D. Campbell. Detailed instructions, illustrations, tables. Also data on bird habitat and instinct patterns. Bibliography. 3 tables. 63 illustrations in 15 figures. 48pp. 5¼ x 8½. 24407-5

BLOOMINGDALE'S ILLUSTRATED 1886 CATALOG: Fashions, Dry Goods and Housewares, Bloomingdale Brothers. Famed merchants' extremely rare catalog depicting about 1,700 products: clothing, housewares, firearms, dry goods, jewelry, more. Invaluable for dating, identifying vintage items. Also, copyright-free graphics for artists, designers. Co-published with Henry Ford Museum & Greenfield Village. 160pp. 8¼ x 11. 25780-0

HISTORIC COSTUME IN PICTURES, Braun & Schneider. Over 1,450 costumed figures in clearly detailed engravings—from dawn of civilization to end of 19th century. Captions. Many folk costumes. 256pp. 8⅜ x 11¾. 23150-X

STICKLEY CRAFTSMAN FURNITURE CATALOGS, Gustav Stickley and L. & J. G. Stickley. Beautiful, functional furniture in two authentic catalogs from 1910. 594 illustrations, including 277 photos, show settles, rockers, armchairs, reclining chairs, bookcases, desks, tables. 183pp. 6½ x 9¼. 23838-5

AMERICAN LOCOMOTIVES IN HISTORIC PHOTOGRAPHS: 1858 to 1949, Ron Ziel (ed.). A rare collection of 126 meticulously detailed official photographs, called "builder portraits," of American locomotives that majestically chronicle the rise of steam locomotive power in America. Introduction. Detailed captions. xi+ 129pp. 9 x 12. 27393-8

AMERICA'S LIGHTHOUSES: An Illustrated History, Francis Ross Holland, Jr. Delightfully written, profusely illustrated fact-filled survey of over 200 American lighthouses since 1716. History, anecdotes, technological advances, more. 240pp. 8 x 10¾. 25576-X

TOWARDS A NEW ARCHITECTURE, Le Corbusier. Pioneering manifesto by founder of "International School." Technical and aesthetic theories, views of industry, economics, relation of form to function, "mass-production split" and much more. Profusely illustrated. 320pp. 6⅛ x 9¼. (Available in U.S. only.) 25023-7

HOW THE OTHER HALF LIVES, Jacob Riis. Famous journalistic record, exposing poverty and degradation of New York slums around 1900, by major social reformer. 100 striking and influential photographs. 233pp. 10 x 7⅞. 22012-5

FRUIT KEY AND TWIG KEY TO TREES AND SHRUBS, William M. Harlow. One of the handiest and most widely used identification aids. Fruit key covers 120 deciduous and evergreen species; twig key 160 deciduous species. Easily used. Over 300 photographs. 126pp. 5⅜ x 8½. 20511-8

COMMON BIRD SONGS, Dr. Donald J. Borror. Songs of 60 most common U.S. birds: robins, sparrows, cardinals, bluejays, finches, more–arranged in order of increasing complexity. Up to 9 variations of songs of each species.
Cassette and manual 99911-4

ORCHIDS AS HOUSE PLANTS, Rebecca Tyson Northen. Grow cattleyas and many other kinds of orchids–in a window, in a case, or under artificial light. 63 illustrations. 148pp. 5⅜ x 8½. 23261-1

MONSTER MAZES, Dave Phillips. Masterful mazes at four levels of difficulty. Avoid deadly perils and evil creatures to find magical treasures. Solutions for all 32 exciting illustrated puzzles. 48pp. 8¼ x 11. 26005-4

MOZART'S DON GIOVANNI (DOVER OPERA LIBRETTO SERIES), Wolfgang Amadeus Mozart. Introduced and translated by Ellen H. Bleiler. Standard Italian libretto, with complete English translation. Convenient and thoroughly portable–an ideal companion for reading along with a recording or the performance itself. Introduction. List of characters. Plot summary. 121pp. 5¼ x 8½. 24944-1

TECHNICAL MANUAL AND DICTIONARY OF CLASSICAL BALLET, Gail Grant. Defines, explains, comments on steps, movements, poses and concepts. 15-page pictorial section. Basic book for student, viewer. 127pp. 5⅜ x 8½. 21843-0

THE CLARINET AND CLARINET PLAYING, David Pino. Lively, comprehensive work features suggestions about technique, musicianship, and musical interpretation, as well as guidelines for teaching, making your own reeds, and preparing for public performance. Includes an intriguing look at clarinet history. "A godsend," *The Clarinet,* Journal of the International Clarinet Society. Appendixes. 7 illus. 320pp. 5⅜ x 8½. 40270-3

HOLLYWOOD GLAMOR PORTRAITS, John Kobal (ed.). 145 photos from 1926-49. Harlow, Gable, Bogart, Bacall; 94 stars in all. Full background on photographers, technical aspects. 160pp. 8⅜ x 11¼. 23352-9

THE ANNOTATED CASEY AT THE BAT: A Collection of Ballads about the Mighty Casey/Third, Revised Edition, Martin Gardner (ed.). Amusing sequels and parodies of one of America's best-loved poems: Casey's Revenge, Why Casey Whiffed, Casey's Sister at the Bat, others. 256pp. 5⅜ x 8½. 28598-7

THE RAVEN AND OTHER FAVORITE POEMS, Edgar Allan Poe. Over 40 of the author's most memorable poems: "The Bells," "Ulalume," "Israfel," "To Helen," "The Conqueror Worm," "Eldorado," "Annabel Lee," many more. Alphabetic lists of titles and first lines. 64pp. 5³⁄₁₆ x 8¼. 26685-0

PERSONAL MEMOIRS OF U. S. GRANT, Ulysses Simpson Grant. Intelligent, deeply moving firsthand account of Civil War campaigns, considered by many the finest military memoirs ever written. Includes letters, historic photographs, maps and more. 528pp. 6⅛ x 9¼. 28587-1

ANCIENT EGYPTIAN MATERIALS AND INDUSTRIES, A. Lucas and J. Harris. Fascinating, comprehensive, thoroughly documented text describes this ancient civilization's vast resources and the processes that incorporated them in daily life, including the use of animal products, building materials, cosmetics, perfumes and incense, fibers, glazed ware, glass and its manufacture, materials used in the mummification process, and much more. 544pp. 6⅛ x 9¼. (Available in U.S. only.) 40446-3

RUSSIAN STORIES/RUSSKIE RASSKAZY: A Dual-Language Book, edited by Gleb Struve. Twelve tales by such masters as Chekhov, Tolstoy, Dostoevsky, Pushkin, others. Excellent word-for-word English translations on facing pages, plus teaching and study aids, Russian/English vocabulary, biographical/critical introductions, more. 416pp. 5⅜ x 8½. 26244-8

PHILADELPHIA THEN AND NOW: 60 Sites Photographed in the Past and Present, Kenneth Finkel and Susan Oyama. Rare photographs of City Hall, Logan Square, Independence Hall, Betsy Ross House, other landmarks juxtaposed with contemporary views. Captures changing face of historic city. Introduction. Captions. 128pp. 8¼ x 11. 25790-8

AIA ARCHITECTURAL GUIDE TO NASSAU AND SUFFOLK COUNTIES, LONG ISLAND, The American Institute of Architects, Long Island Chapter, and the Society for the Preservation of Long Island Antiquities. Comprehensive, well-researched and generously illustrated volume brings to life over three centuries of Long Island's great architectural heritage. More than 240 photographs with authoritative, extensively detailed captions. 176pp. 8¼ x 11. 26946-9

NORTH AMERICAN INDIAN LIFE: Customs and Traditions of 23 Tribes, Elsie Clews Parsons (ed.). 27 fictionalized essays by noted anthropologists examine religion, customs, government, additional facets of life among the Winnebago, Crow, Zuni, Eskimo, other tribes. 480pp. 6⅛ x 9¼. 27377-6

CATALOG OF DOVER BOOKS

FRANK LLOYD WRIGHT'S DANA HOUSE, Donald Hoffmann. Pictorial essay of residential masterpiece with over 160 interior and exterior photos, plans, elevations, sketches and studies. 128pp. 9¼ x 10¾. 29120-0

THE MALE AND FEMALE FIGURE IN MOTION: 60 Classic Photographic Sequences, Eadweard Muybridge. 60 true-action photographs of men and women walking, running, climbing, bending, turning, etc., reproduced from rare 19th-century masterpiece. vi + 121pp. 9 x 12. 24745-7

1001 QUESTIONS ANSWERED ABOUT THE SEASHORE, N. J. Berrill and Jacquelyn Berrill. Queries answered about dolphins, sea snails, sponges, starfish, fishes, shore birds, many others. Covers appearance, breeding, growth, feeding, much more. 305pp. 5¼ x 8¼. 23366-9

ATTRACTING BIRDS TO YOUR YARD, William J. Weber. Easy-to-follow guide offers advice on how to attract the greatest diversity of birds: birdhouses, feeders, water and waterers, much more. 96pp. 5³⁄₁₆ x 8¼. 28927-3

MEDICINAL AND OTHER USES OF NORTH AMERICAN PLANTS: A Historical Survey with Special Reference to the Eastern Indian Tribes, Charlotte Erichsen-Brown. Chronological historical citations document 500 years of usage of plants, trees, shrubs native to eastern Canada, northeastern U.S. Also complete identifying information. 343 illustrations. 544pp. 6½ x 9¼. 25951-X

STORYBOOK MAZES, Dave Phillips. 23 stories and mazes on two-page spreads: Wizard of Oz, Treasure Island, Robin Hood, etc. Solutions. 64pp. 8¼ x 11. 23628-5

AMERICAN NEGRO SONGS: 230 Folk Songs and Spirituals, Religious and Secular, John W. Work. This authoritative study traces the African influences of songs sung and played by black Americans at work, in church, and as entertainment. The author discusses the lyric significance of such songs as "Swing Low, Sweet Chariot," "John Henry," and others and offers the words and music for 230 songs. Bibliography. Index of Song Titles. 272pp. 6½ x 9¼. 40271-1

MOVIE-STAR PORTRAITS OF THE FORTIES, John Kobal (ed.). 163 glamor, studio photos of 106 stars of the 1940s: Rita Hayworth, Ava Gardner, Marlon Brando, Clark Gable, many more. 176pp. 8⅜ x 11¼. 23546-7

BENCHLEY LOST AND FOUND, Robert Benchley. Finest humor from early 30s, about pet peeves, child psychologists, post office and others. Mostly unavailable elsewhere. 73 illustrations by Peter Arno and others. 183pp. 5⅜ x 8½. 22410-4

YEKL and THE IMPORTED BRIDEGROOM AND OTHER STORIES OF YIDDISH NEW YORK, Abraham Cahan. Film Hester Street based on *Yekl* (1896). Novel, other stories among first about Jewish immigrants on N.Y.'s East Side. 240pp. 5⅜ x 8½. 22427-9

SELECTED POEMS, Walt Whitman. Generous sampling from *Leaves of Grass*. Twenty-four poems include "I Hear America Singing," "Song of the Open Road," "I Sing the Body Electric," "When Lilacs Last in the Dooryard Bloom'd," "O Captain! My Captain!"—all reprinted from an authoritative edition. Lists of titles and first lines. 128pp. 5³⁄₁₆ x 8¼. 26878-0

CATALOG OF DOVER BOOKS

THE BEST TALES OF HOFFMANN, E. T. A. Hoffmann. 10 of Hoffmann's most important stories: "Nutcracker and the King of Mice," "The Golden Flowerpot," etc. 458pp. 5⅜ x 8½. 21793-0

FROM FETISH TO GOD IN ANCIENT EGYPT, E. A. Wallis Budge. Rich detailed survey of Egyptian conception of "God" and gods, magic, cult of animals, Osiris, more. Also, superb English translations of hymns and legends. 240 illustrations. 545pp. 5⅜ x 8½. 25803-3

FRENCH STORIES/CONTES FRANÇAIS: A Dual-Language Book, Wallace Fowlie. Ten stories by French masters, Voltaire to Camus: "Micromegas" by Voltaire; "The Atheist's Mass" by Balzac; "Minuet" by de Maupassant; "The Guest" by Camus, six more. Excellent English translations on facing pages. Also French-English vocabulary list, exercises, more. 352pp. 5⅜ x 8½. 26443-2

CHICAGO AT THE TURN OF THE CENTURY IN PHOTOGRAPHS: 122 Historic Views from the Collections of the Chicago Historical Society, Larry A. Viskochil. Rare large-format prints offer detailed views of City Hall, State Street, the Loop, Hull House, Union Station, many other landmarks, circa 1904-1913. Introduction. Captions. Maps. 144pp. 9⅜ x 12¼. 24656-6

OLD BROOKLYN IN EARLY PHOTOGRAPHS, 1865-1929, William Lee Younger. Luna Park, Gravesend race track, construction of Grand Army Plaza, moving of Hotel Brighton, etc. 157 previously unpublished photographs. 165pp. 8⅞ x 11¾. 23587-4

THE MYTHS OF THE NORTH AMERICAN INDIANS, Lewis Spence. Rich anthology of the myths and legends of the Algonquins, Iroquois, Pawnees and Sioux, prefaced by an extensive historical and ethnological commentary. 36 illustrations. 480pp. 5⅜ x 8½. 25967-6

AN ENCYCLOPEDIA OF BATTLES: Accounts of Over 1,560 Battles from 1479 B.C. to the Present, David Eggenberger. Essential details of every major battle in recorded history from the first battle of Megiddo in 1479 B.C. to Grenada in 1984. List of Battle Maps. New Appendix covering the years 1967-1984. Index. 99 illustrations. 544pp. 6½ x 9¼. 24913-1

SAILING ALONE AROUND THE WORLD, Captain Joshua Slocum. First man to sail around the world, alone, in small boat. One of great feats of seamanship told in delightful manner. 67 illustrations. 294pp. 5⅜ x 8½. 20326-3

ANARCHISM AND OTHER ESSAYS, Emma Goldman. Powerful, penetrating, prophetic essays on direct action, role of minorities, prison reform, puritan hypocrisy, violence, etc. 271pp. 5⅜ x 8½. 22484-8

MYTHS OF THE HINDUS AND BUDDHISTS, Ananda K. Coomaraswamy and Sister Nivedita. Great stories of the epics; deeds of Krishna, Shiva, taken from puranas, Vedas, folk tales; etc. 32 illustrations. 400pp. 5⅜ x 8½. 21759-0

THE TRAUMA OF BIRTH, Otto Rank. Rank's controversial thesis that anxiety neurosis is caused by profound psychological trauma which occurs at birth. 256pp. 5⅜ x 8½. 27974-X

A THEOLOGICO-POLITICAL TREATISE, Benedict Spinoza. Also contains unfinished Political Treatise. Great classic on religious liberty, theory of government on common consent. R. Elwes translation. Total of 421pp. 5⅜ x 8½. 20249-6

MY BONDAGE AND MY FREEDOM, Frederick Douglass. Born a slave, Douglass became outspoken force in antislavery movement. The best of Douglass' autobiographies. Graphic description of slave life. 464pp. 5⅜ x 8½.　　　22457-0

FOLLOWING THE EQUATOR: A Journey Around the World, Mark Twain. Fascinating humorous account of 1897 voyage to Hawaii, Australia, India, New Zealand, etc. Ironic, bemused reports on peoples, customs, climate, flora and fauna, politics, much more. 197 illustrations. 720pp. 5⅜ x 8½.　　　26113-1

THE PEOPLE CALLED SHAKERS, Edward D. Andrews. Definitive study of Shakers: origins, beliefs, practices, dances, social organization, furniture and crafts, etc. 33 illustrations. 351pp. 5⅜ x 8½.　　　21081-2

THE MYTHS OF GREECE AND ROME, H. A. Guerber. A classic of mythology, generously illustrated, long prized for its simple, graphic, accurate retelling of the principal myths of Greece and Rome, and for its commentary on their origins and significance. With 64 illustrations by Michelangelo, Raphael, Titian, Rubens, Canova, Bernini and others. 480pp. 5⅜ x 8½.　　　27584-1

PSYCHOLOGY OF MUSIC, Carl E. Seashore. Classic work discusses music as a medium from psychological viewpoint. Clear treatment of physical acoustics, auditory apparatus, sound perception, development of musical skills, nature of musical feeling, host of other topics. 88 figures. 408pp. 5⅜ x 8½.　　　21851-1

THE PHILOSOPHY OF HISTORY, Georg W. Hegel. Great classic of Western thought develops concept that history is not chance but rational process, the evolution of freedom. 457pp. 5⅜ x 8½.　　　20112-0

THE BOOK OF TEA, Kakuzo Okakura. Minor classic of the Orient: entertaining, charming explanation, interpretation of traditional Japanese culture in terms of tea ceremony. 94pp. 5⅜ x 8½.　　　20070-1

LIFE IN ANCIENT EGYPT, Adolf Erman. Fullest, most thorough, detailed older account with much not in more recent books, domestic life, religion, magic, medicine, commerce, much more. Many illustrations reproduce tomb paintings, carvings, hieroglyphs, etc. 597pp. 5⅜ x 8½.　　　22632-8

SUNDIALS, Their Theory and Construction, Albert Waugh. Far and away the best, most thorough coverage of ideas, mathematics concerned, types, construction, adjusting anywhere. Simple, nontechnical treatment allows even children to build several of these dials. Over 100 illustrations. 230pp. 5⅜ x 8½.　　　22947-5

THEORETICAL HYDRODYNAMICS, L. M. Milne-Thomson. Classic exposition of the mathematical theory of fluid motion, applicable to both hydrodynamics and aerodynamics. Over 600 exercises. 768pp. 6⅛ x 9¼.　　　68970-0

SONGS OF EXPERIENCE: Facsimile Reproduction with 26 Plates in Full Color, William Blake. 26 full-color plates from a rare 1826 edition. Includes "The Tyger," "London," "Holy Thursday," and other poems. Printed text of poems. 48pp. 5¼ x 7.
24636-1

OLD-TIME VIGNETTES IN FULL COLOR, Carol Belanger Grafton (ed.). Over 390 charming, often sentimental illustrations, selected from archives of Victorian graphics–pretty women posing, children playing, food, flowers, kittens and puppies, smiling cherubs, birds and butterflies, much more. All copyright-free. 48pp. 9¼ x 12¼.
27269-9

PERSPECTIVE FOR ARTISTS, Rex Vicat Cole. Depth, perspective of sky and sea, shadows, much more, not usually covered. 391 diagrams, 81 reproductions of drawings and paintings. 279pp. 5⅜ x 8½. 22487-2

DRAWING THE LIVING FIGURE, Joseph Sheppard. Innovative approach to artistic anatomy focuses on specifics of surface anatomy, rather than muscles and bones. Over 170 drawings of live models in front, back and side views, and in widely varying poses. Accompanying diagrams. 177 illustrations. Introduction. Index. 144pp. 8⅜ x11¼. 26723-7

GOTHIC AND OLD ENGLISH ALPHABETS: 100 Complete Fonts, Dan X. Solo. Add power, elegance to posters, signs, other graphics with 100 stunning copyright-free alphabets: Blackstone, Dolbey, Germania, 97 more–including many lower-case, numerals, punctuation marks. 104pp. 8⅛ x 11. 24695-7

HOW TO DO BEADWORK, Mary White. Fundamental book on craft from simple projects to five-bead chains and woven works. 106 illustrations. 142pp. 5⅜ x 8. 20697-1

THE BOOK OF WOOD CARVING, Charles Marshall Sayers. Finest book for beginners discusses fundamentals and offers 34 designs. "Absolutely first rate . . . well thought out and well executed."–E. J. Tangerman. 118pp. 7¾ x 10⅝. 23654-4

ILLUSTRATED CATALOG OF CIVIL WAR MILITARY GOODS: Union Army Weapons, Insignia, Uniform Accessories, and Other Equipment, Schuyler, Hartley, and Graham. Rare, profusely illustrated 1846 catalog includes Union Army uniform and dress regulations, arms and ammunition, coats, insignia, flags, swords, rifles, etc. 226 illustrations. 160pp. 9 x 12. 24939-5

WOMEN'S FASHIONS OF THE EARLY 1900s: An Unabridged Republication of "New York Fashions, 1909," National Cloak & Suit Co. Rare catalog of mail-order fashions documents women's and children's clothing styles shortly after the turn of the century. Captions offer full descriptions, prices. Invaluable resource for fashion, costume historians. Approximately 725 illustrations. 128pp. 8⅜ x 11¼. 27276-1

THE 1912 AND 1915 GUSTAV STICKLEY FURNITURE CATALOGS, Gustav Stickley. With over 200 detailed illustrations and descriptions, these two catalogs are essential reading and reference materials and identification guides for Stickley furniture. Captions cite materials, dimensions and prices. 112pp. 6½ x 9¼. 26676-1

EARLY AMERICAN LOCOMOTIVES, John H. White, Jr. Finest locomotive engravings from early 19th century: historical (1804–74), main-line (after 1870), special, foreign, etc. 147 plates. 142pp. 11⅜ x 8¼. 22772-3

THE TALL SHIPS OF TODAY IN PHOTOGRAPHS, Frank O. Braynard. Lavishly illustrated tribute to nearly 100 majestic contemporary sailing vessels: Amerigo Vespucci, Clearwater, Constitution, Eagle, Mayflower, Sea Cloud, Victory, many more. Authoritative captions provide statistics, background on each ship. 190 black-and-white photographs and illustrations. Introduction. 128pp. 8⅞ x 11¾. 27163-3

LITTLE BOOK OF EARLY AMERICAN CRAFTS AND TRADES, Peter Stockham (ed.). 1807 children's book explains crafts and trades: baker, hatter, cooper, potter, and many others. 23 copperplate illustrations. 140pp. 4⅝ x 6.   23336-7

VICTORIAN FASHIONS AND COSTUMES FROM HARPER'S BAZAR, 1867–1898, Stella Blum (ed.). Day costumes, evening wear, sports clothes, shoes, hats, other accessories in over 1,000 detailed engravings. 320pp. 9⅜ x 12¼.   22990-4

GUSTAV STICKLEY, THE CRAFTSMAN, Mary Ann Smith. Superb study surveys broad scope of Stickley's achievement, especially in architecture. Design philosophy, rise and fall of the Craftsman empire, descriptions and floor plans for many Craftsman houses, more. 86 black-and-white halftones. 31 line illustrations. Introduction 208pp. 6½ x 9¼.   27210-9

THE LONG ISLAND RAIL ROAD IN EARLY PHOTOGRAPHS, Ron Ziel. Over 220 rare photos, informative text document origin (1844) and development of rail service on Long Island. Vintage views of early trains, locomotives, stations, passengers, crews, much more. Captions. 8⅞ x 11¾.   26301-0

VOYAGE OF THE LIBERDADE, Joshua Slocum. Great 19th-century mariner's thrilling, first-hand account of the wreck of his ship off South America, the 35-foot boat he built from the wreckage, and its remarkable voyage home. 128pp. 5⅜ x 8½.
40022-0

TEN BOOKS ON ARCHITECTURE, Vitruvius. The most important book ever written on architecture. Early Roman aesthetics, technology, classical orders, site selection, all other aspects. Morgan translation. 331pp. 5⅜ x 8½.   20645-9

THE HUMAN FIGURE IN MOTION, Eadweard Muybridge. More than 4,500 stopped-action photos, in action series, showing undraped men, women, children jumping, lying down, throwing, sitting, wrestling, carrying, etc. 390pp. 7⅞ x 10⅝.
20204-6 Clothbd.

TREES OF THE EASTERN AND CENTRAL UNITED STATES AND CANADA, William M. Harlow. Best one-volume guide to 140 trees. Full descriptions, woodlore, range, etc. Over 600 illustrations. Handy size. 288pp. 4½ x 6⅜.   20395-6

SONGS OF WESTERN BIRDS, Dr. Donald J. Borror. Complete song and call repertoire of 60 western species, including flycatchers, juncoes, cactus wrens, many more—includes fully illustrated booklet.   Cassette and manual 99913-0

GROWING AND USING HERBS AND SPICES, Milo Miloradovich. Versatile handbook provides all the information needed for cultivation and use of all the herbs and spices available in North America. 4 illustrations. Index. Glossary. 236pp. 5⅜ x 8½.
25058-X

BIG BOOK OF MAZES AND LABYRINTHS, Walter Shepherd. 50 mazes and labyrinths in all—classical, solid, ripple, and more—in one great volume. Perfect inexpensive puzzler for clever youngsters. Full solutions. 112pp. 8⅛ x 11.   22951-3

PIANO TUNING, J. Cree Fischer. Clearest, best book for beginner, amateur. Simple repairs, raising dropped notes, tuning by easy method of flattened fifths. No previous skills needed. 4 illustrations. 201pp. 5⅜ x 8½. 23267-0

HINTS TO SINGERS, Lillian Nordica. Selecting the right teacher, developing confidence, overcoming stage fright, and many other important skills receive thoughtful discussion in this indispensible guide, written by a world-famous diva of four decades' experience. 96pp. 5⅜ x 8½. 40094-8

THE COMPLETE NONSENSE OF EDWARD LEAR, Edward Lear. All nonsense limericks, zany alphabets, Owl and Pussycat, songs, nonsense botany, etc., illustrated by Lear. Total of 320pp. 5⅜ x 8½. (Available in U.S. only.) 20167-8

VICTORIAN PARLOUR POETRY: An Annotated Anthology, Michael R. Turner. 117 gems by Longfellow, Tennyson, Browning, many lesser-known poets. "The Village Blacksmith," "Curfew Must Not Ring Tonight," "Only a Baby Small," dozens more, often difficult to find elsewhere. Index of poets, titles, first lines. xxiii + 325pp. 5⅝ x 8¼. 27044-0

DUBLINERS, James Joyce. Fifteen stories offer vivid, tightly focused observations of the lives of Dublin's poorer classes. At least one, "The Dead," is considered a masterpiece. Reprinted complete and unabridged from standard edition. 160pp. 5$\frac{3}{16}$ x 8¼. 26870-5

GREAT WEIRD TALES: 14 Stories by Lovecraft, Blackwood, Machen and Others, S. T. Joshi (ed.). 14 spellbinding tales, including "The Sin Eater," by Fiona McLeod, "The Eye Above the Mantel," by Frank Belknap Long, as well as renowned works by R. H. Barlow, Lord Dunsany, Arthur Machen, W. C. Morrow and eight other masters of the genre. 256pp. 5⅜ x 8½. (Available in U.S. only.) 40436-6

THE BOOK OF THE SACRED MAGIC OF ABRAMELIN THE MAGE, translated by S. MacGregor Mathers. Medieval manuscript of ceremonial magic. Basic document in Aleister Crowley, Golden Dawn groups. 268pp. 5⅜ x 8½. 23211-5

NEW RUSSIAN-ENGLISH AND ENGLISH-RUSSIAN DICTIONARY, M. A. O'Brien. This is a remarkably handy Russian dictionary, containing a surprising amount of information, including over 70,000 entries. 366pp. 4½ x 6⅛. 20208-9

HISTORIC HOMES OF THE AMERICAN PRESIDENTS, Second, Revised Edition, Irvin Haas. A traveler's guide to American Presidential homes, most open to the public, depicting and describing homes occupied by every American President from George Washington to George Bush. With visiting hours, admission charges, travel routes. 175 photographs. Index. 160pp. 8¼ x 11. 26751-2

NEW YORK IN THE FORTIES, Andreas Feininger. 162 brilliant photographs by the well-known photographer, formerly with *Life* magazine. Commuters, shoppers, Times Square at night, much else from city at its peak. Captions by John von Hartz. 181pp. 9¼ x 10¾. 23585-8

INDIAN SIGN LANGUAGE, William Tomkins. Over 525 signs developed by Sioux and other tribes. Written instructions and diagrams. Also 290 pictographs. 111pp. 6⅛ x 9¼. 22029-X

ANATOMY: A Complete Guide for Artists, Joseph Sheppard. A master of figure drawing shows artists how to render human anatomy convincingly. Over 460 illustrations. 224pp. 8⅜ x 11¼. 27279-6

MEDIEVAL CALLIGRAPHY: Its History and Technique, Marc Drogin. Spirited history, comprehensive instruction manual covers 13 styles (ca. 4th century through 15th). Excellent photographs; directions for duplicating medieval techniques with modern tools. 224pp. 8⅜ x 11¼. 26142-5

DRIED FLOWERS: How to Prepare Them, Sarah Whitlock and Martha Rankin. Complete instructions on how to use silica gel, meal and borax, perlite aggregate, sand and borax, glycerine and water to create attractive permanent flower arrangements. 12 illustrations. 32pp. 5⅜ x 8½. 21802-3

EASY-TO-MAKE BIRD FEEDERS FOR WOODWORKERS, Scott D. Campbell. Detailed, simple-to-use guide for designing, constructing, caring for and using feeders. Text, illustrations for 12 classic and contemporary designs. 96pp. 5⅜ x 8½. 25847-5

SCOTTISH WONDER TALES FROM MYTH AND LEGEND, Donald A. Mackenzie. 16 lively tales tell of giants rumbling down mountainsides, of a magic wand that turns stone pillars into warriors, of gods and goddesses, evil hags, powerful forces and more. 240pp. 5⅜ x 8½. 29677-6

THE HISTORY OF UNDERCLOTHES, C. Willett Cunnington and Phyllis Cunnington. Fascinating, well-documented survey covering six centuries of English undergarments, enhanced with over 100 illustrations: 12th-century laced-up bodice, footed long drawers (1795), 19th-century bustles, 19th-century corsets for men, Victorian "bust improvers," much more. 272pp. 5⅜ x 8¼. 27124-2

ARTS AND CRAFTS FURNITURE: The Complete Brooks Catalog of 1912, Brooks Manufacturing Co. Photos and detailed descriptions of more than 150 now very collectible furniture designs from the Arts and Crafts movement depict davenports, settees, buffets, desks, tables, chairs, bedsteads, dressers and more, all built of solid, quarter-sawed oak. Invaluable for students and enthusiasts of antiques, Americana and the decorative arts. 80pp. 6½ x 9¼. 27471-3

WILBUR AND ORVILLE: A Biography of the Wright Brothers, Fred Howard. Definitive, crisply written study tells the full story of the brothers' lives and work. A vividly written biography, unparalleled in scope and color, that also captures the spirit of an extraordinary era. 560pp. 6⅛ x 9¼. 40297-5

THE ARTS OF THE SAILOR: Knotting, Splicing and Ropework, Hervey Garrett Smith. Indispensable shipboard reference covers tools, basic knots and useful hitches; handsewing and canvas work, more. Over 100 illustrations. Delightful reading for sea lovers. 256pp. 5⅜ x 8½. 26440-8

FRANK LLOYD WRIGHT'S FALLINGWATER: The House and Its History, Second, Revised Edition, Donald Hoffmann. A total revision—both in text and illustrations—of the standard document on Fallingwater, the boldest, most personal architectural statement of Wright's mature years, updated with valuable new material from the recently opened Frank Lloyd Wright Archives. "Fascinating"—*The New York Times*. 116 illustrations. 128pp. 9¼ x 10¾. 27430-6

PHOTOGRAPHIC SKETCHBOOK OF THE CIVIL WAR, Alexander Gardner. 100 photos taken on field during the Civil War. Famous shots of Manassas Harper's Ferry, Lincoln, Richmond, slave pens, etc. 244pp. 10⅝ x 8¼. 22731-6

FIVE ACRES AND INDEPENDENCE, Maurice G. Kains. Great back-to-the-land classic explains basics of self-sufficient farming. The one book to get. 95 illustrations. 397pp. 5⅜ x 8½. 20974-1

SONGS OF EASTERN BIRDS, Dr. Donald J. Borror. Songs and calls of 60 species most common to eastern U.S.: warblers, woodpeckers, flycatchers, thrushes, larks, many more in high-quality recording. Cassette and manual 99912-2

A MODERN HERBAL, Margaret Grieve. Much the fullest, most exact, most useful compilation of herbal material. Gigantic alphabetical encyclopedia, from aconite to zedoary, gives botanical information, medical properties, folklore, economic uses, much else. Indispensable to serious reader. 161 illustrations. 888pp. 6½ x 9¼. 2-vol. set. (Available in U.S. only.) Vol. I: 22798-7
Vol. II: 22799-5

HIDDEN TREASURE MAZE BOOK, Dave Phillips. Solve 34 challenging mazes accompanied by heroic tales of adventure. Evil dragons, people-eating plants, bloodthirsty giants, many more dangerous adversaries lurk at every twist and turn. 34 mazes, stories, solutions. 48pp. 8¼ x 11. 24566-7

LETTERS OF W. A. MOZART, Wolfgang A. Mozart. Remarkable letters show bawdy wit, humor, imagination, musical insights, contemporary musical world; includes some letters from Leopold Mozart. 276pp. 5⅜ x 8½. 22859-2

BASIC PRINCIPLES OF CLASSICAL BALLET, Agrippina Vaganova. Great Russian theoretician, teacher explains methods for teaching classical ballet. 118 illustrations. 175pp. 5⅜ x 8½. 22036-2

THE JUMPING FROG, Mark Twain. Revenge edition. The original story of The Celebrated Jumping Frog of Calaveras County, a hapless French translation, and Twain's hilarious "retranslation" from the French. 12 illustrations. 66pp. 5⅜ x 8½. 22686-7

BEST REMEMBERED POEMS, Martin Gardner (ed.). The 126 poems in this superb collection of 19th- and 20th-century British and American verse range from Shelley's "To a Skylark" to the impassioned "Renascence" of Edna St. Vincent Millay and to Edward Lear's whimsical "The Owl and the Pussycat." 224pp. 5⅜ x 8½. 27165-X

COMPLETE SONNETS, William Shakespeare. Over 150 exquisite poems deal with love, friendship, the tyranny of time, beauty's evanescence, death and other themes in language of remarkable power, precision and beauty. Glossary of archaic terms. 80pp. 5³⁄₁₆ x 8¼. 26686-9

THE BATTLES THAT CHANGED HISTORY, Fletcher Pratt. Eminent historian profiles 16 crucial conflicts, ancient to modern, that changed the course of civilization. 352pp. 5⅜ x 8½. 41129-X

THE WIT AND HUMOR OF OSCAR WILDE, Alvin Redman (ed.). More than 1,000 ripostes, paradoxes, wisecracks: Work is the curse of the drinking classes; I can resist everything except temptation; etc. 258pp. 5⅜ x 8½. 20602-5

SHAKESPEARE LEXICON AND QUOTATION DICTIONARY, Alexander Schmidt. Full definitions, locations, shades of meaning in every word in plays and poems. More than 50,000 exact quotations. 1,485pp. 6½ x 9¼. 2-vol. set.
Vol. 1: 22726-X
Vol. 2: 22727-8

SELECTED POEMS, Emily Dickinson. Over 100 best-known, best-loved poems by one of America's foremost poets, reprinted from authoritative early editions. No comparable edition at this price. Index of first lines. 64pp. 5³⁄₁₆ x 8¼. 26466-1

THE INSIDIOUS DR. FU-MANCHU, Sax Rohmer. The first of the popular mystery series introduces a pair of English detectives to their archnemesis, the diabolical Dr. Fu-Manchu. Flavorful atmosphere, fast-paced action, and colorful characters enliven this classic of the genre. 208pp. 5³⁄₁₆ x 8¼. 29898-1

THE MALLEUS MALEFICARUM OF KRAMER AND SPRENGER, translated by Montague Summers. Full text of most important witchhunter's "bible," used by both Catholics and Protestants. 278pp. 6⅝ x 10. 22802-9

SPANISH STORIES/CUENTOS ESPAÑOLES: A Dual-Language Book, Angel Flores (ed.). Unique format offers 13 great stories in Spanish by Cervantes, Borges, others. Faithful English translations on facing pages. 352pp. 5⅜ x 8½. 25399-6

GARDEN CITY, LONG ISLAND, IN EARLY PHOTOGRAPHS, 1869–1919, Mildred H. Smith. Handsome treasury of 118 vintage pictures, accompanied by carefully researched captions, document the Garden City Hotel fire (1899), the Vanderbilt Cup Race (1908), the first airmail flight departing from the Nassau Boulevard Aerodrome (1911), and much more. 96pp. 8⅞ x 11¾. 40669-5

OLD QUEENS, N.Y., IN EARLY PHOTOGRAPHS, Vincent F. Seyfried and William Asadorian. Over 160 rare photographs of Maspeth, Jamaica, Jackson Heights, and other areas. Vintage views of DeWitt Clinton mansion, 1939 World's Fair and more. Captions. 192pp. 8⅞ x 11. 26358-4

CAPTURED BY THE INDIANS: 15 Firsthand Accounts, 1750-1870, Frederick Drimmer. Astounding true historical accounts of grisly torture, bloody conflicts, relentless pursuits, miraculous escapes and more, by people who lived to tell the tale. 384pp. 5⅜ x 8½. 24901-8

THE WORLD'S GREAT SPEECHES (Fourth Enlarged Edition), Lewis Copeland, Lawrence W. Lamm, and Stephen J. McKenna. Nearly 300 speeches provide public speakers with a wealth of updated quotes and inspiration–from Pericles' funeral oration and William Jennings Bryan's "Cross of Gold Speech" to Malcolm X's powerful words on the Black Revolution and Earl of Spenser's tribute to his sister, Diana, Princess of Wales. 944pp. 5⅜ x 8⅜. 40903-1

THE BOOK OF THE SWORD, Sir Richard F. Burton. Great Victorian scholar/adventurer's eloquent, erudite history of the "queen of weapons"–from prehistory to early Roman Empire. Evolution and development of early swords, variations (sabre, broadsword, cutlass, scimitar, etc.), much more. 336pp. 6⅛ x 9¼.
25434-8

CATALOG OF DOVER BOOKS

AUTOBIOGRAPHY: The Story of My Experiments with Truth, Mohandas K. Gandhi. Boyhood, legal studies, purification, the growth of the Satyagraha (nonviolent protest) movement. Critical, inspiring work of the man responsible for the freedom of India. 480pp. 5⅜ x 8½. (Available in U.S. only.) 24593-4

CELTIC MYTHS AND LEGENDS, T. W. Rolleston. Masterful retelling of Irish and Welsh stories and tales. Cuchulain, King Arthur, Deirdre, the Grail, many more. First paperback edition. 58 full-page illustrations. 512pp. 5⅜ x 8½. 26507-2

THE PRINCIPLES OF PSYCHOLOGY, William James. Famous long course complete, unabridged. Stream of thought, time perception, memory, experimental methods; great work decades ahead of its time. 94 figures. 1,391pp. 5⅜ x 8½. 2-vol. set. Vol. I: 20381-6 Vol. II: 20382-4

THE WORLD AS WILL AND REPRESENTATION, Arthur Schopenhauer. Definitive English translation of Schopenhauer's life work, correcting more than 1,000 errors, omissions in earlier translations. Translated by E. F. J. Payne. Total of 1,269pp. 5⅜ x 8½. 2-vol. set. Vol. 1: 21761-2 Vol. 2: 21762-0

MAGIC AND MYSTERY IN TIBET, Madame Alexandra David-Neel. Experiences among lamas, magicians, sages, sorcerers, Bonpa wizards. A true psychic discovery. 32 illustrations. 321pp. 5⅜ x 8½. (Available in U.S. only.) 22682-4

THE EGYPTIAN BOOK OF THE DEAD, E. A. Wallis Budge. Complete reproduction of Ani's papyrus, finest ever found. Full hieroglyphic text, interlinear transliteration, word-for-word translation, smooth translation. 533pp. 6½ x 9¼. 21866-X

MATHEMATICS FOR THE NONMATHEMATICIAN, Morris Kline. Detailed, college-level treatment of mathematics in cultural and historical context, with numerous exercises. Recommended Reading Lists. Tables. Numerous figures. 641pp. 5⅜ x 8½. 24823-2

PROBABILISTIC METHODS IN THE THEORY OF STRUCTURES, Isaac Elishakoff. Well-written introduction covers the elements of the theory of probability from two or more random variables, the reliability of such multivariable structures, the theory of random function, Monte Carlo methods of treating problems incapable of exact solution, and more. Examples. 502pp. 5⅜ x 8½. 40691-1

THE RIME OF THE ANCIENT MARINER, Gustave Doré, S. T. Coleridge. Doré's finest work; 34 plates capture moods, subtleties of poem. Flawless full-size reproductions printed on facing pages with authoritative text of poem. "Beautiful. Simply beautiful."–Publisher's Weekly. 77pp. 9¼ x 12. 22305-1

NORTH AMERICAN INDIAN DESIGNS FOR ARTISTS AND CRAFTSPEOPLE, Eva Wilson. Over 360 authentic copyright-free designs adapted from Navajo blankets, Hopi pottery, Sioux buffalo hides, more. Geometrics, symbolic figures, plant and animal motifs, etc. 128pp. 8⅜ x 11. (Not for sale in the United Kingdom.) 25341-4

SCULPTURE: Principles and Practice, Louis Slobodkin. Step-by-step approach to clay, plaster, metals, stone; classical and modern. 253 drawings, photos. 255pp. 8⅛ x 11. 22960-2

THE INFLUENCE OF SEA POWER UPON HISTORY, 1660–1783, A. T. Mahan. Influential classic of naval history and tactics still used as text in war colleges. First paperback edition. 4 maps. 24 battle plans. 640pp. 5⅜ x 8½. 25509-3

CATALOG OF DOVER BOOKS

THE STORY OF THE TITANIC AS TOLD BY ITS SURVIVORS, Jack Winocour (ed.). What it was really like. Panic, despair, shocking inefficiency, and a little heroism. More thrilling than any fictional account. 26 illustrations. 320pp. 5⅜ x 8½. 20610-6

FAIRY AND FOLK TALES OF THE IRISH PEASANTRY, William Butler Yeats (ed.). Treasury of 64 tales from the twilight world of Celtic myth and legend: "The Soul Cages," "The Kildare Pooka," "King O'Toole and his Goose," many more. Introduction and Notes by W. B. Yeats. 352pp. 5⅜ x 8½. 26941-8

BUDDHIST MAHAYANA TEXTS, E. B. Cowell and others (eds.). Superb, accurate translations of basic documents in Mahayana Buddhism, highly important in history of religions. The Buddha-karita of Asvaghosha, Larger Sukhavativyuha, more. 448pp. 5⅜ x 8½. 25552-2

ONE TWO THREE . . . INFINITY: Facts and Speculations of Science, George Gamow. Great physicist's fascinating, readable overview of contemporary science: number theory, relativity, fourth dimension, entropy, genes, atomic structure, much more. 128 illustrations. Index. 352pp. 5⅜ x 8½. 25664-2

EXPERIMENTATION AND MEASUREMENT, W. J. Youden. Introductory manual explains laws of measurement in simple terms and offers tips for achieving accuracy and minimizing errors. Mathematics of measurement, use of instruments, experimenting with machines. 1994 edition. Foreword. Preface. Introduction. Epilogue. Selected Readings. Glossary. Index. Tables and figures. 128pp. 5⅜ x 8½. 40451-X

DALÍ ON MODERN ART: The Cuckolds of Antiquated Modern Art, Salvador Dalí. Influential painter skewers modern art and its practitioners. Outrageous evaluations of Picasso, Cézanne, Turner, more. 15 renderings of paintings discussed. 44 calligraphic decorations by Dalí. 96pp. 5⅜ x 8½. (Available in U.S. only.) 29220-7

ANTIQUE PLAYING CARDS: A Pictorial History, Henry René D'Allemagne. Over 900 elaborate, decorative images from rare playing cards (14th–20th centuries): Bacchus, death, dancing dogs, hunting scenes, royal coats of arms, players cheating, much more. 96pp. 9¼ x 12¼. 29265-7

MAKING FURNITURE MASTERPIECES: 30 Projects with Measured Drawings, Franklin H. Gottshall. Step-by-step instructions, illustrations for constructing handsome, useful pieces, among them a Sheraton desk, Chippendale chair, Spanish desk, Queen Anne table and a William and Mary dressing mirror. 224pp. 8⅛ x 11¼. 29338-6

THE FOSSIL BOOK: A Record of Prehistoric Life, Patricia V. Rich et al. Profusely illustrated definitive guide covers everything from single-celled organisms and dinosaurs to birds and mammals and the interplay between climate and man. Over 1,500 illustrations. 760pp. 7½ x 10⅛. 29371-8

Paperbound unless otherwise indicated. Available at your book dealer, online at **www.doverpublications.com**, or by writing to Dept. GI, Dover Publications, Inc., 31 East 2nd Street, Mineola, NY 11501. For current price information or for free catalogues (please indicate field of interest), write to Dover Publications or log on to **www.doverpublications.com** and see every Dover book in print. Dover publishes more than 500 books each year on science, elementary and advanced mathematics, biology, music, art, literary history, social sciences, and other areas.